The Write Direction

A New Teacher's Practical Guide to Teaching Writing and Its Application to the Workplace

D1306632

Fred S. Wolff

Lynna Garber Kalna

DeVry University

ALLYN & BACON

Boston   New York   San Francisco
Mexico City   Montreal   Toronto   London   Madrid   Munich   Paris
Hong Kong   Singapore   Tokyo   Cape Town   Sydney

Executive Editor: Aurora Martínez Ramos
Series Editorial Assistant: Kara Kikel
Executive Marketing Manager: Krista Clark
Marketing Manager: Danae April
Production Editor: Annette Joseph
Editorial Production Service: DB Publishing Services, Inc.
Composition Buyer: Linda Cox
Manufacturing Buyer: Megan Cochran
Electronic Composition: Denise Hoffman
Cover Administrator: Linda Knowles

For Professional Development resources, visit www.allynbaconmerrill.com.

Between the time website information is gathered and then published, it is not unusual for some sites to have closed. Also, the transcription of URLs can result in typographical errors. The publisher would appreciate notification where these errors occur so that they may be corrected in subsequent editions.

ISBN-10: 0-205-57033-X
ISBN-13: 978-0-205-57033-1

Library of Congress Cataloging-in-Publication Data

Wolff, Fred S.
    The write direction : a new teacher's practical guide to teaching writing and its application to the workplace / Fred S. Wolff, Lynna Garber Kalna.
        p. cm.
    Includes bibliographical references and index.
    ISBN-13: 978-0-205-57033-1 (alk. paper)
    ISBN-10: 0-205-57033-X (alk. paper)
    1. English language—Composition and exercises—Study and teaching (Secondary)   2. Report writing—Study and teaching (Secondary)   3. First year teachers.   I. Kalna, Lynna Garber.   II. Title.

    LB1631.W585 2010
    808'.0420712—dc22   2008046653

Printed in the United States of America

10 9 8 7 6 5 4 3 2 1   12 11 10 09 08

Allyn & Bacon
is an imprint of

PEARSON

www.pearsonhighered.com

ISBN-10: 0-205-57033-X
ISBN-13: 978-0-205-57033-1

Fred's Dedication

For our future writers, Elisa, Travis, and Jacob.

For LJGK . . . we'll always have Flagstaff.

For Coby, whose patience and support have been appreciated more than she will ever know.

And Uncle Chuck, who always believed in me.

Lynna's Dedication

*To Kaitlin and Reed, I love you all the way around
the world and back.*

*To the "Poker" Ladies and tennis friends,
what's life if it isn't fun.*

*To Sharon, my forever-friend, who makes me feel
very fortunate.*

*And to my dearest friend, with whom I have an
indescribable bond.*

Contents

Conclusion   166

Both Our Worlds   166

Foreword

In writing workshops across the country, I hear teachers say, "The trouble is, no one ever *taught* me how to teach writing." Far too many writing teachers these days feel that way, and the teaching of writing (especially when you're unsure how to go about it) is not only confusing—it's potentially terrifying. Here is a book to calm those jitters, written collaboratively by a veteran teacher who is one of the finest teacher trainers I have ever known, Fred Wolff; and by his remarkable colleague, also a teacher and an expert in on-site corporate professional development, Lynna Kalna. Their complementary skills and perspectives have resulted in a resource that shows us exactly how writing workshop can help students love writing, excel at it, and prepare for the rigorous demands of the workplace.

Teaching writing isn't one of those things a person simply "picks up." We tend to teach—at first, anyway—as we ourselves were taught. And what was modeled for many of us, from elementary years on, was the *assigning and correcting* of writing, rather than the *teaching* of writing. As a six-trait trainer, I always ask my workshop participants how many recall seeing one of *their own* teachers write. It's rare to see more than a hand or two go up. How many of them, I ask, experienced a true writing workshop atmosphere, one in which they felt comfortable writing, conferring with peers, sharing their writing aloud, and choosing their own topics? A few recall *just* such an experience (they're the ones with the smiles on their faces)—but to the majority, this is foreign territory. Heads shake. Eyes meet and roll. And a volcanic eruption of voices releases a flood of memories. Memories of writing assignments in which students had minimal interest. Negative comments (*Your writing reminds me of a porcupine—many points leading in meaningless directions*). Suppression of all collaboration (*That's cheating, isn't it?*). Pathetic attempts at prewriting that seldom stretched beyond outlining (which most of us learned to do *after* the draft was written). Or "revision" that consisted of tidying up a first draft, and adding a title and cover.

If only even a handful of teachers had demonstrated for us those practical, everyday things all teachers of writing need to know: how to manage a student conference, offer comments a writer might actually find helpful, assist student writers in discovering personally important writing topics, or stand intrepidly at the overhead projector and model how to write that first sentence. When we wondered what on earth our writing teachers were looking for as they bled all over our drafts, remarkably few of them thought to offer us examples of strong and weak writing that would have made their wishes clear as the sunrise. And before 1984, the six traits had yet to be discovered, so prior to that time, we had no rubrics, no checklists, and no common language to help us form a writing community. College courses were supposed to fill in *all* these gaps. When they didn't, the truth hit us: Whatever we were going to do as teachers of writing we were going to have to invent.

How much easier that would have been if we'd had this book. Because here it all is: Writing Project, writing workshop, process, portfolios, the six traits, writing topics, conferences, literary mentors—the whole package. And all presented as a lead-in to real-world writing.

In their personable, highly readable blend of strategies and life lessons, Fred and Lynna take us inside the world of public education—*and* professional writing—showing us how the two connect, and how they can and should influence each other. Not only do these writers show us what a successful writing classroom can look like, but through Lynna's invaluable perspective, they also show us the impact that the teaching of writing can have once students enter the workforce.

In a time when corporations increasingly bemoan employees' lack of basic writing skills, it is vital for educators to recognize what employers look for. We are so accustomed to thinking of ways to prepare students for tests that we sometimes forget the far bigger challenge that awaits them: competing for work in corporations that rarely tolerate missed deadlines, jumbled prose, or faulty conventions. In the corporate world, most employees are asked to write frequently, voluminously, spontaneously—and accurately. Academic writing, while important, cannot prepare students for many (if not most) writing tasks that they will encounter on the job. But as this book shows us, by combining academic writing and real-world writing, we *can* give our students the skills and confidence they need to be competitive beyond the classroom walls.

A personal note . . .

I have come to know Lynna through her work in creating writing instruction for professionals in the workplace. I truly cannot state too strongly how important I feel this work is. For many of our students, writing skills will literally pave a personal path to success. It is frequently *the skill* that makes the difference between an upward career course and entrapment at a level well below a student's potential. I am deeply pleased to see the essence of her work captured in this important book.

Fred has been a friend and colleague for many years, and over time I've grown to appreciate his sense of humor, his ingratiating modesty, and his expansive knowledge of literature.

When I first met Fred, I was doing a six-trait writing workshop for a group of teachers in New Hampshire. At that time, Fred was the curriculum coordinator for the district—a job that understandably kept him busy with a vast array of responsibilities. Yet he took time to attend my workshop (which both surprised and pleased me); and he didn't just pop in and out or keep to himself in a corner, making notes. Instead, Fred participated fully and enthusiastically in *all* activities: writing, (good-naturedly) sharing his writing aloud, role playing, putting himself on the line with editing tasks, and offering his perspectives on student writing. I shared sample after sample as we worked our way through the traits, and while many were problematic, Fred found something to build on in every single one. His comments reflected the kinds of feedback that help a writer turn a corner. He heard the tiniest moments of voice and pointed out little details the rest of us had missed. Within a list of generalities, Fred would spot an emerging topic—something on which to build rapport during a later student conference. With such a teacher, students open up. They learn to trust.

This person, I recall thinking, *is truly a teacher—he models what he believes*. For his part, Fred was his usual shoulder-shrugging, matter-of-fact self: "We all need to be writers, you know—otherwise, how can we teach it?" It's that philosophy that drives this book. And here, Fred expands the vision by showing us, through Lynna's work, how everything we do in the writing classroom affects our students' futures. Thank you, Fred, for pulling so many threads of the fabric together—and for continuing to be, through this important book, a teacher of writing.

Vicki Spandel, Author
Creating Writers, 5th edition, Pearson Education
The 9 Rights of Every Writer, Heinemann
Creating Revisers and Editors, Pearson Education
The Write Traits Classroom Kits, Great Source Education

Preface
(And this is one you have to read!)

If you are preparing to be an English/Language Arts teacher in grades 4–12, or you are in the early years of your English/Language Arts teaching career, this book is for you. If you examine your teacher preparation program, you will probably find yourself in the large majority of teachers, myself (Fred) included, who never took an undergraduate course (nor were you offered one!) on how to teach writing. As you enter the classroom, whether in an upper elementary grade, a middle school, or a high school, you will likely find yourself frustrated trying to figure out how to help your students improve their writing. You may work as hard as you can, spend hours poring over your students' papers, correct and suggest until your fingers are calloused, and still not witness much improvement or enthusiasm. That was my situation during my first few years as a teacher. This is the book I wish I had read before I started teaching.

The genesis of this book was simple. For the past fifteen years, Lynna and I have engaged in regular conversations about writing. From Lynna's perspective as a writing consultant for businesses and a professor of technical writing, and from my views as an English teacher in public education and a trainer of writing teachers, we have arrived at similar conclusions. First, people can be taught to become competent writers. Given the time to learn, quality instruction, and ample opportunities to write, almost all individuals can reach a level at which they produce clear, organized, and interesting text. Why then, we often ask each other, are so many individuals reaching the workplace without the ability to write well? Does the fault lie with parents who don't spend time with their children or who don't write well themselves? Or perhaps the problem is the amount of time young people spend IMing and text messaging their friends. Is it possible people spend too much time in front of their computers playing games, surfing the Internet, looking at their friends' MySpace/YouTube/Facebook pages, or reading other people's blogs? We've discussed the possibility that young people don't think that the ability to write well will be important in their lives; thus, why work to become reasonably strong writers? I've heard high school and college students say more times than I can count, "Look, I'm going into computer science/hard sciences/mathematics/research [take your pick!] so I don't need to write that well." If only they understood the reality they will face when they enter their field. Or maybe the problem is the limited amount and quality of writing instruction that takes place in classrooms. We believe it's a combination of all of these issues and more.

We can impact very few of these challenges, but helping teachers do a better job of teaching writing is one area in which we can offer assistance. Research by a host of individuals and our own experiences inform us that most teachers enter the classroom with little if any training on how to teach writing. Most teacher training colleges provide little in the way of instructing future teachers about how to assign writing, grade writing, or teach writing. And so we continue to witness high school and college graduates entering the workplace and finding themselves unprepared for many of the tasks they are required to perform.

Our hope is that this book can be the first in a series of steps that will enable college students in education programs and beginning teachers in grades 4–12 to improve their skills in teaching writing so their students become competent writers. Each chapter (except the last chapter, which only deals with classroom-specific issues) contains ideas and information first from Fred, on classroom applications, and then from Lynna, explaining how Fred's information applies in the world of work.

Many teachers may question the connection to the work world, especially if they teach fourth grade or seventh grade or even ninth grade. However, all of us, to some degree, are helping prepare students for the world they will enter when they leave school. All of us bear some responsibility in this endeavor. Just like we cannot leave preparation for state NCLB tests to the teachers who teach that grade, we cannot "leave it to the high school teachers" to prepare students for the world beyond school. All of us must do our part.

There is another benefit to the work–world connection. As students reach middle school and high school, they tend to ask the ageless questions, "Why do we have to do this? When are we ever going to use this after this class?" Now teachers will have access to the answers.

This book is not intended as *the* comprehensive guide to teaching writing. Such a book would take hundreds of pages, and beginning teachers don't have the time to read such a tome. What it does provide is an overview of the essential components for engaging your students in the art of writing, along with practical assignments and lesson plans that you can use in your classroom to engage your students in developing their writing skills. Numerous books have been written on each of these separate sections, and we encourage you to read further on the topics you find most intriguing. A suggested reading list is included in Appendix E.

This book is not a novel: Please don't feel compelled to read it in the order in which we have presented it. Feel free to skip around! Pick and choose the topics that most interest you. If you're about to begin your career or have just begun your career, you may want to read the book in its entirety.

Please remember that our goal is the same as your goal: to develop graduates who are capable, competent, and confident writers who actually enjoy sitting down to write.

Fred's Acknowledgments

While they don't know it, Vicki Spandel and Tom Newkirk, in their own separate ways, were the catalyst for this book. They have provided the guidance, inspiration, and motivation that enabled me to tackle this project. They have always shared their knowledge, ideas, and humor. I am forever grateful.

While it's been almost twenty years since my introduction to the National Writing Project, those who supported and taught me that summer have not been forgotten. Jack Heath, Don Murray, Don Graves, Les Fisher, Jane Kearns, Jack Wilde, Paula Flemming, Chris Robinson, Dennis Robinson, and a host of others left me with lessons I still carry.

A special thanks to Deb Bamforth, Lynda Beck, Marilyn Gerken, Chris Hobson, Stephanie King, and Coby Troidl, dear friends who willingly read the various drafts and provided valuable feedback and support. Penny Clare, Chris Hobson, Len Miller, and Deb Rutherford provided a wealth of information about writing instruction and planning at various grade levels.

And, of course, the most important thanks to my students during my twenty-four years of teaching. You made this possible.

Lynna's Acknowledgments

Thanks to my colleagues at DeVry University, to those professionals in business and industry whom I have provided training programs, and to my teacher friends who share my passion for education. I'd also like to acknowledge Robert for all the years of stimulating discussions and explorations to places I will always treasure. This book has been greatly enriched by my students over the last twenty-five years. I have learned more from them than they realize; they have fueled my soul with insight, creativity, and humor. And profound gratitude goes to my dearest friend whose brainstorm started this project. You have all made my life richer.

We'd like to thank the reviewers who gave insightful comments to the manuscript: Stayce Baptista, Weston Ranch High School, Stockton, CA; Tamara Doehring, Melbourne High School, Melbourne, FL; Dena Harrison, Mendive Middle School, Sparks, NV; Megan Mahoney, James A. Garfield Elementary School, Brighton, MA; Janet L. Meeks, Fairmont Junior High School, Boise, ID; Susan Stein, Patchogue Medford Schools, Patchogue, NY; and Bonnie Stogner, Weston Ranch High School, Stockton, CA.

CHAPTER 1

The Proverbial Piano Falls on Our Heads

From your perspective

1. *Looking back on your first few years of teaching (or, if you are about to begin, considering your current point of view), summarize in one sentence what you'd most like to accomplish as a teacher of writing.*

2. *What do you need to do to accomplish your goal? Create a list.*

3. *In your current teaching experience, how close have you come to accomplishing that goal—on a scale of 1 (farthest) to 10 (closest)?*

An Overview

For all of us, as we move through our school careers, hobbies, relationships, and work lives, certain events trigger those "a-ha" moments in which questions, challenges, and sometimes answers become clear. If we pay attention to those moments, our understanding of the problem increases and our ability to resolve the challenges improves. Your "a-ha" moments may be very similar to ours.

Fred's World

Just before my twenty-fourth birthday, I signed my first teaching contract. I was going to be an English teacher at a medium-sized high school in southern New Hampshire. I was thrilled. Having finished college two years earlier, I had spent a year traveling around the United States and then a year working a variety of odd jobs. Finally, I was going to use what I thought were my finely honed teaching skills and change the world for my students.

As I looked down the course list my principal had given me, I was confident—at first. Two literature courses. "No problem," I thought to myself. In college, I had taken a course titled *Teaching Literature at the Secondary Level*. Additionally, I had taught literature during my eleven weeks of student teaching. "I'm prepared for that," I said to myself. Next on my list were two sections of ninth-grade grammar. I shook my head in disappointment at having to teach such a boring class (nothing but *Warriner's Handbook of English*) to fifteen-year-old students, but felt fairly well prepared since in college I had also taken a course titled *Teaching Grammar at the Secondary Level*. "I'm ready for that, too," I said to myself. Then, as I read the two courses at the bottom of my list, panic set in. I was to teach two sections of creative writing to tenth- and eleventh-grade students. I had never had a college course on teaching writing. While I had taken a couple of *writing* courses (poetry, creative writing), I had never thought about the concept of *how to teach writing*. Instead, in those writing courses, we simply wrote, received nominal feedback along with a grade, wrote something new, received more feedback and grades, and on and on.

My first "a-ha" moment hit me more as an "uh oh." I realized that while I knew how to assign writing, I didn't actually know how to *teach* writing. I was afraid to ask my department chair for help; after all, the administration had hired me because they assumed I knew what I was doing. If I admitted to having no training whatsoever in teaching writing, they might dismiss me before the school year began.

"Well, *I* can write reasonably well," I said to myself. "So I'll just do to my students what my teachers did to me." I reflected back on my experiences as a student. For sixteen years in school, I had been *told* to write, but not *taught* to write. The teacher had made all the decisions: She (or he) assigned a topic, told us how long the paper needed to be, explained when it was due, and sent us on our way. Simple.

School would end, and then I would go home, eat dinner with my family, and retreat to my room, secretly listening to music when I was supposed to be doing homework. Eventually, my mother would yell up, "Fred, bring down your homework." Remembering that my essay was due, I'd respond, "Mom, give me fifteen minutes; I'm almost done!" Grabbing my pen and notebook, I'd begin to write. I had learned one strategy to begin essays and I used this opening for every essay from junior high school through most of college: an excerpt from *Bartlett's Familiar Quotations*. My formula was simple: I quoted, then I wrote . . . and then I counted . . . and then I wrote . . . and then I counted. I knew when my essay was finished—not because I had arrived at a logical conclusion but because I had accumulated the required number of words. When I hit the magic number, I would proudly take my essay downstairs for my mother's review.

My mother was very adept with language but not the least bit interested in word counts, and, in retrospect, it was from her I learned to write. I was not a willing pupil. I made her climb many hills.

She would begin by reading my essay. Then the sparring began. "Fred, you have too many state-of-being verbs. Let's use some action verbs and bring your paper some life," she would suggest.

Action verbs? My response was honest and simple: "The teacher said she wanted four hundred words; she didn't say what *kind* of words, and I have four hundred words."

Mom would shake her head in disgust. "Fred, you have too many short, choppy sentences. Let's do some sentence combining and the paper will flow better."

"Mom, if I combine sentences, my word count will be less, and I'll have to write even more."

Again, the head shake. "Fred, you've made some interesting statements but you have nothing to *support* the claims you've made. You need to provide some documentation for your statements."

Clearly, mom was not getting into the spirit of word counting. "If I do that," I'd tell her, "I'll have *six hundred words* and the teacher only wants four hundred!"

I won these debates by virtue of stamina. My mother would finally surrender. "Look, it's *your paper*, so do what you want. But if I were you," she'd add, "I'd make the changes." Rarely did I follow through.

The next day, I would hand in my paper and begin the waiting game. I always wondered what grade my paper would receive. I had learned at an early age that a grade was rarely based on the quality of work, but more likely on the person grading. An *A*– in one class could easily be a *C*+ in another. During our elementary school years, if we were assigned one of the "tough" teachers, my friends and I just resigned ourselves to the fact that regardless of how hard we worked, our grades would be mediocre. If we were fortunate to be placed in the classroom of one of the "easy" teachers, we knew we could achieve strong grades with minimal effort. In junior and senior high, my papers were returned with few comments, some corrections in red ink, and a grade. A *C*+ was fairly common with a comment that read, "Work harder and your grade will improve." This made sense to me. If I had spent more than fifteen or twenty minutes, I would have written a stronger paper and probably received a higher grade. On occasion, I would receive an *A*– with the comment "Good job." I never thought I deserved those higher grades; in my mind, my only success lay in fooling the teacher. I also wondered why the minus was there. If I had done such a "good job," why hadn't I received an *A*? What was the difference between an *A* and an *A*–? I never did receive an adequate explanation of that.

I began "teaching" my students to write by following what had been modeled for me. I assigned a topic along with the expected length and due date. And I waited. The papers came in; well, *some* came in. I was stunned that some students chose not to complete my assignment at all. I took the completed papers home, sat at my kitchen table with my red pen, and began to read the papers. This was exciting stuff to a first-year teacher. A sense of purpose, of power—and of total confusion. Most of the papers were terrible. They were fuzzy, loosely focused, poorly organized, and filled with horrendous grammatical errors. Worst of all, many of the students had not even written their papers at home. They had written them on the bus on the way to school, as evidenced by the apparent jerks in their penmanship when the bus had hit a bump!

I was determined to be diligent, even if my students seemed uninspired. I wanted them to know how I felt about their writing and to receive more feedback than I had received over the years. So I covered their papers with comments. In some cases, I wrote more than the students had written. And I thought it was my job to find *all* the mistakes, so I filled their pages with circles, lines, and arrows and their margins with cryptic notes: *awk, mis mod,* or *inc sent*. I assumed that high school students would know that *awk* meant *awkward*. But even those who understood the abbreviation had not the slightest idea what to do about it. I also assumed they knew about misplaced modifiers (*mis mods*) and incomplete sentences (*inc sents*). How wrong I was. They did not know my terminology nor did they care. Worse yet, I did not know what to do about this.

Early on that first year, my second "a-ha" moment hit me, also as an "uh oh." I noticed another problem. Students often received strong grades for what I felt was mediocre writing. Rubrics were unheard of at this time. I, and many of my colleagues, used checklists: 10 points for the cover page, 10 points for the table of contents, 20 points for a bibliography, 10 points for an illustration, and 50 points for the content. I had failed to incorporate the *quality* of writing into my checklist, so as long as students included a cover page, they received 10 points; an illustration, 10 points; and so on. The number of points they received for content was, I finally realized, influenced more by my mood at the moment than by the quality of the students' work. On those days when my principal called me into his office—and there were plenty of those days—to lecture me about another stupid thing I had done (like playing full-speed tackle football after school with the students while no one wore any equipment), even the best papers rarely received more than 30 points for their content. On good days, like when a parent called to thank me for helping a student, even the weak papers might receive 35 or more points for content.

As September rolled into January and January trudged into May, I realized that my students' writing was not improving. I was working my tail off, spending hours grading papers, writing endless comments, identifying virtually every error, and seeing few if any results. I had expected to change lives as a teacher, not to experience constant frustration. I told my students what I had been told: "If you want to become competent writers, you can't write your papers on the bus on the way to school. You have to work *harder!* Spend *more time* on your assignments!" My words sounded eerily similar to my mother's words and teachers' comments from years before. Another "a-ha."

I'm embarrassed to say that very little teaching or learning took place in my writing classes those first few years. I've often thought I should track down those students and apologize. At the same time, I believe I deserved an apology from the university where I spent my undergraduate years. They did not adequately prepare me to be an effective teacher. Fortunately, my university training was not to be the end of my teacher education.

Toward the end of my third year of teaching, two more "a-ha" moments transformed my thinking—and my initially weak teaching style. A significant "a-ha" moment occurred when I realized, "Perhaps the problem isn't with the students. Perhaps the problem is with the way I'm trying to teach them." Then, quite by accident, I came

across an ad for a little-known summer program for teachers: The National Writing Project was about to make its first appearance in New England. I applied and was accepted. My life as a teacher would never be the same.

Lynna's World

My phone rang on a Thursday morning in 1992. The caller, who identified himself as a manager at a local company, sounded angry and frantic. "I need you to come to our company and teach my employees how to write. I am sick and tired of always having to edit the letters they write to our customers. How soon can you get here?!"

I had met Mr. Murphy three weeks earlier at a workshop I had conducted through the American Management Association. The participants were mostly middle-level managers wanting to improve their business writing skills.

After the workshop, Mr. Murphy had returned to his office and started thinking about the three hours a day he spent correcting his staff's customer correspondence. Devoting this amount of time correcting others' work was ludicrous, but he couldn't send out letters that negatively represented the company. I set up a meeting with him for the next day.

As I walked into his office, he seemed a bit calmer than the previous day on the phone. But once he started talking and showing me his file full of letters to edit, I could sense his blood pressure rising. When I glanced at the sample letters, I was shocked! Maybe Fred's first students had found their way to this workplace! Their writing was full of errors—mostly grammatical mistakes and misspellings, but also severe issues with clarity, tone, and organization. I thought to myself, "Don't these people all have college degrees? How does someone get through sixteen years of school and still not be able to write well? When managers hire college graduates, don't they assume that the new employees can write at a proficient level?" Similar to Fred's "a-ha moments," this eye-opening event transformed my thinking about the need to improve the effectiveness of how we teach our students to write.

THE **Classroom–Corporate** CONNECTION

1. True or False: Many workplace memos and letters are never sent because they contain so many errors that the writers' employers can't let the written messages be seen by the public.

2. True or False: Writing skills are an advantage, not a necessity in the workplace.

3. Which of the following do you think is an important element of good writing from a company's perspective?
   a. Clarity
   b. Conciseness
   c. Completeness
   d. Tone
   e. Correctness
   f. All of the above

4. True or False: Writing well may enhance a new employee's ability to be promoted in the workplace, but it won't really make a big difference; in the end, it's the technical knowledge that counts.

5. Which of the following quotes is not accurate?
   a. "One of the most surprising features of the information revolution is that the momentum has turned back to the written word."
   b. "Two-thirds of salaried workers in large U.S. companies have jobs that require writing."
   c. "Professionals spend up to 30 percent of their days—more than two hours daily—writing."
   d. "The price tag to the American public to correct this deficiency [poor writing skills] is nearly $100 million per year."
   e. "One-fourth of applicants for manufacturing positions lack skills to fill out an application form."
   f. "Language is software for the mind."

Although I had previously taught in the public schools, I was now teaching professional and technical writing at the college level. So I knew the level of college students' writing had been on a rapid decline, but for some foolish reason, I thought that they magically grew out of their poor writing skills like it had something to do with maturity. I mean, they cut their hair and put on suits; shouldn't their writing skills also improve?

Seeing the need for someone to train people in industry on professional writing skills, I decided to start my own consulting company, Clear Communications. So for the last fifteen years, in addition to teaching, I have developed and presented training programs for local companies—from small companies to Fortune 500 companies.

I love teaching; I really do. But I also like working with companies. I find it challenging and exciting to meet new people and work in different industries. I also find that it gives me countless real-world examples to use in the classroom.

One company employed me for eight years, training their employees on all types of communication skills, but mostly professional writing. This was an international headquarters whose management had the sense to know that their employees must be empowered with the ability to make decisions and communicate information to clients and customers. I started working with employees in small groups of eight to ten. After meeting with managers and their employees, I identified the major problems in their business documents. The managers loudly insisted, "Grammar, grammar . . . teach it to them, PLEASE." Some shrugged and said, "Shoot, I'd just like them to have an awareness that their writing is important." Although I knew that grammar errors needed to be addressed, I also knew that this written communication problem was more than just grammar errors. But they wanted the grammar errors cleaned up immediately.

After fifteen years of training employees to improve their writing skills, I still ask, "Why don't Americans know basic English grammar?" In the classroom, I've had international students who knew English grammar rules and could use them correctly in writing better than native speakers. When my children were in middle school English classes that used the big grammar text (written in the early 1950s), I made them put it under their pillows at night, explaining to them that the information in that book could make or break them in their careers. So, at least, maybe some of the material would soak into their heads through osmosis.

My kids used to think that it was the worst curse in the world to have a mother who was also a teacher. For twelve years, I insisted that we sit down together and edit their papers. (Sounds a little bit like Fred's mother, don't you think?) My son, who, just like Fred, spent more time counting words than actually writing the essay, would say, "Oh, it doesn't matter. The teacher doesn't care about grammar; she just wants to see twelve hundred words." So thirty-five years later, some teachers are still assigning word-count essays, and some students, like my son and Fred, are still counting words. (Fortunately, most of my children's teachers from kindergarten through high school were exemplary. I know for a fact that their teachers worked extremely hard and did a great job teaching them how to write.)

So, I'm still asking, "Why don't many Americans know basic English grammar?" What made me think that teaching grammar to students at the college level would make a difference in their understanding of correct English usage? Is grammar like multiplication tables? Do we just need to go over and over and over the rules until they get it?

Throughout this chapter (as well as in subsequent chapters), I stress the importance of writing without grammar and spelling errors—from the career benefits of the writer to the respect for the reader. Every company I've worked for during the last fifteen years has insisted that I cover grammar in my training programs. And after reviewing employees' writing over the years, I am disheartened with how weak their writing skills are, particularly the number of grammar and spelling errors in their business documents sent to customers.

Are teachers teaching grammar in K–12? Fred assures me that most teachers are. Therefore, we need to examine how it is being taught and why so many adults in the workforce and students in our classrooms are still struggling with grammar and spelling issues.

Once in a while, I start to question my standards. Do we really need good grammar and spelling skills or am I just an "old dog"? My answer to the first question, even in the age of spelling and grammar checkers, is an astounding "YES" because employers *expect* their employees to professionally represent themselves and the company, and we still need to be smarter than any diagnostic software currently available. In order to convey information accurately and effectively, writers must follow standard usage conventions. (And the answer to the second question *might* be "yes," but I'm not ready to be put out to pasture just yet!)

Because so many students graduate from high school and aren't able to use standard English conventions correctly, we need to explore alternative approaches to teaching these skills (which are addressed in Fred's convention section in Chapter 5). As Einstein said, "Insanity: doing the same thing over and over again and expecting different results."

CONNECTION

In academic and workplace settings, written communication needs to follow the standard English conventions. As the number of errors increases, the consequences become more severe: a grade is lowered or a job is lost.

The more years I taught at the college level and consulted with local companies, while simultaneously helping my own children at home through their twelve years of public education, I started to realize that there's a chasm between some of what we're teaching our students and what they really need to know about writing. This was my second "a-ha moment" that made me question how we can more effectively teach our students how to write. The lessons I learned over the next several years conducting training in the workplace prompted me to reconsider the types of writing that we have students compose in the classroom.

How many of our students will actually use expository writing in their careers? My experience shows me that more than 90 percent of them will be producing a totally different type of writing for the rest of their lives—professional writing—writing that will be used in a career context. This type of writing should be required in all schools. Students need to see how their writing applies to the workplace. I am *not* saying it should replace academic writing, but I do think that some writing assignments should incorporate the concepts of professional writing.

So not only do we need to explore how we teach students to write—whether they are in elementary, secondary, or college—but also we need to introduce them to the types of writing they'll experience in the workplace. Also, we can't just keep teaching writing the same way we did fifty years ago. Technology has changed written communication with advances such as word processing; networking; collaborative writing software; Web sites; blogs; the integration of text, visuals, and sound; and so forth.

But the important core belief to remember is, "Everyone has the capacity to write, writing can be taught, and teachers can help students become better writers" (www.ncte.org, 2004). Absolutely!

Ways to give your classroom the **Corporate Edge**

- Make sure academic writing is balanced with opportunities to experiment with professional genres (e.g., proposals, letters, evaluations, reviews, summaries, etc.).

- With your students, design a take-home questionnaire asking parents what types of writing they do in their careers, how much time they spend per day writing, and what they think the biggest problems are with the writing they see in the workplace. Analyze the results and visually display them in a table. Share the findings with the parents and with other students in your school.

- Ask a local corporation to share samples of typical business writing. Analyze these with your students. Discuss genre, the time your students think might be required to produce each one, and the quality of the writing.

Answers to The Classroom–Corporate Connection

1. True; **2.** False; **3.** All of the above; **4.** False; **5.** a. Accurate. Stated by Hoyt Hudson, vice president of IS at InterAccess.   b. Accurate. Stated by College Board's National Commission on Writing 2004. c. Accurate. Stated by Andrea Kay, columnist. d. Inaccurate. The cost is really $250 million per year, as stated by the National Commission on Writing for America's Families. e. Accurate. Stated by Workforce 2020.   f. Accurate. Stated by David NcNally, author.

CHAPTER 2

Fundamentals

From your perspective

1. What did your best writing teachers have in common? Write down those characteristics. In what ways do you—or could you—incorporate those characteristics into your instruction?

2. Which piece of your own writing makes you feel the most proud? Why are you proud of that piece? Under what circumstances did you create it?

An Overview

If we expect to become competent in any of our endeavors—playing sports or a musical instrument, sewing, horseback riding—it is crucial that we understand the fundamentals and incorporate them into our work. The same is true with writing and with teaching writing. If *we* master the fundamentals of teaching writing, our students stand a better chance of becoming more effective writers. Students need to see and understand the connections between the fundamentals of school writing and the writing they will produce when they leave school.

Fred's World

How the National Writing Project Found and Saved Fred

I had never heard of the National Writing Project (NWP) prior to my participation. Part of the reason, in retrospect, was that it was still in its infancy. It began in 1974 as the Bay Area Writing Project at U.C. Berkeley, and very few people in New England were familiar with it in 1979. As stated on its Web site, "The National Writing Project is a professional development network that serves teachers of writing at all grade levels, primary through university, and in all subjects. The mission of the NWP is to improve student achievement by improving the teaching of writing and improving learning in the nation's schools" (www.nwp.org). NWP has programs in all fifty states and most states have more than one location.

All I knew when I applied was that in exchange for attending class six hours a day, five days a week for a month in the summer, I would receive six graduate credits from the University of New Hampshire and a stipend of $900, an enormous sum for a young teacher at that time. How could I refuse? Jack Heath, chair of the English Department at Phillips Exeter Academy, interviewed me, and I was accepted.

I had no idea what to expect that first day. Surrounded by nineteen other teachers from around our state, as well as a few program administrators, I was curious, hopeful, and somewhat intimidated. Surely, the other teachers present knew far more than I did. I questioned whether I had anything to offer such a group of experienced, quality teachers. The first hour involved typical introductions, a review of our purpose, directions to the bathrooms, and an overview of the daily schedule. After that, nothing resembled what I was used to from my college coursework. We wrote; we worked in groups to listen to what others had written and offer feedback; we listened to quality literature; we thought and thought some more. We began talking about what good writing instruction looked like, and we even engaged in one of those activities.

I left that first day excited and energized. I actually began, for the first time, to see myself not only as a teacher, but also as a writer. Clearly not the best writer in the group, but still, I saw myself as a writer. I wondered why sixteen years of writing in school had never given me the sensation that I *was* a writer as opposed to someone trying *to become* a writer. Just as important, the first inklings of the fundamentals of how a successful writing classroom should look and feel to students and teachers began to swirl in my mind.

As my month at NWP progressed, I realized just how fortunate I was. I received far more than I was capable of giving that summer. My undergraduate experience had not prepared me to teach writing, and I was still relying on the model my teachers had set for me. In addition, I had taught for only three years. Most of my colleagues that summer had far more teaching experience to draw upon. My conversations with them were enlightening. As they shared their ideas, approaches, techniques, solutions, and practical applications—as well as their frustrations—I realized that these were the types of conversations that could have helped me before I started teaching and during my first few years of teaching. Not only could I have avoided many of the pitfalls that I landed in, but I could have been far more successful in helping my students.

The first fundamental of a successful writing classroom became apparent the first week. Teachers must also be writers. I was fascinated that many of the participants at NWP wrote on a regular basis. They talked about articles they had written, editorials they had submitted to local newspapers, stories they had written, books they had undertaken. The notion of teachers of writing actually writing stunned me. Except for occasional letters to family and friends, I had not written a thing since graduating from college. Teachers didn't write, I believed. They taught! I had never considered writing if I didn't have to! Writing was tedious and strenuous. Who in their right minds wanted to write more essays?

Or was there another way to approach writing? I began to rethink why so many students disliked writing. Why was it that I disliked writing and why hadn't I written since I was required to in college? I realized that with the exception of fifth grade and one writing assignment in my senior year of high school, all of my writing assignments were determined by the teachers, and I had no interest at all in their topics. Because I felt so removed from the topics, I had no personal investment in the writing. All I cared about was receiving an acceptable grade. Thus, the second fundamental: If we want students to be engaged in their writing, we must allow them to have input on the topic. Otherwise, they may well be writing about a topic they don't know about or care about.

During the month at NWP, I interacted with people whom I had never heard of at the time, but who have since become household names in the world of writing. Working with us that summer were Donald Graves, Don Murray, Tom Newkirk, Jane Kearns, Jack C. Wilde, and a host of others. The work of Graves and Murray would subsequently become the backbone of our knowledge about how children learn to write. Though I did not realize it at the time, these two would gain a reputation as the godparents of the writing movement in America. As I work with young teachers around the country today, I am amazed and saddened at how many do not even recognize the names of these people. Without their work, we might still be teaching writing not *as a process* but as the *delivery of a product*. How can colleges today move students through their education programs without talking about Graves and Murray?

The third fundamental of a successful writing classroom is that writing must be taught as a process. In my first few years of teaching, writing process meant that I assigned the topic, due date, and length; the students wrote and handed in their papers; I graded the papers and handed them back. On to the next assignment. Process in the sense of planning, rehearsing, self-selecting topics, generating material, and revising text had not been part of my experience as a student and had never been mentioned in my education classes during my undergraduate years. Fortunately, most young teachers I have met in the past few years are aware of following the writing process and revising drafts, but I still meet some teachers who grade the first draft and move on. I meet others who talk about process, but when I observe their work with students in the classroom, there isn't much substance to the process. I have found that many teachers know the concept of process, but lack clarity on how to implement the process in a meaningful way in their classrooms.

The rest of the summer at NWP was an awakening experience. We explored the purpose of a student conference, when to conduct one, and what to do. We discussed the challenges of conferencing with students when, as a middle school or high school teacher, 150 students or more walked into our rooms every day. Elementary teachers faced the challenge of finding time to confer with twenty-eight students when teaching six or seven different subjects. We also talked about what good writing looked like and why we had such different reactions to the same piece of writing. It was as if I could hear some of my former teachers arguing in my head. How confusing this inconsistency must be for our students, I thought.

Perhaps my most important lesson that summer was the power and value of encouraging students to write from experience. This notion has gained a sense of common knowledge over the years, but for me, that summer, it was a stunning and fascinating idea. While the topics I had assigned my students were important to me, most of the subjects held no fascination for them. No wonder their writing was listless and distant.

This concept also led me to examine my own attitudes toward writing. My experience with writing for school had always centered around teacher-selected topics. As a result, my own writing for school was lackluster and distant. Writing felt like a chore, just like mowing the lawn and taking out the trash. I put it off as long as possible and did only what was required, nothing more. But when my piece about Mr. Klein and Tank emerged that summer, I became fully aware of the power of writing from experience.

Mr. Klein was my ninth-grade teacher from religious school, and Tank was the one true juvenile delinquent in our class of twelve. Their confrontations with each other were inspiring and, at times, frightening. I admired Tank for his courage and bravado. I had not thought about either one of them for many years, but the NWP prompt to write about "a memorable teacher" sparked memories of suffering through a year with a teacher who rivaled Attila the Hun and the student who was determined to overthrow him.

I approached this writing with a vigor and joy I had never before experienced. Each peer conference raised more questions, more recollections, and more laughs. I thoroughly enjoyed creating the story and was actually saddened when it was finished. Tom Newkirk, now in charge of the writing program at UNH, and I still talk and laugh about that piece. The experience taught me volumes about how people write successfully. I discovered the purpose and value of sharing my work with others and receiving their feedback. The notion of writing for an audience other than my teacher had never before occurred to me. I began to understand why we revise and what we can learn from our audience. My final draft delighted the entire group and provided me with a sense of accomplishment I had never before felt from my writing.

During my first three years of teaching, I had not once written with my students. Writing with students had never been modeled for me, and therefore, I assumed it was not necessary or valuable. In my previous experiences, students wrote; teachers graded. However, through NWP, I discovered that writing, sharing my work with a small group of colleagues, listening to their response to my writing, revising my work based on that feedback, and sharing again was a powerful learning tool.

I was able to share my work because of the trusting environment we enjoyed at NWP. How would I go about creating that trust in my own classroom? I was experiencing firsthand what my students needed if they were to become proficient writers, and now my challenge was to recreate the same atmosphere for them. How would I create an environment in which my students would feel safe and secure enough to take the risk and share their work with their peers? Would my students find topics to write about that would energize them like Mr. Klein had energized me? Did they have the experiences from which to draw upon? Was I willing to let the students become the assessors instead of me? Most important, was I willing to trust my students enough to let the magic of writing take place in my classroom? Not knowing what it would look like, and realizing I would be losing some control, this was an enormous step to take, but one I knew was essential if I wanted to change my instruction. The change had to begin with me. In reality, it had already begun.

Steps to take right now

- Go to www.nwp.org on the Internet and find out who sponsors Writing Project in your state. Call or email the contact and request information about next summer's program.

- Reflect on how your teaching of writing has changed from your first year to the present. If it hasn't, what are you doing well? How do you know? What is your biggest challenge in improving your students' writing?

- Speak with your colleagues about how they teach writing. Many of them possess a wealth of information and ideas and will be very willing to share with you. How do they motivate their students? Do they allow their students to create additional drafts in order to improve the grade? Do you? How do they—and you—determine the grade?

Lynna's World

As Fred learned, the fundamentals to teach writing include writing with students, engaging students in their topic selections, exploring writing as a process, and encouraging writing from experience. There are also some fundamentals in writing itself. First, and key to all learning, is motivation—a person has to want to do well. This section will address the issue of motivation and highlight the other fundamentals of professional writing: reader-centeredness, clarity, completeness, accuracy, conciseness, objectivity, document design, style, tone, and elimination of errors. This overview will provide you with a basic understanding of what professional writing is so that you feel more comfortable incorporating this type of writing in your classroom.

Why We Need to Write Effectively in the Workplace

According to T. A. Murphy, former Chairman of General Motors, "The common denominator in business and in management is people and relationships with people . . . in the final analysis, communication is all important . . . effective communications can make the difference between success and failure, or at least it can determine the degree of success" (www.oe2u.com, 2008). The University of Pittsburgh conducted a survey of recruiters from companies with more than fifty thousand employees; communication skills were listed as the most important criterion in choosing managers (www.mindtools.com, 2008). Do your students know this?

THE Classroom–Corporate CONNECTION

1. True or False: Many students' personal lives are filled with writing—Facebook messages, email messages, blog entries, instant messaging, and text messages.

2. True or False: Professional writing is basically the same as academic writing with only minor differences that aren't significant.

3. True or False: In Ohio, a person faced foreclosure of his home due to a government worker's one-letter spelling error on a title search.

4. Which of the following sentences best reflects effective writing for the workplace?
   a. Anyone eating in this area will be dealt with accordingly.
   b. The intrinsic labyrinth of wires needs disentangled.
   c. The liquid contents of the container should be disgorged via the spout by the operator.
   d. Illumination is required to be extinguished on these premises on the termination of daily activity.
   e. i will give u the report this monday btw what time's good for u
   f. None of the above.

5. True or False: "U.S. employers said that a fourth of workers fail to meet the writing requirements of their positions."

Communication skills can be divided into three categories: oral, written, and interpersonal. Organizations expect their employees to be able to run meetings; give presentations; and work well with customers, coworkers, and supervisors. Likewise, organizations expect that the employees can write emails, memos, letters, and reports that are clear, concise, complete, and accurate. The writing needs to represent professionally the organization as well as the employee.

Companies that I've worked with over the years value good communicators because they know that they *save* the company money as well as *make* the company money. Communicating clearly the first time eliminates costly errors: Inaccurate information can result in the improper operation of a machine, a poor tone can result in an angry customer. Students need to understand that it's in their best interest to improve their writing skills. If they want to be promoted, they need to realize that they will hit more than a glass ceiling climbing the career ladder if they can't write well.

For example, at one company, the president told me that their technical director, Mike, was a superb employee but his writing skills were so poor (as evidenced by several emails) that he could not promote Mike any higher in the company. I met Mike and the president was right; he was an exemplary employee: a hard worker with great people skills and sharp technical skills. In fact, he probably knew more than anyone in the company when it came to technical expertise on the automated equipment. But I understood why the president thought Mike couldn't professionally represent the company to potential customers. Mike's poor writing skills gave customers the impression that he and the company weren't conscientious about their work, didn't pay attention to detail, weren't hard workers, or just didn't care enough about them as customers.

CONNECTION

In academic and workplace settings, possessing strong writing skills has benefits. In the classroom, writing effectively will result in higher grades, access to higher-level classes, and increased achievement in content areas. In the workplace, strong writing skills will result in employability and promotions, resulting in higher salaries.

Sell your students on the fact that refining and improving their communication skills will provide them with the power and knowledge to communicate effectively as well as put more money in their pockets.

Differences between Professional Writing and Academic Writing (Purpose, Audience, and Format)

While your students currently may not create much workplace correspondence, accuracy and effectiveness are crucial components of writing in your classroom as well. So although I would like different types of workplace documents added to the English curriculum, it's also important to see that many of the skills taught in academic writing also apply to professional writing. But first we'll examine the differences between the two.

Professional writing is a *specialized* field of communication whose purpose is to convey information accurately and effectively. It differs from other types of writing in purpose, audience, and format. I think it's important to understand these basic differences so that we can write accordingly. Journalistic writing is different from poetry, which is different from academic writing, and so on.

Purpose

In school we used to read a book and then sit around and discuss it. One person thought the bell tower symbolized the passing of time. Another person thought it stood for the pendulum of life. That type of discussion usually has no place in an organization. We have to write so clearly that there's only one interpretation. In school, students may have the opportunity for creative writing, but that type of writing usually doesn't exist in the workplace. The students' persuasive essays and compare-and-contrast essays are more like the types of writing that will be required of them in their careers. Clarity, however, is an essential component of all types of writing.

An example illustrating lack of clarity that I frequently use in my courses is the sign that's in most classrooms or areas in the workplace: "No food or drink in this area." I ask the participants to come up with different interpretations of this sign. Groups usually come up with some of these versions:

1. You can't have any food and drink in the area right by the sign, but you can have food and drink in other areas of the room.
2. You can't bring any food or drink into the room (no crackers, no water bottles, etc.).
3. You can bring food and drink into the room, but there's no eating or drinking (even though the words *eating* and *drinking* aren't in the sentence).
4. No food or drink is offered in this room, so you'll need to bring your own.

Another example of lack of clarity I use deals with the fiasco in Florida during the 2000 presidential election. Many counties had recently changed to the large-print ballots. Naturally, the new ballots had more pages than the original ballots. However, the instructions had not been changed. They still said, "Mark a vote for a candidate on each page." Since the large-print version made the presidential candidate roster expand to two pages, some voters marked a candidate on the first page and another one on the second page. Now, you might be thinking, "What idiot doesn't know that you can only vote for one person for president?" My point though is why display directions for people that we really don't mean for them to follow? (Poor document design also interfered with the clarity of the ballots.)

Audience

In expository writing (i.e., academic essays), the audience is almost always the same: the teacher. In professional writing, the audience varies: in the industry/not in the industry; in the organization/not in the organization; colleagues; subordinates; superiors; customers; technical/nontechnical; knowledgeable/less knowledgeable; and so forth. Students, therefore, need opportunities to write for different audiences on a regular basis.

We write differently for these diverse types of audiences. For example, with a less knowledgeable audience we should

- Use a common term, not a technical term.
- Define terms.
- Use an analogy with a term or concept.
- Give specific examples.
- Incorporate visuals where needed.
- Use transitions and headings and subheadings.

We need to analyze our audience by asking these questions: What do they already know about the subject? What do they need to know? How are they likely to react? What is my relationship with that person? These questions help us as writers to identify the appropriate tone, language, information, and channel of communication. We also use more basic psychology in professional writing than in academic types of writing by being sensitive to our audience's needs. In professional writing, if we think the audience will be hostile toward our message, we need to anticipate and answer the opposing objections. Additionally, we need to take cultural differences into account—cultural expectations and practices—by keeping our messages simple and avoiding idioms or other figures of speech. Someone from another country probably won't know what it means to "get a company back on its feet." Basically we need to look at the demographics (gender, age, income level, education, etc.) and psychographics (attitudes, personality, and other psychological characteristics). In organizations we expect writers to modify their writing for the audience. So a good question to ask ourselves is, "Do students have opportunities in the classroom to write for different audiences, or is the audience always the same?" (Fred will talk more about audience in Chapter 5.)

We analyze the audience before we write because the reader is the most important person: The reader determines whether or not our message has achieved its purpose. We can't take the attitude of "Well, it's your fault if you can't figure it out." Or "Get over it if it offends you . . . too bad . . . move on." As writers in the workplace, we need to be professional and courteous at all times. Even if we're angry with how stupid people can be, we can't vent our anger; it rarely improves the situation. Student writers also need to be courteous when they write. So another good question to ask ourselves is, "Do we teach our students to express their displeasure, anger, or resentment tactfully?"

CONNECTION

In both settings, there are times when the writer must follow a specified format. Whether the writing occurs for a science lab in school or a performance review in the workplace, writers must learn to adhere to the teacher's or employer's structure. Failure to do so could result in negative consequences.

Format

In expository writing, writers have more freedom to structure their writing than writers in the workplace. In organizations, we need to follow their format. For example, one company I worked for wanted their associate minutes (performance reviews) done a certain way. Now, personally I thought it included some unnecessary information, but it didn't matter what I thought. We had to follow the company's format. Many of us may think that this is too restrictive; we want our students to be more creative. But this is how it's done in industry. We can be creative within the company's structure, but we have to follow the company's format. Similarly, students in your classroom use your format for spacing, margins, and placement of names, date, title of assignment, and so on. And students should be held accountable for following your format. So I would suggest that some of your assignments be flexible and others more structured with strict guidelines.

Sins of Professional Writing

Professional writing and academic writing need to meet high standards due to the consequences that can result. In professional writing, decisions are made from what is written, and therefore, money is involved. Also, we can be sued for what we write. In the classroom, students' level of writing determines what grade they'll receive.

The first sin of professional writing is **Neglecting the Reader**: failing to analyze the knowledge level; leaving information out so that a decision is based on incomplete information; using a poor tone that is offensive to the reader; or having poor organization so that someone has to work hard to figure out what's being said. It is, in essence, just a general disrespect for the reader.

The second sin is **Fuzziness**: using vague words or the wrong words. For example:

Anyone caught smoking in this area will be dealt with accordingly.

In the workplace, we can't write company policy that can be interpreted in different ways. This statement is too vague. What will happen to the people who are caught smoking? Will they be written up, fired, or given an evil eyeball? (Let alone the problem with "this area," which was discussed earlier.)

And then there's the type of fuzziness that includes using the wrong words. Too many times, writers don't trust the vocabulary of their own voice. They think they need to impress people with their important vocabulary so the readers will think the document was written by someone really smart. The writer then ends up using words incorrectly. For example,

The intrinsic labyrinth of wires must first be disentangled.

Nobody should have to work hard to read a sentence or have to read it twice to try to guess the meaning. You'd be surprised how many people don't know the meaning of *intrinsic*. When I use this example at companies, participants usually say that *intrinsic* means complicated. And, why not just use the everyday word *maze* instead of the ten-dollar word *labyrinth*? And where did the word *disentangled* come from?

My son always liked to use a thesaurus so he could insert several ten-dollar words in his high school essays. (And with word processing programs today, repeatedly using a thesaurus requires nothing more than a click of the mouse.) His writing usually ended up sounding awkward: Sentences didn't make sense, I had a hard time reading it, and his writing didn't sound natural. In the workplace, this type of writing is very dangerous.

People could interpret directions differently, resulting in lost time, money, and energy. Likewise, in schools, teachers want students to have clarity in their writing so the reader has a clear understanding of the message.

The next sin is **Wordiness**: being redundant, using meaningless words, having unnecessary repetition, or using wordy phrases. For example:

> The liquid contents of the container should then be disgorged via the spout by the operator.

I believe it would be simpler to say, "Empty the container." Now granted, if it's important that it be the operator who empties the container, then that information needs to be included. And, if there are solids and liquids in the container and only the liquids are to be emptied, then, yes, that information needs to stay in the sentence. Additionally, if there is more than one opening on the container and we want the liquids to go through the spout only, then, yes, we also would include that information. Another example:

> Illumination is required to be extinguished on these premises on the termination of daily activity.

When I show this sentence to groups at companies, I always have a handful of people who think this sentence is talking about putting out a fire rather than referring to turning out the lights at the end of the day. There is no reason to write like this. If it's so imperative for people to make themselves feel important and build up their egos, they need to do it in another manner, not in professional writing.

Wordiness also includes phrases like "due to the fact that" and "the point of the matter is." Going back to counting words, my son loves these phrases. He can use five words instead of one (*because*) and six words instead of zero (since the entire phrase should be deleted). In professional writing we need to eliminate all unnecessary words. For example, "on a daily basis" should just be "daily." We also need to eliminate redundancy like "in the year 1996" instead of just writing "in 1996."

People in the workplace are busy; they don't have time to read our autobiographies. Say what has to be said and no more. Yes, I know, this is easier said than done. But trim sentences are like trim bodies; it takes a lot of hard work! We, as teachers, are also busy people. So let's start when kids are young and teach them to be specific and concise in their language, so maybe we'll have more time to do something fun on the weekends.

The fourth sin is **Awkwardness**. Again, no one should have to work hard to read our writing or have to guess at the message. We can avoid awkwardness by writing the way we talk and reading our messages slowly out loud. I'm a professional writer and I am still amazed at how many errors I catch on email messages before clicking "send"—just by reading the message slowly out loud.

Here's an example of an email I received recently from a college student:

> Prof I have nown about the test but would like to know in the event that its necessary to at that time. Please advice if that's okay.

Now, you tell me . . . what does the writer want? Your guess is as good as mine. How many times have we read a student's paper and scratched our head, muttering, "What?"

Passive Voice is the fifth sin, though some experts debate this point. The active voice ("I performed the evaluation") is more concise and direct than the passive voice ("The evaluation was done by me"). Passive voice makes writing wordy or evasive. I don't think it's a mortal sin to write in passive voice; in the workplace there are times when it is appropriate to write using the passive voice. (Shoot, I hear government officials say this all the time: "Mistakes were made.") However, we should write in active voice whenever possible. I understand many students have difficulty understanding the difference between passive and active voice, but let's begin the discussion at a young age so eventually it starts to make sense for them.

The last sin is **Errors**: grammar, spelling, mechanics, and accuracy. These, I believe, *are* mortal sins in professional writing. Stephen King, in his book *On Writing* (2000), states that to be a good writer we need a toolbox, and one of the tools on the top shelf should be grammar and spelling skills. Grammar rules apply so that our meaning is clear.

Use these sample emails as examples of how poor grammar affects communication in both the understanding of the message and the impression of the writer.

> . . . last time i talk to you and i email for you to take the exam earlier but i never herd from you or they cant find the exam can you please tell me what need to do.

> I had a family emergency and had to leave out of town. I'm not sure if i can make it to class tommarow. if I am unable to make it to classI am forwarding you my resume. I would really appreciated if you evaluate the resume for me. Plz replay back asap. If that's okay. . . . Thank you.

> . . . I wanted u to check if the imformation i put in my clain letter is accurated and i if i did correctly format vise. And, information vise once again thanks for understanding the issue.

Let's not spare any words: These writers look illiterate! In reality, they are bright students, but they don't understand how important writing is when communicating with others. When this attitude and skill level carries over into the workplace, the consequences can be very detrimental to their careers.

CONNECTION

The same sins apply in both worlds. Neglecting the reader, fuzziness, wordiness, awkwardness, passive voice, and errors need to be avoided in school writing and in workplace writing.

Effective Characteristics of Professional Writing

After reviewing what not to do, it's important to flip the coin and look at what we should be doing in professional writing. Essentially, the effective characteristics of professional writing are listed in Figure 2.1, as well as their corresponding characteristics in academic

Figure 2.1 Effective Characteristics of Professional and Academic Writing

Professional Writing	Characteristic	Academic Writing
Write from a position of knowledge, check all figures, and spell names correctly.	ACCURACY	Ensure that information is accurate; include a bibliography; and (for older students) cite sources using MLA format.
Write so clearly the message is easy to read and there's only one way to interpret it.	CLARITY	Write so clearly the reader understands the message and all questions are answered.
Include all the information that the reader needs.	COMPLETENESS	Meet all requirements of the assignment and include evidence that supports the statements or positions.
Say what needs to be said and no more; avoid redundancy and unnecessary repetition; and eliminate wordy phrases. (However, never sacrifice completeness for conciseness.)	CONCISENESS	Aim to substantiate all statements rather than meet a word count. Use precise language in place of vague language (e.g., *good, nice, thing*).
Choose quality paper, print, and layout; use headings/subheadings and bulleting of information; include visuals.	DOCUMENT DESIGN	Confirm that handwriting is easily legible or word-processed documents are appropriately spaced; use margins, as well as charts/graphs, when useful.
Correct grammar, punctuation, and spelling errors.	ELIMINATION OF ERRORS	Ask others to proofread the writing.
Make no assumptions; use facts and logic.	OBJECTIVITY	Unless requested in the assignment, avoid "I think."
Meet the readers' needs; use the appropriate style and tone; and be courteous and respectful.	READER-CENTEREDNESS	Consider who the reader will be (teacher, student, community person, etc.) and use language and tone appropriate for that reader.
Use a conversational style and positive tone.	STYLE AND TONE	Consider the reader throughout the paper.

writing. (A more in-depth explanation of these characteristics appears in Chapter 5 in relation to Fred's discussion of the six traits of writing.)

Not surprisingly, the characteristics of both worlds are very similar, so if you're teaching these skills, you have already taken the first steps to prepare your students for writing in the workplace.

Ways to give your classroom the **Corporate Edge**

- Assign students to interview three adults (relatives or neighbors), asking if they recall times when poor writing impacted their work or their coworkers'. Provide an opportunity for students to share their findings with the class.

- Require students to bring in samples of writing errors from newspaper articles, Internet sites, blog entries, and other popular sources. They can also take pictures of signs with usage errors. Have students design a visual display of the items.

- Provide students with an article and ask them to decide what graphics would help highlight the information being presented. Then ask students to revise the information by inserting bullets, headings, and subheadings.

- Have students examine the differences between academic and workplace writing. For example, assign a piece of writing that is meant for an audience outside of school. Incorporate email assignments that deal with one issue and have students write emails to a classmate, teacher, and principal.

- Go to http://owl.english.purdue.edu. Select a grade level and then click *Grammar and Mechanics*. Ask students to read the information in one of the areas listed under *Grammar and Mechanics,* write a summary of that information, and develop an exercise for their classmates. In small groups, students can present their information and administer the exercise.

Answers to The Classroom–Corporate Connection

1. True **2.** False **3.** True ("Clerk's error jeopardizes family's home," *Columbus Dispatch,* May 31, 2008, by Sarah Pulliam) **4.** f **5.** False. According to College Board's National Commission on Writing, 2004, "US employers said that a third of workers fail to meet the writing requirements of their positions."

CHAPTER 3

Writing Environments

From your perspective

1. *During your school years, which classes made you comfortable and which ones made you nervous? What caused your comfort or anxiety?*

2. *On a scale of 1–10, low to high, how would you rank your own classroom as a safe and comfortable place for students? How do you think your students would rank your classroom? If you're courageous, ask your students to score you anonymously and compare their scores with what you predicted.*

3. *Identify three strategies for making your classroom even safer.*

An Overview

The environment in which people write often determines the quality of their work. If we expect students to take risks with their writing in the classroom, they must feel safe and respected. How do we create such an environment? And while classroom and workplace environments differ significantly, both impact a person's writing. While schools often provide a safer environment than the workplace, students should at least be aware of how the workplace environment functions so they won't be caught by surprise.

Fred's World

Miss Beavers and Miss Hudson

I've often thought about my fifth-grade teacher, Miss Hudson, and my eighth-grade English teacher, Miss Beavers. I worked my tail off for Miss Hudson, and it wasn't because I was young and afraid not to. I knew she truly cared about my work, my success, and me. Miss Beavers, on the other hand, would have been happier if I had spent the year at home or in suspension. Granted, I wasn't the model student during my junior high years, but for some of my junior high teachers I did work hard.

When I think about the writing I produced for those two teachers, I'm not surprised by the differences. For Miss Beavers, I was writing only to complete an assignment. I did the minimum required, plagiarized when possible, and waited until the last minute to begin and complete my assignments. I particularly remember the book reports we were required to complete for her every other Friday. The best part was that the "reports" required that we fill in two boxes, each about two by four inches, on a sheet of mimeographed paper. In one box we described the plot, and in the other box we explained what we liked and/or disliked about the book. This biweekly assignment, in retrospect, may have been the most uninspiring writing assignment I ever received, and I've spent a number of years in formal schooling. I doubt Miss Beavers ever read our entries and, even worse, I didn't care if she read mine or not.

In retrospect, Miss Beavers was nearing retirement, and there is no doubt in my mind that she was just passing the time until her magical day arrived. She rarely smiled, never laughed, and complained bitterly about what miserable students we were. Her shrill voice, yelling or lecturing us on some irrelevant topic, was painful. I left eighth grade thinking writing was a boring task that students were forced to endure throughout our remaining years of school. No wonder some students dropped out of school once they turned sixteen!

With Miss Hudson, however, it was a different story. She spent time in class explaining what she expected in a quality piece of writing. And while she mentioned items like a table of contents, bibliography, illustrations, and so forth, she spent most of the time talking about quality work, helping us find interesting information to write about, and showing us how to organize our reports so that they proceeded in a logical manner. She provided us with time to figure out our topics, to research our topics, and to talk with other students about our reports. Additionally, she met with every one of us, over and over, asking us questions, offering suggestions, and encouraging us to do our best work. Every writing assignment I produced was the result of hours of work. I asked Miss Hudson and my mother for help and suggestions, and I took pride in the end result. When I received my paper back, it contained Miss Hudson's impressions of my writing: what she liked, what she thought needed further development, and careful attention to the details of spelling and grammar. While my grades did not always reflect the effort, I knew I had done my best and took pride in that knowledge. I also knew Miss Hudson had read my paper with sincere interest and had taken time in offering her feedback.

Miss Hudson remains one of my models for good teachers. She was strict yet fair; she also maintained a sense of humor that let us know she was human. She had high expectations for every student, expected quality work, and showed her disappointment when she received less than a student's best effort. She loved teaching writing and accepted the hard work that it requires from a teacher.

So what can we learn from Miss Hudson and Miss Beavers? How do we create writing classrooms in today's schools in which students strive for excellence and are willing to do the work excellence requires? How do we create an environment in which students seek input and are willing to revise? And how do we create classrooms in which students desire to write and become competent writers?

Teacher as Writer

Dynamic writing classrooms begin with a teacher who is also a writer. This may be the single most powerful strategy in our toolbox to encourage students to write. Not writing with my students may have been my single, biggest mistake my first few years of teaching. In her book *Radical Reflections,* Mem Fox (1993) writes, "If we are so foolish as to dare to teach writing without even writing ourselves, we are treading with arrogance on shaky ground."

Consider the message we give to students when we assign writing to them and then either walk around the room or, worse, sit at our desk and grade papers or check email. Subconsciously, or perhaps consciously, they realize that writing is something students do and adults do not. Students ask, "If this is so important, then why don't I ever see adults writing?" But when teachers assign writing and then say to the students, "Unless it's an emergency, no questions for me for the next fifteen minutes because I'll be writing," students begin to understand that writing is important for all of us. They learn that writing is a skill we all continue to develop.

As Don Graves (1994) wrote in *A Fresh Look at Writing,* "Students can go a lifetime and never see another person write, much less show them how to write. Yet it would be unheard of for an artist not to show her students how to use oils by painting on her own canvas, or for a ceramist not to demonstrate how to throw clay on a wheel and shape the material himself. Writing is a craft. It needs to be demonstrated to your students in your classroom, which is a studio, from choosing a topic to finishing a final draft. They need to see you struggle to match your intentions with the words that reach the page."

Our struggle, as I've heard from so many teachers and myself as well, is where do we find time to write? As teachers, our days are packed. We provide instruction; design lessons; grade papers; counsel students; discipline students; modify lessons to meet the needs of our special education students; return phone calls to parents; work with struggling students during our plan period; and attend far too many meetings before, during, and after school. I do realize that we may not be able to write *every* time our students do or during *every* plan period, but it's crucial that our students see us write. So when do we find time to write?

First, we have to ask ourselves whether or not we believe writing with our students is valuable enough to make it a priority. In a writing classroom, next to having students write, it should be our number one priority. When I began writing with my students, it changed the entire nature of our discussions. No longer was I the "wise, all-knowing teacher." For the first time, I understood their struggles as writers because I was experiencing the same ones.

"How do I get started?"

"I don't have anything to write about."

"I don't know how to conclude."

"This topic is stupid."

"Is my paper any good?"

Each day my students witnessed their teacher working not as a teacher but as a writer and the interactions we had as a result were remarkable. They gained a sense of confidence and importance they had never experienced in a classroom.

If we believe in the value of writing with our students, we will find the time to write. I found it in three places:

1. At the same time my students were writing. Students don't like to be interrupted when they're writing. Likewise, I told my students not to interrupt me. I reserved the first ten to fifteen minutes for myself and only then made myself available to students who had questions or problems. As tempting as it may have been, I didn't grade papers; I didn't finish my weekly Plan Book; I didn't walk around the room. I sat and wrote.

2. During my plan period. When I was not required to attend a meeting, I often spent most of my plan time talking with colleagues, grading papers, or reading the newspaper. I realized that I could talk with colleagues during lunch and after school, and I could read the paper at home. Even if I tried to grade papers, I was often distracted by a variety of interruptions (intercoms, colleagues, phone calls, etc.), so I wasn't accomplishing that much. I decided to commit part of my plan period to writing. And it worked. I stayed in my classroom, closed the door, and devoted at least twenty minutes to writing.

3. At home in the evening. This was simple. The TV went off; the writing went on. And I'm not suggesting that I never watched TV or that I wrote every night. But I tried to devote some time two to three evenings a week to writing. I was stunned by how much I could produce in just twenty to thirty minutes. Moreover, my students were impressed as well and began coming to class asking, "What did you write last night, Mr. Wolff?"

We all know how easy it is to find excuses for why we don't have time to write. But if we are determined to improve our teaching and, therefore, improve our students' learning, we will find the time.

Sharing Our Writing

After we begin writing with our students, the next crucial step is to share our writing with them. I learned the value of this twice. The first, as I discussed earlier, was during my summer with the National Writing Project.

My second awakening was a surprise. The school year after NWP, I began to write with my students and share my writing with them. I initially anticipated they would be impressed, students would tell me what a great writer I was, and I would feel great. I was not prepared for what transpired. First, I found myself nervous. Preparing to read my writing to my students actually made me perspire! And I NEVER perspire. "What must it be like for the students to share their writing with their peers?" I wondered.

At first, they liked my writing, but then they started to ask me questions! Slowly and cautiously at first; after all, how often do students have an opportunity to question a teacher? After a few days of the cautious questions, the real ones arose. "Why did you have the character do that, Mr. Wolff?" "That doesn't seem real to me. No kid would do that!" Or "What did Mr. Klein do with Tank's hat? We want to know!" I was stunned. Oftentimes, I didn't have answers to their questions. Amazingly, they had the answers for me. The students began to direct my writing. Suddenly, we had gone from a teacher with students to a group of readers and writers. They began to ask each other questions about their writing, and for once, no one felt offended or defensive.

While I didn't realize it at the time, I had served as the model for how to share a piece of writing and how to listen and respond to my readers. If I intended to ask my students to trust each other with their writing, I had to trust them as well with my own writing. And it worked. Conference groups took on new lives that were productive, invigorating, and focused.

In both instances, I learned that sharing my writing was a motivating factor for producing my best work. It enabled me to hear what my reader wanted to know. And it provided me with the information I needed in order to begin my revision.

I'm not suggesting that we complete every assignment we give to our students every year. That is probably not realistic. But I encourage you to complete some of your own assignments each year. If for no other reason, it enables us to determine if our assignments are reasonable. If *we* struggle with the assignment, imagine what it is like for our students who lack the background knowledge we possess. If I had tried to complete some of the research papers I assigned to my first students, I would have known very quickly how foolish the assignments were.

Allowing Students Privacy Not to Share

With all that I've just said, I need to acknowledge that there were times I allowed my students to choose not to share their writing. I found out early on that when students write in a trusting environment, they will write about topics that will startle adults and children alike. Abuse of all kinds, fears, dreams, and a host of other topics often create powerful writing. But at the same time, many students—and many adults—for obvious reasons prefer to keep these events private. I told my students, "You are allowed to refrain from sharing on one condition. Before the week is out, you need to share your private writing either with me or with one other person (adult or peer) who will provide you with feedback. Then you must share the feedback you received with me."

This approach guaranteed two things. First, if the writing addressed a topic or situation that was potentially harmful to the student or others, someone would now know about it and, hopefully, report it to those who needed to know. I have come to believe that if students write about something that is potentially damaging, that is their way of asking for help. Instead of acting out as some students may do, many students will choose to write about it.

The second guarantee was that every week, all my students received feedback about their writing and I was able to monitor what type of feedback they received and who provided it. Even if the writing was personal, the writer shared, received feedback, and reported to me.

Setting Rules for Feedback

I've spent time in many classrooms where students read their writing to a group of peers, ask for feedback, and receive comments such as, "That was really good, April. I liked it a lot." Maybe April walks away thinking she's done a great job, but deep down, she knows the truth: The feedback she received was useless.

Other times, students receive a written comment from a teacher like the one my fifth-grade friend Kathleen received: "I'm really impressed with this work! Your talent as a writer is growing very strong! Bravo!" Now what is Kathleen supposed to do with that information? As Kathleen said to me, "Ever since first grade, all my teachers have told me what a good writer I am. None of them ever tell me how to improve." In this instance, Kathleen didn't even know what she had done well or why her teacher was impressed!

Here are a few clues for helping students—and teachers!—provide honest and useful feedback.

1. Model what it means to give feedback!   If we don't teach them, students often do not know what to say other than "I liked that" or "That was boring." Provide students, through modeling, with the tools and terminology they need in order to provide feedback that is worth listening to. Talk with your students about various aspects of the writing to respond to (e.g., details, clarity and focus of the work, the impact the writing had on you as a reader, quality of verbs, images conveyed, crafting of sentences, organization of the writing, etc.). In Kathleen's situation, her teacher should have told her that he was impressed with her verbs and which verbs impressed him. Thus, Kathleen would have known what she had done well in her writing so she would know what to continue doing. Furthermore, he could have shown her how to modify her sentence structure, since she began most sentences with the same word (*the*). A more detailed discussion of modeling appears in Chapter 5.

2. Provide students with plenty of opportunities to practice.   Students need to practice offering feedback on samples written by students (or adults) from outside the class. This is safe; no one in the class is embarrassed by hearing negative reactions to their writing; and students are able to hear how others, including the teacher, would respond to a piece of writing. Practice, practice, practice! Then they can try with peers.

So where do you find papers for students to practice providing feedback? This year, save papers your students write for use in future years. In the meantime, swap papers with other teachers and just remove the names. Or write some of your own that are purposefully weak and/or strong in specific areas, and tell your students these were written by students from previous years. The intent is for all students to have a chance to practice offering feedback before they provide feedback to their peers.

3. Help students develop specific comments or questions.   After a student has read a piece aloud to a group of four or five peers, have the other students in the group write a specific positive comment and either a suggestion or a question about something that was unclear. Then students turn in these papers to the writer. Eventually, before the period is over, collect the written slips so you can review what students are writing and monitor the feedback. Initially, you and your students may want to develop a basic list of possible comments for students to use. For example:

- Great verbs! (Students identify the verbs.)
- Terrific focus on one incident and exploding that moment.
- You may want to change some of your sentence beginnings. Almost all of them begin with a pronoun or an article.
- You created great suspense on page X. I had to keep reading.

4. Help students obtain feedback.   Teach your students how to focus on a specific skill or passage they wish to improve and how to ask for feedback on that section. The writer's job, prior to sharing the writing, is to inform the other students what feedback would be helpful. A student may say, "I'd like your input on whether or not I'm clear about my meaning in paragraph one" or "I want to know if my arguments are convincing you to side with me." Now the readers have something on which to focus.

5. Encourage discussions.   Once the written feedback is completed, have the students provide oral feedback with plenty of discussion from the group. Three to four minutes per paper is usually sufficient to get across the key points. Again, we need to model what those discussions look and sound like.

6. Help students create feedback guidelines.   The students, with your guidance, can create their own rules about this. But generally, ban "That's stupid" or "That's boring" or other comments that only discourage and embarrass the writer.

In God—and the Teacher—We Trust

If you want to create a climate like Miss Hudson's, the simple truth is *you* have to lead the way. *You* have to find ways that will allow your students to trust you. After all, how many of us are willing to trust a stranger? For our students, starting on the first day of school, we are strangers to them. By going out on a limb and being the first to write, the first to share, the first to ask for and listen to feedback, the first to take that feedback and infuse it into our next draft, the first to show genuine care and concern for our students and their work, we can create classrooms in which students feel safe enough to write powerfully about important topics. Our students need, and deserve, more Miss Hudsons.

- Reflect upon teachers who wrote with you and shared their writing with you. What was it like for you, as a student, to see and hear your teacher's writing? How was that classroom different from others? Write one of those teachers a letter—or place a phone call—and ask that teacher for some hints in teaching writing. Think about classrooms in which you were encouraged to take risks with your writing. How did your teacher encourage those risks? What did it feel like? Were there times when taking risks in writing resulted in negative consequences (e.g., a low grade)? What did you learn from those experiences?

- Ask your students if they feel comfortable trying new approaches in writing. Ask them to give you examples of times they have taken risks in writing. Do you model *how* to try new approaches in front of your students? How does that feel? What happens when those approaches are not successful for you? For your students?

Lynna's World

What does it mean to be a confident and competent writer in the workplace? To start, it means that employees can write from a position of knowledge, meet deadlines, be an independent writer, and incorporate all the characteristics of effective communication.

However, I don't think we should duplicate the workplace in a school; after all, the classroom is supposed to be an environment that is conducive to learning. Albert Einstein said, "I never teach my students; I only attempt to provide the conditions in which they can learn." So, as teachers, what are these conditions? Well, first of all, we need to provide an atmosphere where one mistake won't make a student fail the course. Second, we need to provide students with the proper tools and the opportunity for practice and feedback so that they have the knowledge and experience to feel confident in their writing ability. Third, we need to maintain rigor and standards in the quality of the writing we want the students to produce. And fourth, we need to motivate them to want to write well by showing them how they will benefit from developing strong writing skills.

Basically, we need to prepare students to feel confident, proficient, and positive about their writing skills so they can be successful in any school or work environment.

I am a technical writer, so I do understand the challenges students/employees experience when they write. Those struggles are fresh in my mind when I work with them on their writing assignments: What do I want to write about? How do I organize it? How do I start? What will others think about me? How will the readers react? These are the same questions that Fred's students raise.

Writing Documents in the Workplace

I frequently show students samples of manuals I've written or examples of written documents I've composed for companies' letter libraries. This certainly gives me more credibility from the students' perspective. Either they've never seen teachers show samples of their own writing, or it dispels the myth "Those who do, do; those who can't, teach." Either way it helps me engage and identify with the students/participants. So, as Fred discussed earlier in this chapter, sharing your writing with your students is a powerful strategy.

Models

In the workplace, employees may have the opportunity to see sample documents that others have written, giving them an idea of what a specific type of business communication should look like. However, there will also be situations where writers will have no model to follow and they must be original in the creation of the report. Sometimes managers will assign a report and give a lot of guidance; sometimes they will give no direction at all, so the employees must figure out how to write the document. Likewise, students on state tests receive a prompt and then must figure out how to respond. Thus, one of the goals for schools is to create independent writers who know how to locate or determine the information they need to convey their message. Teachers, therefore, should provide students

---

THE **Classroom–Corporate** CONNECTION

1. True or False: With today's technology, students' writing on Facebook, instant messaging, email, and blogs is not private.

2. Match the following terms with their definitions.

   Blogs   a. collaborative tool where users can modify content; access can be limited

   Wikis   b. audio and video files may be included so that users can download to listen and/or see speaker

   Podcasts

        c. postings, usually written in journal style, are listed in reverse chronological order; writer shares information and readers comment

3. True or False: The main difference between the previous Web 1.0 era and the current Web 2.0 era is the increased ability to interact.

4. Which of the following statements is inaccurate?
   a. By 2009, half of the companies around the world will be using wikis.
   b. Companies are increasing the number of project teams, requiring more employees to be skilled in working collaboratively.
   c. Writing emails in all capital letters is the equivalent of shouting.
   d. None of the above.

with a variety of writing opportunities—some with actual samples to preview, some with no samples to preview, some with a detailed format to follow, and some where students have to determine the appropriate format.

Privacy

There's no such thing as guaranteed privacy in workplace communication. Your email could be forwarded to the CEO, pinned on the bulletin board because of a careless mistake, or leaked to an outside audience.

In the case of a fast food restaurant, an employee put this message on the sign in front of the store for all to see as they drove by.

Wanted: Losers
Apply within

(I believe they really meant "Closers." But what do I know?)

Even CEOs' emails aren't private. An article in the *New York Times* by Edward Wong (2001) detailed the ramifications of a CEO's leaked email, which was posted on *Yahoo!* I'm sure the CEO didn't want the whole world to have access to his raving message to his employees. The email, which was an attempt to improve productivity, included statements such as:

You have a problem and you will fix it or I will replace you. . . . Hell will freeze over. . . . You have two weeks. Tick, tock.

The result? After analysts and investors read the message, "In the stock market, the valuation of the company, which was $1.5 billion on March 20, plummeted 22 percent in three days."

While students who seek privacy at school can generally be assured that their writing assignments won't be shared with the class (although their writing could be shared with another adult), we need to talk to them about their writing outside of school (e.g., Facebook, email, and blogs). Their writing in these forums is out there for the world to see. So students are beginning to learn about privacy already. Sometimes the hard way.

C O N N E C T I O N
In both worlds there is no guarantee that electronic communication will be kept private. Once a writer hits the *send* or *post* button, there's no telling who or how many people will see what was written.

Feedback

I've learned over the years that people, at all levels in an organization, often keep their writing to themselves, infrequently showing their written correspondence to others for feedback. In organizations, colleagues will discuss strategic planning and industry trends, but seldom discuss their writing. They'll develop training programs and marketing strategies, but rarely develop their writing. Just like Fred's initial fear of sharing his writing at the NWP, business managers, while they may assign and correct written documents, may hesitate to share what they've written with their coworkers.

Managers may give their employees feedback, and they will hopefully train their staff in professional writing. Employees may give their colleagues an important letter or memo to critique, but most of the time workers can't ask their peers to review their correspondence before they click *send* or mail it. There's just not enough time. Coworkers have their own work to complete. Consequently, employees are forced to check it over themselves. Likewise, students should practice editing their own work.

Independent Writers

In the classroom we need to create an atmosphere where students will gain confidence and competence in their writing skills so when they get to the workplace they can function under different situations: time pressures, collaborative environments, angry customers, international audiences, and so forth.

We need students to become independent writers so they don't need their hands held when they are told to write a proposal or letter. They need to have the confidence that they are well prepared with basic writing skills and the ability to find out how to approach the proposed assignment.

But this should not be a false confidence. Not every piece of student writing is brilliant. Teachers must give students constructive criticism when appropriate and then develop a plan to help them improve and also hold the students accountable for applying the specific skill set. Nor should teachers promote the philosophy that it's the process, not the end product, that counts. In organizations, the end product is the only thing that counts. As we all know, in the long run, grade inflation hurts our students.

Safe Environment

Unfortunately, many workplaces are not safe environments. People usually don't get hired or promoted when they display poor writing skills. They can even be fired due to their unsuccessful written communication. For example, a woman I know, an outside contractor for a major consulting firm, missed a proposal deadline by two hours for a huge contract. The company representative told her that it was unacceptable to submit a proposal late and that the report itself was "crap." Needless to say, she lost work immediately and was cut loose soon after—all due to just one mistake. In industry rarely are there rewrites or second chances, and extensions are frowned upon if accepted at all. So we need to prepare students to be held accountable for what they write. Here are a few actions to consider:

CONNECTION

Holding students responsible for deadlines, appropriate language, plagiarism, and other expectations prepares them for what they'll experience in the workplace.

- Hold students accountable to deadlines (except for excused absences).
- Establish early in the year what language is unacceptable (e.g., IM language, slang, incorrect grammar, profanity).
- Explain the school's regulation for plagiarism and adhere to it without exception. (Make sure your school has one in place.)
- Clearly explain to students your grading rubric and follow it. In other words, establish and maintain rigor in the classroom. Students will rise to the occasion if the bar is set reasonably high.

Time Limits

Many people are surprised by the amount of time per day workers spend writing on the job. Writing is part of almost every job, and the higher you advance, the more you will write.

A couple of years ago at my tennis club I ran into a student from my Professional Writing class (and, no, I really haven't spent over $10,000 for my backhand). She and I talked for a minute and then her husband joined us. When she introduced us, he said, "Oh, you're the one who gives her all the work!" I replied, "Well, we do write two emails, a memo, two letters, a proposal, a progress report, and a ten-page formal report over the fifteen-week term." With his mouth agape, he looked at his wife and then back at me and said, "Are you serious? As an engineer that's what I write in one day!" When entering the workforce, many people are surprised by the amount of writing that is required of them daily.

We can't take four hours to write a one-page memo. Let's say a worker makes $45,000 per year (approximately $22 per hour). So, that one memo would cost the organization $88!! But we do need to take the time to write so that readers can understand the message and so that we professionally represent ourselves and the organization. We can't exclude editing and revising just because we're in a hurry to get the message out. Professional writing must be a careful process because we'll spend more time in the end trying to straighten out the mess.

However, time allotted to written communication varies. Some documents may be written over a period of months while working on a major project. Others may contain urgent information so they need to be sent out immediately. Or they could be sent out the next day. One company I consulted for had problems with the tone of their business letters. Once customers received the letters, they called the company to complain. This issue was time consuming, hurt customer satisfaction, and required finely tuned skills to overcome the customers' negative attitudes. I suggested that the writers should wait one day after writing the letters, reread them that second day, and then decide if the tone was appropriate before sending out the letters. The employees were a bit shocked by the tone of the letters when they reread them the second day compared to their initial reaction. They couldn't believe the angry, sarcastic, and blunt tones in their writing. Students, like adults, can benefit from reading their work a day later to determine if any problems exist.

Ways to give your classroom the **Corporate Edge**

- Search for an article about the importance of writing in the workplace. Have students read and discuss the article.

- Write with students and show them samples of your writing.

- Bring in guest speakers from various professions to talk about the kinds of writing they do at work.

Collaborative Writing

As Fred stated, sharing our writing is important, but we need to go one step further—and that's by writing together, not separately. To mimic another type of writing environment in the workplace, we can have the students work collaboratively on written projects.

Much business writing is done in a team environment—either face to face, over the telephone, or via the Internet. Collaborative software, or groupware, can be used in electronic conferencing. Shared workspaces are set up as virtual offices. Lotus notes (featuring group scheduling, for example), collaborative media (e.g., wikis), and Microsoft Office make collaborative meetings, writing, and editing more efficient.

Collaboration in the workforce can operate in various ways:

- One person writes the draft and then shows it to others in the company (e.g., a lawyer, HR director, manager), which is similar to peer conferencing in the classroom.
- The report is divided into different topical sections. (Each person writes a different section and then the group edits and assembles it as one document.)
- Each person completes a different task of the project (e.g., creating hardware, software, documentation, an instruction manual) and then presents the report as a team or with one representative. All members may not be involved in the actual writing of the report.
- All team members write the report together (which is very time intensive).

C O N N E C T I O N

In both schools and organizations, people work in teams. Teachers can explore an additional team concept: *writing* as a team.

In groups we depend on each other's expertise, experience, and viewpoints. Writing collaboratively in groups is *supposed* to make writing easier—producing a higher-quality end product. Yet in several companies I've worked with, few employees have received guidance on how to work successfully in a team environment.

In the classroom, when you form team projects, it's important to discuss group dynamics and team roles. Also, talk about suggestions to deal with problem team members. I suggest the following guidelines to improve collaboration:

- Select a leader. (Someone needs to be driving.)
- Divide the tasks. (Ensure equal participation.)
- List all the tasks with staggered due dates and list who is responsible for which task.
- Address conflict resolution techniques such as proaction, compromise, and collaboration.
- Identify the expectations of the group (attending meetings, meeting deadlines, submitting quality work).
- Determine consequences for not meeting group guidelines, such as losing a specific number of points on the assignment.
- Establish relationships/build rapport. (This aids cohesiveness and unity.)
- Set up important milestone dates along the way.

- Become familiar with collaborative writing tools that help multiple users to edit and review documents. Such tools include:

    Wikis: software that allows users to create, edit, and link Web pages.

    Aspects: software for collaborative writing, peer editing, and discussions on a network.

    Whiteboard: sharable, Web-based text documents that allow users to compare edits.

    Google Docs: a free, Web-based application offered by Google, allowing users to create and edit documents online while collaborating synchronously with other users.

- Teach students how to work in teams by helping them establish rapport with team members, state a clear purpose, develop guidelines, enhance interpersonal skills, and give short feedback loops (staggering due dates).

- Provide collaborative writing assignments. (Some example assignments are provided in Chapter 7.)

In a school setting, the final point allows teachers to monitor students' progress. It also allows students to learn skills during the collaboration process instead of dealing with issues at the end of the project.

Since much of the work in organizations is completed through teamwork, educational settings need to include collaborative projects in all their courses, including writing classes. However, we can't just put students in groups and say, "Duke it out." We need to teach them how to successfully work in a collaborative environment and to remind them that they will need to communicate in this manner in the workplace.

Electronic Communication

We can mimic another common type of workplace writing environment by requiring students to use technology in their written communication. As we enter into the Web 2.0 era (which is much more interactive than the previous Web 1.0 era), we'll be communicating more in the workplace environment through blogs, wikis, and podcasts. For example, an organization's monthly sales reports can be recorded as digital audio files and posted on an intranet site for employees to listen to on their MP3 players as they run on the treadmill at the gym.

Technology can help improve our writing in many ways: collecting and organizing information, adding graphics, designing documents and Web pages, checking for grammar and spelling errors, and using collaborative software for teamwork. Therefore, in classrooms, students should have opportunities to learn about these mediums, practice these mediums, and use them as part of their writing assignments.

Wikis

According to the Technology Initiative Grants Program, a wiki is "a website that includes the collaboration of work from many different authors. A wiki site allows anyone to edit, delete, or modify the content of the Web." A common example of a wiki is Wikipedia. Students, however, should be aware that one of the challenges of using wikis as a resource is that because anyone can modify the content, information may not always be accurate.

Wikis can increase the effectiveness of communication and encourage teamwork in the workplace. They can aid businesses by allowing customers to be more interactive and by making information more accessible. Wikis allow users to add and edit content, provide an arena to collect employee knowledge, and enhance workplace productivity.

Why use wikis in the classroom? Well, for one, using wikis involves skills students will need in the future. Wikis are becoming commonplace in the workplace as we use different types of technology to communicate. A report from Gartner, Inc., in Stamford, CT, states that by 2009, half of the companies around the world will be using wikis. Second, wikis allow opportunities to engage writers beyond the classroom. Many times I see students write far more in a wiki environment than they would in a traditional environment. Additionally, probably the most important reason is to help facilitate on-line collaboration among students. We need to provide new learning experiences to adapt to the new generation of learners and a new generation of learning environments. Many students are very comfortable with blogs, podcasts, and wikis and are excited and motivated to use this type of communication.

C O N N E C T I O N

The academic and workplace worlds will require twenty-first-century literacy skills. For schools to keep pace with the way written communication is utilized outside of the classroom, they must incorporate the use of electronic communication in collaborative writing on a regular basis.

How can we use wikis in the classroom? Here are some examples:

1. *Collaborative writing projects.* Students can use wikis to suggest links, research topics together, and record findings in one place so everyone has access.

2. *Collaborative study sites.* Each group can write and post a segment on what they've learned on a particular topic in preparation for an exam.

3. *Threaded discussions.* Students can continue the dialogue on a specific topic.

4. *Collaborative projects between schools.* Students can learn from peers across the country.

5. *Interactive stories.* Students can write the next part of a story or provide multiple endings.

6. *Daily articles.* Students can take turns being a reporter, writing about what happened in the classroom that day. Pictures can also be included.

7. *Classroom portfolio.* Teachers can showcase students' writing.

8. *"About Me" page.* Students can introduce themselves to fellow classmates.

9. *Webliography.* Students can read articles brought in by an RSS feed. (To learn about a good RSS feed reader, go to www.google.com/help/reader/tour.html.)

How can teachers learn to set up and get ideas for their own wiki? It doesn't have to be complicated. Here are some great sites to get you started:

- http://pbwiki.com or www.wikispaces.com: provides great sites to host wikis (designed for education); offers free accounts (with additional features that can be added with a subscription fee); sends monthly newsletters with tips; makes it very easy to set up a wiki.
- http://sbwikicamp.pbwiki.com/: includes a wonderful site, especially designed for teachers; is very easy to understand, with example wikis. (Check out the video *Wikis in Plain English* from Common Craft.)
- http://edtechtalk.com/: provides interesting webcasts that can teach you a lot about wikis, blogs, and podcasting. (Check out EdTech Weekly, Women on the Web, and 21st Century Learning.)

Email

Email has revolutionized the way we communicate in the workplace. However, the guidelines for using email and Instant Messaging in an organization are different from personal use, and students need to learn the differences. Some of the main benefits of these mediums of communication also create their worst problems. Here are a few of the drawbacks:

- Instead of saying, "You've got mail," business email programs should say, "You've got evidence." Not only can email be used as evidence in court, but employers have the legal right to monitor their employees' email.
- Because email (as well as Instant Messaging) is so quick and easy to use, people tend to overuse it. A performance-improvement company in Boston found that only 25 percent of the emails people receive actually facilitate job performance.
- Just because someone sends an email doesn't mean that it will actually be delivered (and don't always count on getting an undeliverable message notice). Or, if it is delivered, it may not be read at the appropriate time, if at all. I hate it when clients email me an hour before our meeting to explain that they have to cancel. I'm not always "wired" to receive messages 24/7.
- Because of the usual immediacy of email writing, we tend to think of emails as quick conversation and don't take the time to craft the messages or revise and proofread them before we click *send.* Consequently, the result can cause embarrassment, offense, confusion, wasted time, and so forth. In the workplace we should never write the following: *Gtg ttyl blos.* (Translation: "Got to go; talk to you later. Boss looking over shoulder.") Nor should our business emails be full of emoticons:

Surprised	:-O or :o	Tongue out	:-P or :p
Wink	;-) or ;)	Sad	:-(or :(
Confused	:-S or :s	Disappointed	:-| or :|
Crying	:'(	Embarrassed	:-$ or :$

It is essential to remember that there is a difference between work and personal email. And once again, students need to learn the difference between personal writing and writing that's appropriate for the workplace/classroom. IM language with friends is different from IM language used with the teacher or in the professional arena. Here are some guidelines to discuss with students. They apply to the workplace as well as the classroom.

- Keep them short and simple. One popular format: here's what I want; here's why; and here's specifically what you need to do.
- Care about correctness. Follow the standard rules of grammar and punctuation; spell it right. Proofread before you hit *send*.
- Don't send copies to everyone in your address book. I'm not just referring to the spam emails promising to enhance body parts, to ensure a killing in the stock market, or to help me claim my fortune from a long lost cousin in England. I'm talking about the pointless, long-winded messages that I don't need to know anything about. For example, one manager thought his emails were so important he would send them to *all* employees whether or not the message pertained to them. One such email announced a staff meeting at a local German restaurant. It stated, "The meeting will be held at 1:00 . . . ; we'll have plenty of brats and beer." He was fired the next day for providing alcohol during work hours. Sometimes it's better if not everyone knows everything we're doing!
- Don't write in all capital letters; IT'S LIKE YOU'RE SHOUTING!
- Follow the organization's email policy.
- Avoid emotional outbursts. Email is a monologue, not a dialogue, and hostilities can escalate.
- Maintain a businesslike tone and conversational style.
- Write subject lines that include signal words (e.g., *information on, recommendation to, notice of*) and a do/know statement (for example, Information on New Hiring Process). Because we receive so many emails (many of which are spam), subject lines often determine when the reader will read the message or if it will be read at all. For example, one student sent me an email with this subject line: "Weather Bug." When I looked at the *from* line, it read: studmuffin@aol.com. Needless to say, I thought it was spam and deleted it without opening it. Unfortunately, the student was trying to let me know that he was ill and would need to make up the test that was scheduled that day. Maybe a better subject line would have been: "Request to Retake ENGL227 Test #1."

It is also essential to make employees and students aware of proper netiquette. For example, at one company, a customer in Detroit emailed an employee to state that the equipment was finally up and running. That employee forwarded the message to his boss, adding, "It's about time they realized it was them, not our equipment." The boss replied, "It's about time they got their head out of their ass." Then the employee forwarded the entire email—with all the previous threads—back to the customer, saying, "We're so glad that your [*sic*] pleased with the performance of our equipment. Please let me know if you need any farther [*sic*] assistance." (Not too sure about repeat business in this case.)

It's important that students understand the strengths of different types of technologies, but we have to teach them how to use these technologies effectively. Writers need guidance and opportunities to experiment in writing for print, Web, audio, and video; writing in the workplace requires being able to successfully write in all mediums.

You may have noticed that some of the practices in the workplace and classroom don't always align. Nor should they. If we develop successful students now, they will have a better chance of being successful later in their careers. Throughout the next few chapters you'll notice different views expressed on other points. So what should we teach? We need to teach both aspects so that students can match their writing to their purpose and audience in a variety of environments.

Ways to give your classroom the **Corporate Edge**

- Ask students to examine, analyze, and use electronic channels of communication such as Web sites, blogs, email, wikis, and so on. Have them write an email to their parents or other adults about the advantages and disadvantages of each medium and identify tips on how to use each one effectively.

- Direct students to http://owl.english.purdue.edu, selecting the grade level and clicking *Internet Literacy,* and then *Email Etiquette.* Discuss the article with the class. Ask students to find other articles on email netiquette, and then, in a PowerPoint presentation, display guidelines for using email appropriately.

- Have students create a written document about what they are studying in class and email the information to you or set up a blog where others can comment on the information (and use it as a study guide).

Answers to The Classroom–Corporate Connection

  1. True   **2.** blogs—c., wikis—a., podcasts—b.   **3.** True   **4.** d.—None of the above.

CHAPTER 4

Keeping It Simple
Writing as a Process

From your perspective

1. *What do you think of when you hear the term writing process? Write a brief summation of what writing process means to you and what it looks like in a classroom.*

2. *On a scale of 1–10, low to high, rate yourself on your ability to teach each phase of the writing process.*

   Drawing upon experience
   1 2 3 4 5 6 7 8 9 10
   Prewriting
   1 2 3 4 5 6 7 8 9 10
   Drafting
   1 2 3 4 5 6 7 8 9 10
   Conferencing
   1 2 3 4 5 6 7 8 9 10
   Revising
   1 2 3 4 5 6 7 8 9 10
   Editing
   1 2 3 4 5 6 7 8 9 10
   Publishing
   1 2 3 4 5 6 7 8 9 10

3. *What else do you currently need to help your students through the process?*

An Overview

All of us, hopefully, have learned that writing is a process, and we think we know the various stages of that process. Writing process is nothing new; it's been around for as long as people have written. What has changed in the past three decades is our *understanding* of what the process looks like in classrooms and how we can utilize it to help our students. Unfortunately, many of the posters that supposedly depict the writing process are not the full story, and those of us who write on a regular basis know that. So how many of us fully understand the process and how it takes place, whether it be in the classroom or the workplace?

The Musical Connection

My friend Brad is a gifted musician and music teacher. He is one of those rare individuals who can hear a song on the radio and a few minutes later, play it on the piano. A few years ago, as part of his graduate work at the University of New Hampshire, he started composing for school bands. Already, he has had a number of pieces published. While it's time-consuming and difficult work, he enjoys composing. When I asked Brad how he creates a piece of music, his answer was remarkably similar to what I've heard for years when talking about writing.

He explained that an idea for a new piece of music comes into his head from a variety of sources. Sometimes, sounds he hears, such as brakes or tires squealing or the sound of a copy machine or even doors slamming, trigger an idea for a melody. Other times, he will use a musical tool to find a melody. And other times he hears a cadence in words or phrases he overhears in a conversation. He pulls from his experiences in everyday living to begin a piece of music.

Then, Brad thinks about two issues: What is the purpose of the piece, and who is the intended audience? He decides if the piece will be used as a concert opener—which requires something upbeat and fast—or if it will be used as a ballad, which requires a slower pace. When he thinks about his audience, he decides who he thinks will play the piece: an advanced middle school band, a quartet of advanced high school players, a marching band, or some other group. He gives thought to audience before he puts pen to paper.

Finally, Brad decides upon a structure for the composition. In music, structure is form. In music, there are numerous forms: no form; binary (a section and b section); aba form; rondo (abaca); sonata; theme and variation. Form is an architectural plan for how the whole piece will fit together. What sections will be repeated? What themes will be introduced and when?

Once all this is decided, Brad begins to write. As he goes along, he revises constantly, because the music may take him in a different direction than he expected. Often, he writes the ending before the middle and then decides how to move smoothly from his beginning to his ending.

After Brad has finished his draft, he listens, thinks, and "sits on it." As he explained to me, "I need time to let the piece settle inside of me for a while, to see how it feels, how it sounds. That helps me decide what changes I need to make. While the basic structure of the piece remains the same, I may change the rhythm or add a complementary part. But before I know what needs to be done, I need to give it time."

Eventually, Brad shares the music with musical colleagues whom he respects and trusts. They offer feedback in the form of questions, such as:

- Why did you change the rhythm at this place?
- Why did you change the harmony?
- Why didn't you play the second theme fully, like you did the first time through?
- How do the percussion parts relate to the main theme?

Based on their feedback, he chooses either to modify the music or, at times, to leave it as it was.

The more I thought about Brad's explanation, I realized it is the same for writers. Although creating music or creating a piece of writing is hard work and takes time, the process is relatively simple. An idea pops into our head, we think about it, and we let it percolate. We ask ourselves many questions:

- Who is the audience?
- What is the purpose? Am I writing a letter of complaint to a local business owner? A thank-you note to my grandmother? An essay for my English teacher? A journal entry for myself? A research paper for history?
- What is my timeline?
- Approximately how long should the paper be?
- What information do I already have?
- What information do I need to gather?

We begin to write, adding and deleting words, phrases, and entire ideas as we go, and then we go back and ask ourselves questions like, "What's missing? Is my message clear? Does it proceed along at a reasonable pace? Is the ending satisfying?" Obviously, the list of questions can go on for a while.

The reality is, however, that some pieces we write may never go beyond an initial draft, and that draft may well be incomplete. We started it just to put down our thoughts, our anger, our passion, our dreams. It was not meant to be revised or seen by anyone except ourself.

Eventually, if we like what we've written, we share it with someone we respect and trust and ask their opinion. Hopefully, they respond with more than, "Wow! That's really good. I like it!" Hopefully, they offer some suggestions, raise some questions, and are specific about what they like. As a result of their input, we go back and make some changes to our draft. We may seek input from other friends and colleagues, making adjustments to our writing based on their feedback. Eventually, we make sure our spelling, punctuation, and grammar are correct, and we call it "good enough for now." The point when a piece of writing is finished, like a piece of music, varies. As Brad told me, "I know when I'm done when I run out of energy, time, or both. There are times when I'm thoroughly satisfied with a piece and I know it's done. It just feels right."

That's writing process.

Do we allow students the same opportunities that we afford ourselves when *we* write? In many classrooms I've visited over the years, the only time students have a chance just to write for writing's sake is through journal writing. Often, the teacher determines every assignment, and it is due, in completed, polished form, within a very few days if not the next day. Why do we demand something of our students that we do not do ourselves? Why do we talk about writing process but often, when it comes to high-stakes writing— writing that will be graded—do we change our practice? Shouldn't our students have at least the same opportunities that professional writers have? One of my favorite lines of all time comes from Mem Fox, a prolific writer. In *Radical Reflections*, she writes, "I have about four ideas a year, and I'm a proficient, professional, published writer, yet we ask children to write story after story."

Figure 4.1 Traditional Writing Process Model

> **Writing Process**
>
> Prewriting ➡ Drafting ➡ Revising ➡ Editing ➡ Publishing

If we believe in writing process, we must allow our students to practice it in all their writing.

Over the years, writing process has gained some magical, mysterious persona that intimidates both younger teachers and their students. Many teachers display posters in their rooms showing a picture of the writing process. Those posters usually look something like the one shown in Figure 4.1.

Unfortunately, this model has two problems. First, it is inaccurate. Second, too many teachers interpret this model literally and in a linear fashion. I wish I had a dollar for every time I heard someone say, "When you've finished your first draft, come and see me so I can help you with your revisions." As if revision didn't begin until the first draft was finished!

So let's uncover what writing process should look like for our students. Figure 4.2 offers an accurate poster for Writing Process.

Figure 4.2 New Writing Process Model

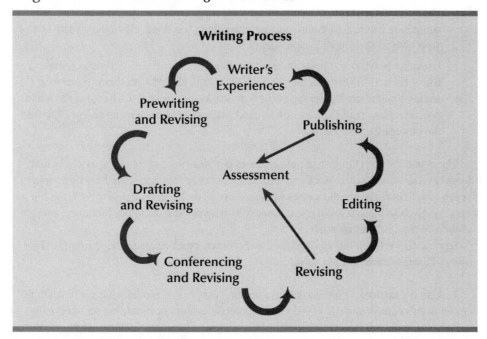

Source: From Vicki Spandel. *Creating Writers Through 6-Trait Writing Assessment and Instruction, 4e.* Published by Allyn and Bacon, Boston, MA. Copyright © 2005 by Pearson Education. Reprinted by permission of the publisher.

Experience

The writing process begins not with prewriting activities, but with the experiences a writer brings to the table. Most writers agree that the strongest writing usually occurs when writers write from experience. If you ask me to write about fly fishing, I'd be in serious trouble. I don't fly fish. Never have. So if you ask me to write about a topic on which I have no background knowledge, the writing I produce will be distant, vague and lackluster. Even Stephen King writes from experience. In his book *On Writing*, King (2000) explains how his inspiration for the character Carrie emerged from his knowledge of two girls with whom he went to high school.

Roni Schotter (1997), in her book *Nothing Ever Happens on 90th Street,* does a magnificent job of discussing both the writing process and the notion of writing from experience. This picture book, with a reading level for third or fourth graders, follows a girl who has been given an assignment to "Write about what you know." However, as she ponders the assignment from her front steps, she realizes that, in her eyes, nothing ever happens on her street. Very soon, various neighbors—each of them quite unique—appear and inquire what she is doing. When she tells them and explains her frustration, each offers a suggestion about how to craft her writing. Eventually, a remarkable story unfolds as she begins to see the story in everyday events. The book could be used in a number of ways:

1. Discuss with students Eva's initial frustration about "nothing to write about" and any connections they have to how she feels.

2. Ask students to think about two or three adult neighbors and/or relatives and then list their interesting/funny/unusual habits or behaviors. Ask students to write a short character sketch about one of these people and provide a short narration of something interesting/funny/unusual the person has done. Obviously, write one of your own to share with your students.

3. Open the book to any page and read the page to your students. Together, make a list of the action verbs on the page. Each page is loaded with them. Have your students substitute the strong verbs with weak ones or state-of-being verbs when possible. Now read the new version and listen to how the writing sounds. Discuss the power of action verbs.

The challenge is to tap into the experiences our students possess—experiences that, oftentimes, they don't see as worth writing about because they are such daily occurrences. Our job is to help them see the stories in their daily lives. Even on the new SAT, the top scores are given to papers that make connections between the question, literature, and events from the student's own life.

So how do we teach our students to use their own experiences as the springboard for writing? I suggest three simple ways.

1. Use literature.   Find books, articles, and essays that model what we're teaching. Gary Paulsen's *Harris and Me* (1993) is a wonderful example of building on one's own life events to create an engaging book. Essays by Anna Quindlen (in *Newsweek*) or editorials by Maureen Dowd (in *New York Times*) can offer further examples of using our own experiences to shape our writing.

2. Model ourselves.   By allowing our students literally to watch us write, talking as we move through the writing, we increase their understanding. Are we courageous and confident enough to stand at the overhead or computer, projecting onto the screen, and let our students watch us write based on some of our own everyday experiences? If we're really brave, we can allow a student to determine the topic. After all, we ask students to do this all the time!

3. Take mind walks.   Sometimes, when I'm feeling stuck in my writing, I walk outside into the woods and down to the pond behind my house. I just need to clear my head and gain a fresh perspective. Unfortunately, at school, we can't allow our students to leave the classroom or the building. But we can take them on a mind walk. Psychologist Richard Wiseman (2007) says, "It seems that just a few moments' thinking time can prime you to perform either better or worse than normal at both mental and physical tasks." Help them to take an experience and walk them through what the story or essay could look like. Ask questions, make suggestions, have other students do the same. The purpose is to clarify details, events, and images in the writer's mind before the writing begins.

For example, in one writing program, I was asked to write about a memorable experience (watching a fellow student being paddled when we were in second grade). The instructor asked me to close my eyes and consider the following questions: What did the room smell like? What color were the walls? What could I see out the windows? What sounds could I hear before the girl was paddled? What was it like watching the teacher walk across the floor? What color was her dress? Her shoes? Could I smell anything distinctive about her? And many more. By the time I was asked to write, I could clearly visualize the entire scene and the writing was easy.

There is little doubt that our students will produce the most powerful and engaging writing when it's based on their experiences. My own best writing emerged from my experiences with certain teachers I had in school, the four hours I spent at the 1964 NFL championship game at Municipal Stadium in Cleveland, or playing underneath my grandmother's dining room table.

When our students write from their own experiences, their writing gains energy. The further removed they are from the topic, the flatter their writing becomes. When we ask them to write about topics they don't know about, they don't care about, and they have absolutely no connection to, we create a situation that is difficult for even our strongest students to overcome. I understand that there are times when all of us must write about topics we don't particularly care about. I also agree that our students need opportunities to practice writing on such topics. But how often should this happen? Can we engage our students in conversations about the challenges and frustrations of such assignments before they begin writing? The more they understand why some assignments are more challenging than others and the purpose of such assignments, the more likely they are to stretch themselves to be successful.

Prewriting and Revision

During my years as a student, including my public school years, undergraduate years and graduate years, and during my first few years as a teacher, I never heard of prewriting. All I knew was that teachers gave an assignment and students were expected to write. But the more I thought about the notion of prewriting, the more sense it made. I realized that in almost every activity, people "warm up" before they actually begin. They warm up to prepare themselves better for the game or concert or speech. During my years playing baseball, we didn't just show up at the field and have a game. We threw the ball around, took some fielding and batting practice, ran the bases, talked about players on the other team and, as we got older, discussed how we would pitch to certain players. The coach would give his pep talk and discuss strategies for the game, telling us which outfielder had the strongest or weakest arm, whether or not the catcher had a decent throw to second, and what pitches the pitcher could throw with control. We warmed up and prepared for the game.

Writing is the same. Over the years, I have arrived at the belief that prewriting may be the most critical stage in the writing process. The time and thought given to prewriting has a direct correlation to the quality of a first draft. While we talk about prewriting in classrooms, many teachers provide only limited time and focus to this stage. One of the most remarkable first drafts I've ever seen was a result of significant time spent on prewriting. A class of second-grade students and I spent approximately thirty minutes prewriting before they began their draft. In about fifteen minutes after the prewriting, Griffin wrote his draft:

Cookies

Once when I was six years old I went to my pantry and stole the Milano cookies! I wasn't allowed to eat anymore cookies until lunch was over. So I ran and hid. I ate almost every Milano cookie! I said to myself I know this is wrong but I can't resist. Later on my mom was walking down the hall where the closet was. That's where I was hiding! I heard her walking down the hall making a click clack click clack sound with her high heels. So I ate the cookies as fast as the cookie monster could eat cookies. Right when I was about to eat my second last Milano cookie my mom opened the door right when the cookie made the sound crunch. She laughed and said no more cookies you cookie monster.

Most intermediate grade teachers would be ecstatic to see writing like this. And how many middle school teachers would be thrilled to see their students writing with such power? Had I not watched Griffin write this, I'm not sure I would have believed it was a first draft. Such is the power of prewriting.

Students need a chance to warm up for the writing they are about to undertake. It helps them answer questions like "What do I want to say?" and "What's the most important thing I want my reader to think about?" and "How should I begin?" There are a variety of possibilities for what this warmup looks like, but regardless of what format it takes, for many writers a time to prewrite is essential if they are going to produce their best work. When you consider what prewriting looks like, think about how you could incorporate these ideas and others into your students' writing:

1. Draw before they write.   Drawing gives children time to think about their writing, to let their ideas percolate for a while before the pencil hits the paper. It helps them to find a focus for their writing, identify the details they may want to include in their work, and consider how they want to organize the writing once they begin. Oftentimes, it helps them think of ideas that otherwise might never have entered their minds. By encouraging our students to add details to their drawings; to include expressions on the faces of the people, animals, or characters; to use some vivid colors; and to think about where on the page they draw their items, we help them to think about details, voice, and organization. And drawing should not be limited to elementary students. Many high school students relish the opportunity to draw or sketch as part of their prewriting work.

2. Pantomime their work before they begin writing.   Oftentimes, when I have students practice the notion of "show, don't tell," I ask a student to go to the front of the room and act out an emotion without speaking. The class has to guess which emotion the student is acting out and then discuss what the person did in order to show that emotion. After we've completed a few of these acting scenes, the students then write in less than twenty-five words about a person "doing" that emotion. They may not use the word for that emotion (e.g., *nervous, worried, happy, sad*) in their writing. Understandably, many students need to see or act out an event or moment in order to comprehend fully what that event or moment will look like. Only then can they successfully write about it. Clearly, this approach is more effective with students in some grades than others, as many middle school students will be very hesitant to try this. (Although a few can't wait to have the stage in front of their peers!)

3. Engage in conversations to find and/or focus their topic.   When we give students in-class time to talk with their peers about a possible topic for writing, or to begin telling the story, their minds begin to hear the story they want to tell. These conversations, in which their peers ask questions, debate points of view, or offer new perspectives, help writers shape their work. Many times students need to think through their thoughts out loud to help them determine what they want to say and how they want to say it. Five minutes of talking can lead to an onslaught of writing. And don't forget the value of modeling this for your students.

4. Make lists of possible topics.   One of the most powerful and simple prewriting activities I've observed and used came from my friend Vicki Spandel. Ask students to make a list of important or memorable places in their lives. Provide a few minutes of time and then have a few students share their lists with the class. Make sure you share your list as well. Then, ask them to select one of those places with the most vivid recollections and make a list of sensory images of that one place (e.g., what do they see, hear, smell, taste; how do they feel; etc.). Again, ask a few students to share their lists, and share yours as well. Finally, ask them to write about that one place, using some of the sensory images they have identified. Intriguingly, when I ask children or adults, "How many of you wrote about the first place on your list?" only about 20 to 30 percent have selected the first place on their list. And yet most students, when faced with the pressure of the state or local writing assessment, read the prompt and immediately begin to write about the first thought that comes to their mind. Many writers, especially young ones, need to take time to find their topic. If they write about the first idea that pops into their minds, it is often not what they are most ready to write about. But given time to consider possible topics, writers will eventually find the one that is right for them at the time. More information about the local and state assessments appears in Chapter 8.

These are just a few methods of prewriting that help students better focus and organize their work. Five or ten minutes spent with prewriting often leads to much more productive writing and quality writing. Young writers need even more time to prewrite, often as much as twenty minutes.

Let's not forget that the first phase of revision often begins during prewriting. Revision, the act of adding, deleting, or changing something one has written or thought about writing, is not something students do once they've finished their first draft. Most of us, as we tell stories, modify the facts somewhat to appeal better to the audience. We might add a detail that never really occurred, or we may leave something out. As our students consider what they're going to write, this process takes place for them as well. Thus, we want to convey to them that they're actually revising before they're writing! By modeling this for our students, we can help them gain a firm grasp of the concept.

Drafting and Revision

Once our students determine their purpose (entertain, persuade, inform, etc.) and their audience, they actually begin to create a draft. As teachers, we want to encourage students to "just write!" I avoid telling my students, "Don't worry about spelling, don't worry about punctuation," as this conveys the wrong message. When my students are drafting, my mantra is, "Spell the best you can right now. Punctuate the best you can right now. We'll edit later on." Often our students are so concerned with "doing it right" the first time that they spend more time and energy struggling to "do it right" than they spend actually writing!

When students are struggling with "How should I begin?" I suggest they forget about the first paragraph for the time being and start right in with the second paragraph. Unbeknownst to them, this often becomes their first paragraph! My goal for them is to get something down on paper. And to just keep writing.

When drafting, we need to let our students know that it is fine to cross out, squeeze in, move words or sentences around, or whatever they need to do to move along with their work. All writers revise as they write, and we want our students to know that this is typical of what writers do.

There are times, when teaching a mini-lesson, that I will tell students, "You must write nonstop for five minutes. You cannot stop writing. I don't care what you write, just don't stop!" My goal is for students to experience what it's like to write nonstop, just to let the pencil flow, and to see how much they can produce in a short amount of time. It also provides students with a chance to practice writing and writing and writing.

Conferencing and Revision

Next to grading, conferencing is the greatest challenge for teachers. During my workshops, teachers often raise the question, "I teach 160 [and I have heard as high as 205!] students a day. How am I supposed to conference with all of them?" Or, for an elementary teacher, "I teach seven subjects to twenty-eight students. When am I supposed to conference?" My simple answer is, "YOU don't have to conference with every student on every draft of every paper."

First, let's clarify the purpose of a conference. Many teachers think they should read the entire paper, make corrections, and offer suggestions for how the paper should be revised. These conferences are teacher-led and teacher-focused, and the teacher does most, if not all, of the talking. Nothing could be further from what a successful conference should look like. The purpose of a conference is for a writer to gather specific information about what is working (e.g., clarity of purpose, plot development, persuading a reader, etc.) and what needs to be strengthened (e.g., use stronger verbs, vary sentence structure, rework the lead to create more curiosity, etc.). The writer should come to a conference with questions for the reader. What does the writer want to know about the writing? The writer should provide the focus and direction for the conference, not the teacher or other students.

Second, let's clarify who should be involved in a conference. If we want our students to become strong, independent writers, we need to let go of our control over conferences and teach our students how to conference with each other. Clearly, when time allows, I want to conference with as many students as possible, but with twenty-five to thirty-five or more students in a class, it is not possible to conference with each student on any given day. So let's examine a teacher-student conference and a student-student conference.

Teacher-Student Conferences

An approach that came from Roy Peter Clark (1987) in *Free to Write* is very effective in keeping conferences to a reasonable time, allowing the writer to lead the conference, and focusing on clear and specific issues. The conference is based on three answers that the students must determine before they approach the teacher's desk.

1. In one minute or less, what is your paper about? This question allows students to practice the art of summarizing and helps the teacher to find out the content of the paper. If students can't finish their summaries in less than a minute, then it's back to their desks for some further contemplation.

2. Which part of your paper satisfies you? Explain why. This question provides the writer with an opportunity to self-assess on a positive note. Writers can ask themselves, "What did I do well?" "What's good about it?" As a teacher, I want my students to be asking those questions, and others like them, as a way to become independent writers. If students always rely on the teacher to tell them what they've done well, they will always remain dependent and never become fully aware of what good writing looks like.

3. Which part of your writing are you struggling with or needs work? This question is the key to the conference. Once again, students must self-assess, focusing on one key issue that they feel needs improvement. The teacher's role is to guide, not tell, the students to find their own solutions to the problems. Asking the students "What are some possible ways to improve this section?" allows the writer to determine the solution, which leads to independence as a writer. The high level thinking that takes place during this phase of the conference is precisely the type of thinking we want our students to engage in on a regular basis.

Other questions a teacher could ask include:

- What bothers you about this section?
- What are you trying to convey to the reader?
- Is there anything we've done in class that could help with this?
- What is it you're trying to say?

This model for a conference has a number of advantages. Most important, it places the responsibility on the writer, not the teacher. Writers take responsibility for their writing and for identifying and determining strengths and weaknesses. Second, from a teacher's perspective, it keeps the conference focused and short. This eliminates the days of a fifteen-minute conference with each student, and the teacher can spend time with more students.

Logistics of Student-Teacher Conferences

Teachers have many questions about the "how to" component of conferencing. Where do I conduct the conference? How often should I conference? What are the other students doing while I'm conferencing? How do I record the information from the conference? Here are some helpful hints.

Where Do I Conference? In reality, wherever your classroom allows room for this. It may be at the student's desk, your desk, or a corner of the room set aside for conferences. Ideally, I prefer a table not littered with student papers and notices from the principal. Keep possible distractions at a minimum. Clearly, you will want easy access to certain resources (e.g., a computer, dictionary, thesaurus, some favorite books, etc.). Please, find a table or desk at which you and your student can sit side by side. Avoid sitting across from your student with a desk or table separating the two of you. You and your student are going to *confer* with each other, not interrogate each other. Sitting side by side says, "Let's tackle this together." Finally, remember that you will need a space at which you can keep one eye on the other students. Even elementary students will disrupt others if they sense the teacher isn't looking!

How Often Do I Conference? This is a difficult question, because the answer varies greatly from classroom to classroom and from time to time. On average, I try my best to meet formally with each student every five to eight school days—as often as time allows. Short, informal conferences or discussions take place much more frequently, often at the student's desk or just standing by the door. If you're teaching in a school in which you see the students every day for eighty to ninety minutes, you may be able to conference more often for longer periods of time. If students are changing classes every forty-three minutes, your goal may easily elude you. In an elementary setting, in which students remain in your classroom most of the day, you have more flexibility than your secondary counterparts.

Keep in mind that as assignment deadlines approach, students will be clamoring to see you much more frequently; it's important to ensure that all students have equal access to you. Trust me, you will have some students who will monopolize huge chunks of your time on a daily basis if you allow them. Additionally, some struggling writers require more of our time than some of our more capable writers. Thus, we may need to conference with them more often than every eight days.

What Are Other Students Doing While I'm Conferencing? Again, the answer will vary greatly. A few guidelines:

Don't . . .

1. Have them engaged in "busy" work.
2. Have them sitting around with little or nothing to do.
3. Have them use the time for homework in other classes.
4. Tolerate disruptive behavior (often brought on by a lack of engaging work).

Do . . .

1. Post a list of constructive tasks students need to complete during class.
2. Provide students with options (e.g., read, edit a peer's paper, work on a writing assignment, complete a short writing activity, etc.).
3. Organize and begin small-group conferences of peer writing.
4. Make sure that students are on task.
5. Display an easily visible list of students you will be conferencing with that day in the order you want to see them.

How Do I Document Conferences? In the age of computers, recording and maintaining records of conferences has become relatively easy. Early in your school year, create an electronic folder for each class of students. Within that folder, create a separate folder for each student. Within each student's folder, create a spreadsheet that lists the following information:

Date	Paper Reviewed	Strengths	Areas Needing Improvements	General Comments

After each individual conference, I take one minute and complete the spreadsheet for the student's conference. I can easily refer back to it over time and determine what, if any, patterns are apparent in the strengths or weaknesses of the student's writing.

Student-Student Conferences

Another powerful conference model involves only students. Whether we use a one-on-one approach or small-group conferences, students who have been taught HOW to conference can provide powerful feedback to their peers. Historically, the problem has been that students don't know what to do in a conference. We put them in groups, and students, individually, read their paper or part of the paper, and everyone says, "That was really good, Elise" or "I really liked that a lot, Travis." The writers go back to their seats without learning anything of value.

As I work with students, I begin by teaching them to raise questions. As they listen to the writing, what questions emerge for them as readers? Questions may be simple, like "What was the pet's name?" or much more complex, like "Why would the character's brother treat her that way? Isn't that unrealistic?" In nonfiction writing, students often notice a change of perspective or a major hole in a peer's defense.

Raising questions requires reflection by the reader and the writer. The writer does not have to answer the question at the conference, only to consider it. My students use a half sheet of paper to write down at least two aspects of the writing they enjoyed and at least one question they are left with. Then they have the discussion with the writer. The writer collects the papers as a tool to refer back to during revision. I also look at the papers or a master copy of all the input. This allows me to monitor what type of feedback the students receive from their peers. Time-wise, by placing four students in a group and limiting each student to five minutes of reading and discussion time, I ensure that every student in the class has completed a conference within twenty minutes, and I've had time to meet with individual students who may need additional help with their writing.

In order for this approach to be successful, the teacher must model a number of times how to ask interesting and valuable questions. Select a short piece of writing, written by someone not in the class, share it with your students, and show them the questions you would ask. Raise simple questions (e.g., What is the pet's name?) and more complex ones (e.g., Of all the events you mentioned about your trip, which was the most interesting and what made it the most interesting?). Provide your students with opportunities to ask questions in a practice piece many times before you place them in a peer conference when the pressure to perform is increased.

Another approach to these conferences is for the writer to come to the conference with a question or two for the other students to consider while reading the paper: Which verbs seem strong and which ones need to be changed? Does anything seem out of order? Do I have enough details to really paint a picture in the second paragraph? When the writer asks readers to listen for a specific detail or issue, the readers are able to focus better on the paper, and it transforms them from passive to active listeners.

I usually involve four students in a conference group, with one person reading and the others providing feedback. That way, the writer has a greater chance of gathering valuable feedback. However, one-on-one conferences, student to student, can also work very well if you have students who are able and willing to provide strong feedback.

Overall, here are some general rules to consider for successful conferences:

- Focus on the writing, not the writer (e.g., "Your paper needs . . ." instead of "You didn't. . . ."
- Accompany each suggestion or criticism with something positive about the paper.
- Ask questions that lead to clarification.
- Focus on a few areas for improvement, not everything all at once.
- Be specific in your comments.
- Make sure the writer comes to the conference with specific questions for the reader.

Revision, Revision, Revision

Revision is not editing. Revision is when a writer, after conferencing with others about the writing, goes through the first draft and decides what to add, what to delete, what to change, or what to move around. It is not correcting for errors in spelling, grammar, punctuation, or usage. While correcting these areas may occur during revision, it is not the main purpose or thrust of the time spent revising.

For many writers, revision is the painful part. How often do our students say, "I already wrote it once; why do I have to write it again?" or "It's good enough the way it is." Revision IS hard work. It is tedious. For most writers, it's NOT fun!

One reason students abhor revision is they lack passion for the paper or the reader or both. This usually occurs when the topic is teacher-selected (and not of interest to the writer) and/or the reader is either someone they don't know or don't particularly care about. Again, Mem Fox (1993): "If the children in our classes don't care about their readers, how can they develop as writers? They can't because they won't care about what they're writing and they won't want to revise."

A second reason many students despise revision is they don't know what to do. If they have not been provided with enough quality feedback about their writing, they are stymied. If no one has helped them figure out the problems, or if they have not figured out the problems themselves, much less the solutions, how can we expect them to look forward to revision? Confidence and success in revision result only when the writer knows what to do.

Some friends of mine told me that their high school daughter was in the midst of her fifth draft of a seven-page typed paper. This revision was not her decision but her teacher's. My friends explained how frustrated their daughter was and how she had "had enough of that piece." Fifth draft? I was stunned. Why do we do this to students? For what purpose?

I wanted to visit the teacher because I was genuinely curious about the teacher's motive. Perhaps a good one existed and I was missing it. My friends stopped me: "She has to live with the teacher the rest of the year, Fred. The last thing Jess needs is you going in making trouble!" I understand the value of revising a short section of a piece more than once, but I have a difficult time seeing any value in revising an entire seven-page paper five times. Instead, after the paper has been revised once or twice, the teacher can point out how the student could improve the paper, suggesting, "Next time you write a paper, please try this in the first draft. Then we won't have to deal with it in revision."

So how can we teach our students what to do during revision? My first suggestion revolves around practice revisions that are not threatening. I have always found that students are more willing to revise someone else's paper than they are their own. Therefore, provide students with a short piece of writing that has numerous problems. Perhaps it's a piece that you have written with specific problems you purposely created. First, give the students time to confer with each other to identify the paper's problems (e.g., weak verbs, poor organization, lack of detail, redundant sentence structure, etc.). After this small-group discussion, ask the students to work either with a partner or independently—they both have their merits—and revise the paper for just one of the areas they have identified. Follow with a class discussion and encourage students to share their changes. The entire activity lasts only fifteen minutes and can be repeated on the following days for other problems the students have identified. Obviously, instruction should be blended into this activity to teach students how to fix the problems. For example, you may need to teach students how to rewrite sentences to avoid a subject-verb-object structure over and over and over!

A quick reminder to teachers: Not all pieces of writing need to be or should be revised. Some pieces, depending upon their purpose, have one draft and one draft only. There's nothing wrong with that. Others may be revised entirely once only. And others may have only a section or two revised. We always need to ask ourselves the simple question, "What is my purpose?" Let the purpose of the writing (along with your curriculum if you have one!) determine how often and to what length revision needs to occur.

Editing

I wish I had a dollar (the day of the penny is LONG gone!) for every time I said, or heard a teacher say, "We just went over this two days ago! How could you miss this?" The issue of editing is the bane of every teacher's existence. We ask our students to edit (proofread) their work before they turn it in. They do and, not surprisingly, they never find any mistakes. Honestly, they are not doing this to make us crazy, even if it appears so. The reality is that if we want students (and most adults as well) to edit their own work, they need to wait at least three days before they can accurately edit. Prior to this, the writing is "too warm." Writers see what they think is there, not what actually is there. If you doubt this, pull out one of your old college papers and you'll be amazed at what you find.

Most of us don't have the luxury of waiting three days for a paper to be edited. So we have the students peer edit. The results are not much better. Depending on which students are editing the paper, they may find some errors. But often they miss just as many as they find. Again, the students don't miss the errors because they want to see us break down and cry. (Although they relish the thought!) Most students, and again the same is true with adults, are not able to edit for all conventions simultaneously. For most individuals, the task is too daunting and requires focus on too many areas at once. If we ask students to edit a paper just for end punctuation, they will do quite well. Or just for capitalization; they will accomplish this with great success. But trying to edit for everything all at once is almost impossible. During my workshops with teachers, I ask them to count the number of convention errors in a sixty-five-word passage that I provide. I give them two minutes.

The range of responses is always remarkable, usually from around twenty errors to thirty-five errors. Sometimes, the range is even greater. When I tell them the correct answer is thirty-one, they are stunned and often embarrassed. When I review the piece with them, they can't believe some of the simple errors they glossed right over. Even the teachers who teach this every day and admonish their students for missing some of the more obvious errors in their writing miss some fairly simple mistakes.

So what do we do with regard to editing?

Keep in mind that the politician's rhetoric is very different from reality. We can create independent writers who can edit reasonably well but not perfectly, or we can create dependent writers who will create polished work with help from the teacher. The notion that the typical student can become an independent writer who produces error-free work without outside help is simply false.

The answer to the editing issue is not for the teacher to edit each student's paper in total. I firmly believe in self-editing and peer editing. But it needs to be focused. A student who has been studying end punctuation can edit a paper quite accurately for end punctuation marks. Another student who has been studying the use of punctuation in dialog can edit for punctuation in dialog quite effectively. But ask students to edit for every convention and you doom them to failure.

There is a solution. Instead of asking one student to edit for all errors, ask different students, who have been studying different components of conventions, to edit just for the convention they have been studying. When a paper is edited by three or four students, with each student editing for a different convention (e.g., capitalization, end punctuation, apostrophe to show possession, subject-verb agreement), the process creates a number of advantages:

1. A student has a chance to practice editing on real papers.
2. A writer receives valuable editing feedback.
3. A teacher's life is lengthened!

Obviously, older and more skilled students may be able to edit for more than one convention at a time. But even our highly skilled fourteen-year-old students will struggle if they attempt to correct everything.

Understand, please, that if you want a paper to be error-free, the teacher will most likely need to conduct the final edit. And while, in my opinion, it's fine to display a student's work that has some errors, it is not okay to mail out writing for publication or to people in the community (e.g., business people, politicians, school officials, etc.) that contains glaring errors. Thus, the publishing stage.

Publishing

The year after my NWP experience, I had the good fortune to work with some very talented seventh- and eighth-grade writers. We decided that we should publish a book of our stories. It was my first experience in any model of student publishing. One thing became very clear early on: Knowing their work was going to be seen by friends, family, community members, and total strangers was an enormous motivator. The students, without prompting from me, wanted their work to be as strong as possible. Finally, they had a purpose to revise and edit. The finished product, which was printed and bound by professional printers and binders, was impressive. The writing was sophisticated, enjoyable, and memorable.

Similarly, in his book, *No Place But Here,* Garret Keizer (1998), a brilliant teacher and writer in the Northeast Kingdom of Vermont, tells the story of the year he taught a high school English course for students who struggled with reading and writing. He decided the students should write a book, which they did, and, as a result, the students gained accolades they would otherwise never have received. He writes, "Years later I still get questions about 'them guys that wrote the book.'"

Whether students are high achievers or perched on the bottom rung, when they are faced with the opportunity to do something real—something beyond the school walls, such as publishing in a newspaper or a magazine or on the Web—they become excited and motivated by the challenge, by the possibility of doing something great.

I always encouraged my students to submit pieces of writing for publication in either the local newspaper or regional or national magazines. In order to submit their writing, they also had to learn to write a business letter to accompany their submission. While few were published, students almost always received a notice informing them that their writing had not been accepted. The energy and joy that they exuded when they bounded into the classroom with their rejection letter was something I will always remember. They had been recognized by someone outside the school. It was magical.

However, classroom publishing has taken on an almost crazed atmosphere today. I walk into classrooms, especially primary classrooms, and teachers tell me with pride that each student "has published twenty-seven books" or "the class published eleven books" or some number that astonishes me. Upon examination of the material, I see that some of the books are polished and impressive, but I am often stunned by the poor quality of some of the writing, by the numerous errors that appear, and by the glitz without substance.

To my mind, pride in publishing should be a result of the effort required to create a solid, polished piece of writing. Publishing is hard work and, as many professional writers have learned, not everything we write is published just because we finished it. I would far prefer to see a young writer publish two or three or four solid stories than fifteen or twenty-two mediocre ones that are filled with errors.

Whether publishing occurs through a professional printing company or through a school's computer department or with ribbon and a plastic cover, it should be reserved for children's best pieces, the ones in which they take great pride. I want students to learn that publishing is not easy, but once a piece is published, the writers can take pride knowing they earned it. Publishing, in any format, deserves a time-out from our daily routine so we can stop and honor a student who has done something remarkable. If this happens for every child every week, it loses its significance and its lessons. I want every child to publish, but I also want everything published to be worthy.

A Final Thought

As a teacher relatively new to the profession or as an experienced teacher looking for ways to improve instruction, you may think that you can keep your students relatively aligned with where they are in the process. "Okay, this week we'll get through prewriting and their first draft, and next week we'll conference and begin work on the second draft." We all wish it were that simple. While final-draft due dates are appropriate and often essential, the reality is that writing is messy, and keeping all your students near the same point in the process is almost impossible. Prepare yourself for the fact that while some students are diligently working (or sometimes not so diligently working!) on their first draft, others may still be organizing and planning what they're going to write. At the same time, other students, those who love to write and spend time at home working on their draft, may be ready to conference after two days, well ahead of your expectations and the rest of the class. You can't very well ask those students to wait for the others; nor can you tell the others to "hurry up!" Flexibility and planning are essential.

Success revolves around two ingredients. First, teach your students that not everyone will finish at the same time and that you expect students to be ready to conference or revise or edit or publish at different times. This alleviates the "fear factor" that some students encounter when they believe that they should be working faster or that there is something wrong because almost everyone else in the class is ahead of them. Students need to expect that some of their peers will be conferencing while they're still drafting or planning. A seamless approach needs to be encouraged in the classroom. Thus, the second ingredient is strong teacher management of the process. You will need to help some students organize a conference group while others are still drafting. Be prepared to have some students who are editing a peer's paper while others are conferencing. And be prepared to help some students submit a polished piece for publication while others are still drafting. I often used magnetic boards to monitor visually where students were in the process. This way I could easily assist students directly or help them find other students who were ready and able to brainstorm ideas/conference/edit and so forth.

Remember, if everyone is at the same place at the same time, something is probably wrong!

Steps to take right now

- Consider the activities in which you have participated that require a process. Learning a language? Playing an instrument or a sport? Creating a piece of art? What does that process look like? How were you taught the skills required to be successful in that endeavor?

- Write about those who taught you about the writing process. How did they teach you? Was their model an accurate one? How have you taught the process to your students? In what ways do you model this for your students?

- If you haven't read anything by Donald Graves, Don Murray, Lucy Calkins, Tom Romano, or Vicki Spandel, hop on the Internet, or go to your local bookstore and order one of their books!

Lynna's World

Professional writing seeks to express information, not impress people with a big vocabulary or the length of our documents or the number of emails we distribute in a day. In the workplace our writing needs to solve problems and convey information, clearly and concisely, and be reader-oriented. In organizing and developing the message, we need to be proactive rather than reactive. In other words, we need to take the time to construct the message so that the customer isn't calling our boss to scream about us or having a lawyer call us. Both instances would require far more time to deal with after the fact than the time spent initially to avoid those types of problems.

In the workplace, the writing process is in some ways similar to the classroom, but it also has distinct differences. The boss isn't going to give the employees handouts and edit

THE **Classroom–Corporate** CONNECTION

1. True or False: There is only one right way to write a business message.

2. Match the following channels of communication with their descriptions.

Oral communication	a. is delivered quickly, can incorporate audio and video, and often lacks privacy
Written communication	b. is appropriate for sensitive issues, provides immediate feedback, and allows limitless nonverbals (gestures, facial expressions, eye contact, etc.)
Electronic communication	c. is appropriate for complex messages, provides a permanent record, and shows more formality

3. True or False: Some business messages will be routine and brief while others will be more complex, involving research, analysis, and careful organization.

4. True or False: In determining the purpose of an effective business message, the writer's needs should relate with the reader's needs.

5. Using the writing process in composing a business message provides which of the following advantages:
   a. Saves time
   b. Produces a better-quality end product
   c. Makes writing less difficult
   d. All of the above

6. Fill in the Blank: Two major organizational patterns of letters and memos are _____ and _____ strategies.

sheets. But there may be samples of similar documents to look at. For example, when employees need to write a proposal, they *may* find other proposals to look at for guidelines. In any case, the writing process takes hard work and thoughtful effort.

Process

When I teach students and employees about the writing process, I use the three-part process shown in Figure 4.3. Together, we look at the fundamentals of planning, drafting, and revising.

Most participants appreciate an explanation of the writing process. They look at writing as a huge task: They don't know where to start or what to do next. This process helps guide them as they write workplace documents. It gives them a road map to get to their destination.

F i g u r e 4 . 3   **Business Writing Process**

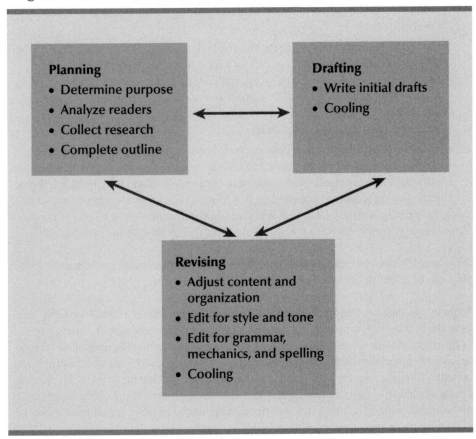

But I often wonder, "Why don't they know about the writing process by the time they get to this level?" Many of my college students tell me they were taught the writing process but were never forced to use it—until they entered my classroom. Several students, with a look of amazement, comment on how much easier it is to write since they actually started using the writing process in planning, drafting, and revising their documents.

CONNECTION

When upper elementary students, middle school students, high school students, college students, and people in the workplace use a process to write, they become more competent writers. The earlier they learn to use the writing process, the easier it will be for them to write more effectively.

Planning

When I introduce the planning stage to groups of employees, I explain the process I used to create an email to members of a communications committee to announce an upcoming meeting, a very simple business message:

- First I had to determine the purpose: to announce a meeting.

- Second, I had to consider my audience: Who were the people I was writing to? They were long time members of the committee, so I didn't need to go into a lot of detail, and I could use our specialized terminology with which they were all familiar.

- Third, I needed to do my research. I had to look at everyone's schedule to see when everyone was available so I could set up a time for the meeting. (There's no use holding a meeting if half the members can't attend.) Then I needed to reserve a room so I could include the room number in the email (versus sending a second email later on). I also needed to determine what the agenda would be so I could include that information in the email.

- Fourth, I needed to create an outline. Now, I could have done this in my head or quickly jotted one down on paper, but either way, it was important. Otherwise the information in the email would have been hard to follow and I might have left out important information. I decided on this format: First section—announcement of the meeting with the date, time, and place; second section—the agenda of the meeting; third section—a list of what they needed to bring to the meeting.

This example shows writers how going through the process can make our writing more efficient and effective. This section explores each step in detail.

Purpose   In the planning stage, it's important to understand the purpose: to inform, to persuade, to entertain, or to promote goodwill. This is true in professional writing just as it's true in classroom writing. Types of informational documents in the workplace include those that explain procedures, announce meetings, answer questions, or transmit findings. Examples of persuasive types of writing in the workplace include those that sell products, convince managers, motivate employees, or win over customers. Writing that entertains can be found in the advertising industry through humorous ads that persuade us to buy products or use a service. Promoting goodwill is usually a secondary purpose in all workplace documents. We write differently for different purposes, so important questions to ask are, "Why am I sending this message?" and "What do I hope to achieve?" The responses will determine how we organize and present our information, either directly or indirectly, and the amount of information we include.

Channels of Communication Writers also need to determine the appropriate channel of communication (assuming it won't be oral). Printed media includes memos, letters, reports, and proposals. Electronic media includes email, faxes, Instant Messaging, Web sites, wikis, blogs, and so on.

Writers need to select the medium that best fits the message and situation. This is obviously true in the work world, but opportunities to write using different mediums should be provided in the classroom as well (e.g., PowerPoint, emails, class blogs, etc.). Written communication has its advantages and disadvantages over oral communication. For example, oral communication provides instant feedback, but you can't revise and edit the message (nor do you have a permanent record of the message and discussion). So if you say to an employee, "You're lazy," you can't take it back and say, "I really meant to say you are accomplishment challenged." Printed communication, on the other hand, takes more time to create and has limited nonverbals (facial expressions, gestures, body language), but it can be carefully crafted and revised. Additionally, electronic communication can reach a large audience very quickly and can use rich multimedia formats. But, there is lack of privacy and they tend to be overused. Many managers start the day by looking at more than a hundred emails.

There are differences in how printed documents and emails are written. Electronic messages have a greater need to state the main point early in the message and require even more care in writing the subject lines.

In professional writing, the communication channel should suit the level of formality, the complexity of the information, the time restraints, and so forth. Writers should select the best medium for their situation, purpose, and reader(s). One company made the news lately when a supervisor wrote an email to several employees to announce that their jobs were being eliminated. The right channel? I think not!

Audience Next, writers need to analyze the reader because we write differently for different audiences. Analyzing the audience helps writers to identify the appropriate tone, language, and channel. There are several ways to adjust the writing to the type of message and reader:

- Spotlight reader benefits. Show them how you're going to save them time and money or help them reach their goals.
- Use bias-free language.
- Accentuate the positive. Eliminate negative words. Tell people what you can do, rather than what you can't do.
- Be courteous.

C O N N E C T I O N
So in both school and the workplace, writers need to consider the notion of audience, purpose, and channel of communication for writing to be effective. These are key issues for schools to address in their writing assignments, so when students enter the workforce, they'll be better prepared to perform the types of writing their employers will require.

- Simplify your language. Use short, everyday words; avoid pompous and pretentious language; and use jargon with discretion.

- Promote the "You Attitude." Use more *you* and *your* instead of *I* and *we*. In academic writing we avoid writing in second person. However, frequently in professional writing, we write in second person in letters, memos, emails, and proposals to talk directly to the reader. For example, in an essay, students wouldn't write, "When you lose your job, you'll find that . . . " But in organizations, employees might write, "This property would give you a profitable site for university housing." Once again, it's all about the purpose!

- Use precise, vigorous words: strong verbs and concrete nouns.

Research   Also, to avoid reader frustration and inaccurate messages, we need to write always from a position of knowledge. This means that we must do research; collecting the necessary information may take five minutes or five months. So in the classroom we need to ask, "Is it reasonable to expect students to complete the research paper in the time the teacher has allotted?"

One manager received a letter from an angry customer who insisted that he should not have to pay the sixty-dollar late fee because he had mailed the payment ten days before it was due. Instead of just firing off a letter to the customer, the manager did some research. He found the customer's cancelled check, and sure enough, the company had received it before the due date. However, the check was postdated after the due date. So when the manager wrote back to tell the customer that he would have to pay the late fee, he was able to include a copy of the check. It would be unreasonable for a customer to remain angry with this decision when the evidence clearly showed that the check was dated December 10, five days past the due date of December 5. This is just a simple example of how important it is for writers to write from a position of knowledge, whether they are writing to customers, suppliers, vendors . . . or even teachers.

Teaching students effective research skills is an essential part of preparing them to write in the workplace. When researching, students need to focus on identifying the specific information they need, locating the information, gathering it, analyzing it (is it reliable, relevant, current, etc.), and putting it into their own words.

Outlines and Organizational Patterns   After the research is completed, writers need to create an outline. Professional writing, such as letters, proposals, and reports, usually require a specific format. Completing outlines forces us to think before we write and to organize our writing. I know we all teach that to our students, but in my experience, few writers actually create an outline when they write (unless the teacher requires it, and then students will just create it after they write the rough draft). Outlines also help employees to follow the company's required format. The actual design of the outline is not important, so visual learners can create their outline any way they want as long as the end product follows the company's guidelines.

One company I worked for wanted their credit reports done with ten particular headings in a specific order. I thought it was a bit redundant, but again, it didn't matter what I thought; I had to follow the company's format. Outlining saves us time in the long run.

It also makes us more comfortable and confident when we move forward to write the rough draft.

I understand that in the classroom, stressing creativity and individuality is important, but there should also be times when students have to follow a format, thus modifying their writing to match the purpose and audience. An outline can help them stay on track.

When we communicate we don't just throw a mass of ideas at people; we present an organized whole. In the workplace, people are busy, and they can't spend time trying to piece together information to get the message. Likewise, teachers are busy, and we should teach our students how to organize information effectively. A business document should not be fragmented like a jigsaw puzzle that needs to be put together to get the picture. Nor should organizing a document be like playing Pin the Tail on the Donkey—just randomly inserting information. Rather, writers of well-organized messages group similar ideas together so that readers can see relationships and follow logical arguments.

Most workplace documents can be arranged in conventional patterns of organization. (See Figure 4.4.) You can also use these organizational patterns when you create students' writing assignments.

CONNECTION

All writers, regardless of their ages, need to take time to become knowledgeable about their topics. Writers also need to create an outline or a graphic organizer so that they have a structured approach to writing. We need to continue to teach this and require students to do it so they can be more successful writers. Please keep in mind that some individuals can visualize what their writing will look like, but they are a small minority.

Figure 4.4 **Organizational Patterns**

Letters/Memos	Instructions	Progress Reports	Proposals	Formal Reports
I. Opening	I. Introduction	I. Introduction	I. Introduction	I. Introduction
II. Body	II. Main Step 1	II. Work Completed	II. Discussion	II. Facts/Findings
III. Closing	a. Substep	III. Present Status	a. Description of Problem	III. Conclusion/ Recommendations
	b. Substep	IV. Work Remaining	b. Significance	
	c. Substep		c. Methods	
	III. Main Step 2		d. Staffing, Cost, Resources	
	a. Substep		e. Work Schedule	
	b. Substep		III. Conclusion	
	c. Substep			
	IV. Closing			

Drafting

After the planning stage (which included determining the purpose, selecting the channel of communication, analyzing the audience, researching, and outlining), writers move into the drafting stage. In this stage, I strongly encourage employees to write the way they talk. When I mention this in training programs, people often snicker, thinking that concept is crazy. They don't believe that their own natural voice is good enough or professional enough. Now in the classroom setting, I understand you will need to adjust this approach because you are dealing with a different group of writers. Many students do not speak using standard English or modify how they speak to different audiences (i.e., they speak in the same manner to the principal, teachers, and friends). We need to teach students that they should speak appropriately to different people, and, therefore, they can't necessarily write the way they talk.

Essentially there are three styles of writing and speaking: street style, conversational style, and scholarly style. The street style usually includes incorrect grammar, profanity, slang, and so forth. It has its place, but not in the workplace or in the classroom. The scholarly style is on the other end of the spectrum, with its big words that most people don't understand and long, flowery sentences, which makes the information hard to read and even more difficult to comprehend. In organizations, we want a conversational style; it excludes both the incorrect grammar and profanity of the street style, and the pompousness of the scholarly style. When we don't use our natural voice (conversational style), our writing ends up being awkward. So when we write our first draft, we shouldn't worry about tone, vocabulary, grammar, or spelling (which is my version of Fred's earlier statement, "spell the best you can right now"). At this stage, we should just follow the organization of the outline and write the way we talk. (We'll worry about the other aspects in the next stage.)

Revising and Proofreading

This stage is where we really get down to the basics: reexamining content, organization, style, tone, and usage. It's like we're already dressed, but we need some finishing touches and polishing—a last look in the mirror to make some modifications. Here are some questions to ask:

- *Content:* Does the content need adjustment? Is there enough information included for the reader to understand the message clearly? Is any information unnecessary? Is the information accurate?

- *Organization:* Is the information easy to follow? Is there a logical order to the information? Have I followed the company's format?

- *Style:* Have I inserted transitions for fluency? Is there variety in the sentence structure? Does the vocabulary contain any terms that the reader wouldn't understand?

- *Tone:* Have I eliminated as many negative words as possible? Have I told people what I can do rather than what I can't do? How would I feel if someone wrote this to me? Is the tone appropriate for the purpose and audience?

- *Usage:* Have I corrected all errors in grammar, spelling, and mechanics?

Finally, it is vital to proofread before we click *send* or distribute the written document. Professional writing MUST be error-free. Otherwise, writers appear unprofessional, unconcerned about detail, and lackadaisical about their work. Proofreading needs to be done at least twice. Use a spell checker, but recognize that you are smarter than any spell checker or grammar checker out there on the market today. For example, a spell checker will not identify *their* as misspelled when it really should be *there*. Several years ago I tested a grammar checker by entering one hundred sentences, all with different types of errors. Only fifty of the sentences were marked as incorrect, and out of those, 50 percent were "corrected" incorrectly. Remember, a poorly written message can cause embarrassment, poor decisions, loss of job, and other dire results.

CONNECTION

These basic criteria are stressed in school writing and in workplace writing: Content/Ideas, Organization, Style/Word Choice, Tone/Voice, and Usage/Conventions. They are the key components to making messages clear for readers and, therefore, should regularly be examined in the revision process of all writing.

One employee sent his boss and colleagues an email beginning "Hell, Craig" instead of "Hello, Craig." For six months, every time he walked into a meeting, everyone yelled, "Hell, Dave" just like the Cheers' patrons used to yell, "Norm." Another employee told me he emailed all the members of his church about an upcoming fundraiser. He wrote, "We will be selling shits, so everyone can wear theirs this Saturday at the retreat." He kept referring to the "shits" instead of the "shirts" throughout the entire email.

Although short emails and other documents can't always be reviewed by another reader in the workplace, sometimes it's a good idea to know when you need another pair of eyes to look at a document. One of Fred's favorite stories is about a school administrator who ran off fifteen hundred copies of a letter to send home to parents, welcoming them to the new school year. One of the people at the school realized there was a spelling error in the first sentence. The administration, however, decided to go ahead and send out the letters. As one person said, "We've already printed off fifteen hundred copies! We're not going to print it again."

Proofreading is absolutely, totally necessary!!!

This revising process also includes a cooling off period in which the writer puts the document aside and reviews it later. All in all, the revising process varies considerably depending on the situation and complexity of the document.

Ways to give your classroom the **Corporate Edge**

- Direct students to http://oregonstate.edu/dept/eli/buswrite/Business_Writing_Help.html, where they can click on various types of business documents (e.g., memos, letters, instructions). Ask them to examine the organizational pattern of each type of document and highlight the pattern in the sample documents provided.

- Direct students to www.powa.org, where they can review the interactive writer's guide. Ask students to select topics for help in revising/editing their work and complete several of the online exercises.

- Invite guest speakers to discuss how they create PowerPoint presentations in the workplace, explaining how they storyboard their ideas and how they determine the wording of the key points to put on each slide.

- Provide students with plenty of practice to edit and revise various documents.

- Create an assignment in which students design a brochure identifying the different types of electronic communication (e.g., email, Instant Messages, video and teleconferencing, faxes, blogs, wikis, and Web sites) and highlighting their advantages and disadvantages.

Answers to The Classroom–Corporate Connection

1. False **2.** oral—b; written—c; electronic—a. **3.** True **4.** True **5.** (d) All of the above
6. direct (main message first in document) and indirect (main message in middle of document)

CHAPTER 5

Six Traits

From your perspective

1. Which component of writing do you emphasize most with your students? Why?

2. Which component of writing would you like to spend the most time teaching? What would you do with that trait if you had more time each day?

3. Create a list of resources in your school that can assist you in teaching the traits of writing.

An Overview

Whether you've heard of Six Traits, Write Traits, or 6+1 Traits, they all refer to the same concept: the components of strong writing. The traits, in both schools and businesses, provide clear and consistent expectations of quality for readers and writers. But what do these traits look like, how do we teach them, how do we use them to help improve writing, and are they valued components of business writing? This chapter explores the basic highlights of the traits and how they're used to improve writing.

Fred's World

Albert Einstein's Short-Lived Golf Career

A few years ago, I read an article in a golf magazine about Albert Einstein's short-lived golf career in America. The story goes that Einstein, having lost a bet to some colleagues, was going to have to play a round of golf with them as payment for his loss. He requested that he be allowed to take a lesson with a pro before undertaking the round of golf. The pro, telling Einstein that he wanted to see his swing, put down a ball and told him to hit it. Not being very athletic, Einstein swung and missed. "No, no," said the pro. "Put your feet a little closer together and bend your knees. Now hit the ball." Einstein swung and missed again. "No, no," yelled the pro. "Keep your head down over the ball and don't be looking down the fairway. Now hit the ball." Again, Einstein swung and missed. "Listen to me," urged the pro. "Your right arm should be like a pendulum. Straight back and straight through. Now hit the ball." Once again, Einstein swung without success. "This time," said the frustrated pro, "rotate your hips as you bring your arms through. Just hit the ball." Again, Einstein missed. As the pro began another round of instructions, Einstein, frustrated, picked up four golf balls, threw them to the pro, and told him to catch the balls. The pro missed all four. "Why didn't you catch them?" asked Einstein. "Throw them to me one at a time and I will," replied the pro. "Exactly," responded the scientist. "When you teach me, teach me one thing at a time."

When I finished the article I realized that while I was reading about a golf lesson, I was also reading about how writing is often taught. In an attempt to help our students improve their writing, we provide feedback about everything all at once, and much of that feedback is about conventions. For student writers, this is far too much information for them to process at one time.

In good teaching, we break the concept into its components and teach one skill at a time, allowing our students to process that one skill, practice the skill, and become reasonably proficient in that one area before we tack on additional components. This is what the traits are all about. Athletic coaches, musicians, artists, and others learned and perfected the approach of teaching one skill at a time years before the proverbial piano finally dropped on the heads of English and Language Arts teachers. When I coached baseball, I thought about what hitters need to do to hit well. Some of it is natural: Some people have better eyesight, faster reflexes. But the other aspects include shifting weight from the back leg to the front leg; positioning the arms correctly; extending the arms as they move over the plate; rotating their hips; and so on. In teaching hitting, we worked on one or maybe two components—or traits—each practice. Players practiced arm extension over and over and over until it became instinctive. Over time, we started connecting arm extension with hip rotation and on and on until all areas had been practiced and pieced together to form a smooth, effective swing that, hopefully, connected with the ball! The few players I coached who possessed both the natural instincts and the ability to process what I was teaching became exceptional ballplayers. Those who did not have those lightning-fast reflexes and great eyesight at least became reasonably good hitters. I hold the same expectations for our students and their writing. Some will become exceptional writers. The others, I believe, can become competent writers. Right after writing process, knowledge of the traits is at the top of my list about what I needed to know when I started teaching. It certainly would have made my life, as well as the lives of my students, much easier.

No one "invented" the traits. They've always been around. The traits are the components of strong writing. But it took Vicki Spandel and a group of middle school teachers from Beaverton, Oregon, in the early 1980s to formalize them into a structure that could benefit both teachers and students. Whether you have heard of Six Traits or Write Traits or 6+1 Traits, they all are based on Vicki's work with the Beaverton teachers.

The traits of writing are Ideas, Organization, Voice, Word Choice, Sentence Fluency, and Conventions. While Ruth Culham (2003) adds her "+1" of "presentation and layout," the original model includes that within conventions. The traits give teachers the structure to help our students develop each skill of writing and then put them together to create one strong piece of writing.

Detailed books have been written on the traits, such as *Creating Writers* by Vicki Spandel (2009), so for an in-depth examination I encourage you to read one. For our purpose, I offer an overview.

1. *Ideas:* clarity, focus, quality details.
2. *Organization:* leads, sequencing, transitions, pacing, conclusions.
3. *Voice:* reader-writer connection, audience, enthusiasm.
4. *Word choice:* strong verbs, precise language, everyday words used in unique ways.
5. *Sentence fluency:* rhythm of language, variety of sentence length and beginnings.
6. *Conventions:* grammar, usage, mechanics, presentation, layout.

Six Traits is not a program you can buy or a curriculum you can just stick into an English/Language Arts department. The traits are a vision, a philosophy, and an approach to teaching writing that builds upon writing process and also provides some structure to guide us.

Key Ingredients

The traits model offers teachers a common language to discuss writing, a consistent rubric for evaluation, and a gateway into revision.

Common Language

The traits provide a common language we can use to discuss writing with our students, our colleagues, our students' parents, and our administrators. The language remains constant with first graders and with high school seniors taking honors English. This is especially helpful for our students who struggle with writing and with school in general. When the traits *aren't* used, many of these students spend part of the year floundering before they realize that what Mr. Heatherly called "beginnings" or "grabbers" last year is what Ms. Abramovitz calls "leads" this year. When a common language is in place, students' understanding of instruction about writing is clear from the first day. After two years of working with the traits, one group of teachers commented, "Last year was so easy. We couldn't believe the students' progress after just one year of using the traits. They were able to engage in discussions about writing, using the language of the traits, at a much higher level than ever before. It made everything so much easier!" The common language that students can carry from year to year and from content area to content area provides clarity for students and their teachers as they discuss writing.

Rubrics

The traits provide us with a reasonably consistent and reasonably objective way to answer the question, "How good is this paper?" If our desire is to help students produce quality writing regardless of content area, then we need to provide them with a clear and consistent vision of what success looks like. Students need to know where the target is and what is needed to hit the bull's-eye. This vision of success needs to maintain common expectations and criteria of strong writing.

Through the use of well-designed rubrics, the traits help establish the criteria by which a paper is assessed. They offer teachers and students a valuable tool for assessing writing, and they provide students with a clear understanding of what good writing looks like. Unlike most state writing rubrics, which are holistic (one rubric that incorporates all aspects of writing), trait rubrics are analytic. There is one rubric for each trait; thus, a student could receive as many as six scores for a piece of writing. Before you panic and think, "You mean I have to score each paper six times?" let me assure you that not all papers have to be graded for all six traits. We merely ask ourselves, "What was the purpose of the writing and who is the audience?" to determine which traits are most useful in assessing the paper. For once, all teachers can use the same set of criteria and have the same expectations for defining good writing.

Consider the differences between the following analytic rubric and holistic rubric. Table 5.1 shows an analytic rubric from Vicki's book *Creating Writers* (4th edition). It examines the trait of ideas, which is all about clarity, focus, and quality details.

The rubric in Table 5.1 provides the teacher and student with clear and concise expectations for success in this area. Consider the wealth of information students gain about their writing, both their strengths and weaknesses, and the knowledge teachers gain about where to focus their instruction and how to help students improve their writing. Students know what is needed for improvement if their initial score is low, and the same expectations exist for every class every year. A rubric exists for each of the traits.

Holistic rubrics, on the other hand, cram everything into one score. For example, Table 5.2 shows a four-point holistic rubric similar to those used by many states to assess student writing.

Table 5.1   Analytic Rubric: Trait of Ideas

6	Clear, focused, compelling—holds reader's attention Striking insight, impressive knowledge of topic Takes reader on a journey of understanding Clear main idea and significant, intriguing details
5	Clear and focused Reflects in-depth knowledge of topic Authentic, convincing info from experience/research Clear main idea well supported by details
4	Clear and focused more often than not Writer knows the topic well enough to write in broad terms Some new info, some common knowledge Main idea can be easily inferred, quality details outweigh generalities
3	Clear, focused moments overshadowed by underdeveloped, rambling text Writer needs greater knowledge of topic—gaps apparent Mostly common knowledge and best guesses Generalities dominate, writer has a weak grip on the main idea
2	Writer lacks clear vision—still defining topic, key questions Writer struggles with insufficient knowledge—writing is strained Broad unsupported observations, invented details Filler dominates—main idea wanders in and out of focus
1	Very foggy—no "land in sight" yet Main idea never emerges due to writer's lack of knowledge Hastily assembled notes, random thoughts Bits of info wander in search of a main idea

T a b l e 5 . 2 Holistic Rubric

4 Develops and maintains a clear and focused purpose that is aligned to the topic.

Incorporates specific details to support and clarify the central idea and contains little if any extraneous information.

Revolves around an organizational structure that connects ideas.

Uses transitions effectively.

Contains a variety of sentence structures and lengths that enhance the readability.

Uses vocabulary that is precise and helps clarify the writer's message.

Contains few if any errors in mechanics, grammar, punctuation, or spelling and any errors that do occur do not impact the reader's ability to understand the text.

3 Generally develops and maintains a clear and focused purpose that is aligned to the topic although a lapse may occur.

Contains details that usually support and clarify the central idea but may contain some extraneous information.

Revolves around an organizational structure that usually connects ideas.

Uses some transitions effectively.

Contains some variation in sentence structure and length.

Uses vocabulary that is usually precise and usually helps clarify the writer's message.

Contains some errors in mechanics, grammar, punctuation, or spelling but they do not impact the reader's ability to understand the text.

2 Demonstrates little understanding of the purpose and often loses focus.

Contains few details to support or clarify the ideas and includes extraneous information.

Revolves around a loose organizational structure that often does not connect ideas and leaves the reader confused.

Uses few transitions but they often fail to connect main ideas.

Includes limited variation in sentence structure or length.

Exhibits minimal vocabulary that is precise and helpful to the reader. Most language is simplistic and often vague.

Contains numerous errors in grammar, punctuation, or spelling and they sometimes impact the reader's ability to understand the text.

1 Relates somewhat to the purpose but has little if any focus and is often confusing.

Contains few if any details and those that are present do not support or clarify the ideas. Extraneous information confuses the reader.

Lacks an organizational structure and the reader is often confused about where the paper is heading.

Does not use transitions to connect ideas.

Uses a sentence structure in which run-ons, repetition, or incomplete sentences cause the reader to lose focus.

Includes vocabulary that lacks precision and may be irrelevant, incorrect, or overly simplistic.

Contains numerous errors in grammar, punctuation, or spelling that interfere with the reader's understanding.

I have a number of concerns with this rubric, but the greatest is the lack of connection to student writing. How do you score a paper that "Develops and maintains a clear and focused purpose that is aligned to the topic" (4), "Revolves around an organizational structure that usually connects ideas" (3), and "Includes limited variation in sentence structure or length" (2)? What score does this paper receive? Many students possess strengths and weaknesses with various aspects of their writing; furthermore, they do not maintain similar levels of quality in all components throughout a piece of writing. Thus, the single, holistic score does not provide an accurate representation of the writer's skills and does not provide the teacher with adequate information to help guide instruction.

Too often rubrics are the "end point" of a piece of writing. A student writes a paper and turns it in; the teacher reads the paper and offers comments and rubric scores. Then they're off for the next assignment. Instead of an end point, rubrics should be the springboard for discussion about the strengths and weaknesses of a piece of writing. Most important, rubrics should be used throughout the various drafts to help a student understand what needs to be done to improve the writing on the next draft.

When we provide our students with copies of our rubrics, explore what they mean, and demonstrate what various scores look like in writing (establishing benchmark papers), we empower them to become self-assessors, which leads to competent, independent writers—our ultimate goal.

When faced with the dilemma "So do I use the state holistic rubrics or someone else's quality analytic rubrics?" I suggest that teachers use analytic rubrics for instructional purposes in their classrooms. If students can perform at high levels on analytic rubrics, they will do exceptionally well on their state rubric.

More information on rubrics is available from a variety of sources, but I would suggest the work of Grant Wiggins or Jay McTighe for those who wish to pursue this topic further.

Revision

The third component of the traits is that they provide a gateway into revision. Let's be honest. Unless we have taught our students about what to do when they revise, most of them are left guessing. Most of them know to correct the "mistakes" marked on the paper, but once that is accomplished, many of them don't have the slightest clue what to do next. The traits help them get started. Students, after a conference with the teacher or peers, know where to focus their attention. They know that they need to focus on their verbs (word choice) or that they lack details that would create a picture (ideas) or that all their sentences begin with a pronoun and they need to revise some of them to create variety (sentence fluency). Additionally, students can use the rubrics as a guide that tells them what to do to improve their writing.

These three components—common language, analytic rubrics for assessment, and a gateway into revision—make the traits a powerful tool to guide our teaching of writing and to help our students improve their writing so they can become both competent and confident.

Let's take a quick look at each of the traits. If you would like more in-depth information, please read Vicki Spandel's book *Creating Writers*.

Ideas

Good writing begins with three key concepts: focus, clarity, and quality details. These concepts are the heart of the trait of *ideas*. The rubrics for the writing assessment in many states focus on topic development, but ideas goes beyond that. While it's true many students struggle with topic development, the problem stems from something greater: a lack of focus on their topic. How many times have we seen students write papers on "The Civil War" or "Ancient Egypt" or "The Civil Rights Movement in America" or "The Solar System" or "A Famous Mathematician"? Or write a short story about "A Long Year for My Family" or, even worse, "My Summer Vacation"? We sometimes assign these topics and then we wonder and complain about their lack of quality details and topic development. The problem, I believe, is simple: They write on topics so broad that it prevents them from focusing on specifics. Until students are able to narrow their topics, their writing, in all likelihood, will be general, superficial, and bland. Our task, as Stephen King writes in his book *On Writing*, ". . . is to help students find their topic."

Often teachers' assignments prevent students from focusing in and developing their topic. Some of the assignments I've seen in the past few years include this tenth-grade history assignment:

> Select three forms of government that exist in the world. Write a paper, two to four pages in length, explaining each form of government, its core principles, the advantages and disadvantages of each, and discuss at least one country in the world that uses that form of government.

All that in two to four pages? Sounds more like a dissertation to me! And we want to see topic development and quality details? A more reasonable and effective assignment that would provide an opportunity for strong writing would be a paper, two to four pages in length, on *one* form of government. A logical follow-up would be to team together three students who wrote on different governments and have them create a collaborative paper that would compare and contrast the governments they researched.

Another broad assignment came from a math class. The teacher, to her credit, was having the students write as part of their math curriculum. Unfortunately, the teacher was not familiar with what strong assignments looked like in math and had not been provided with any training by her school. She gave the following assignment:

> Select a famous mathematician from the list I've given you. Write a one- to two-page biography making sure to include his or her contributions to mathematics.

Most of the papers looked like something out of the encyclopedia and contained nothing about the importance of the contribution. Here are a couple of segments from one paper.

> Henri Poincare's father, Leon Poincare, was a professor of medicine at the University of Paris. Henri had a sister named Aline who married a well known philosopher named Emile Boutroux. (Jules Henri Poincare) His cousin was Raymond Poincare, the President of France from 1913–1920. (Knapton 530)

Some of Henri Poincare's other contributions to mathematics are his contributions to algebraic topology, the theory of abelian functions, algebraic geometry, number theory and the theory of electromagnetism. Poincare had many more triumphs in his math work; these are only a few.

When we assign a biography, this is often what we get. The writer provides a list of facts, many of which either lack relevance or are beyond the comprehension of anyone without a doctorate in the field. Here, the assignment created the problem. To create an assignment that could provide some meaning and relevance in relation to the class, the teacher might instead ask students to select one of the mathematicians from the list, research the mathematician's contributions to the field, explain one of those contributions in relation to both the material covered in class during the year (which requires that the teacher list only mathematicians whose work is relevant to the course) and to the student's day-to-day life. How is the contribution used in the world outside of school? In the world within school?

The ability to develop a topic and incorporate quality details begins with a narrow topic. Our job, as teachers, is both to assign narrowed topics and/or to make sure that the student has selected a narrow topic about which to write. Clearly, students often need to conduct significant amounts of research before they are able to narrow their topic. Fifth-grade students who want to write about "Ancient Egypt" will need to read a great deal about the broad topic before they determine what is of greatest interest to them. Then, with help, they can begin to narrow their topics to ones that are manageable for the students' age and the amount of time they have to complete their assignment. Our challenge is to ensure that each assignment, each topic, provides students with opportunities to incorporate intriguing details so both the writer and reader are engaged.

I talk with teachers about teaching their students to "explode moments." It's a powerful concept that students remember, especially if we provide models from literature to show what exploded moments look like. But students can only explode moments when they have narrowed the topic.

Exploded moments, both in fiction and nonfiction, often take three or four pages to describe a thirty-second scene. Consider this passage from Gary Paulsen's (1993) book *Harris and Me*, in which the author and his nine-year-old cousin attach the motor from the washing machine onto a bicycle to see how fast the bike would travel.

> I checked the clock numerous times as I heard Harris trying to start the motor back in the yard.
>
> Put-n-put-n-put . . .
>
> And it would die. I found later that the motor died because Harris had already unhooked the governor and it was getting too much gas and was choking out. I also decided still later that it was probably God trying to save Harris from himself. But even divine intervention didn't work, and in truth Harris was so determined probably nothing could have saved him. Or, as Harris put it later, speaking of God: "At least He could have stopped me from unhooking that stupid governor . . . "
>
> The motor started, finally, with a stuttering put-n-put-n-put and as soon as I saw Harris begin to move I looked down at the clock. I couldn't have had my

eyes down for more than three seconds, but when I brought them up I was surprised to see that Harris had already moved toward me some distance.

Several other things were happening by this time that would determine Harris's fate. The engine, starved of gasoline all its life on the washing machine by the mechanical governor, responded in explosive gratitude for the chance at freedom. It went from the subdued put-n-put-n-put to a healthy BAM-BAM-BAM that I could hear easily from the end of the driveway.

Then, too, there was the further bad luck that somehow, in some way, everything held together. Bolts, belts, the bicycle—everything miraculously stayed in one piece and all of the gasoline that poured into the wide open throat of the little Briggs and Stratton engine was translated into power at the back wheel.

Power and speed.

From that point on everything came in flashes, flickering scenes of disaster, like watching a stop-action film of a flood or a hurricane hitting the coast of Florida.

To give him his due, Harris was plucky. Early on the Bendix brake had jammed and the chain—and therefore the pedals—had turned with the back wheel. Harris kept his feet on the pedals, or tried to, but as the speed went up and the pedals began to turn faster, much faster than they'd ever turned, his legs became at first a blur, then he held them up, the pedals slapping the bottoms of his bare feet as the bike approached something like terminal velocity with Harris just along for the ride.

It was amazing that nothing fell apart. As he got closer, his knees up alongside his cheeks, I could see that sense had at last come into his mind and his eyes were wide, huge with fear. His tongue hung out the side of his mouth, spit flying, and he turned into a blur.

Fifteen, twenty, thirty, forty—the bike had to be doing close to fifty miles an hour when he passed me standing at the end of the driveway.

"Helpppp meeeeee!" he yelled, the Doppler effect changing the pitch of his plea as he cleared the end of the driveway, flew across in front of me, and hit the ditch on the far side of the country road like a meteorite.

It was then, as he put it later, that he realized he was in trouble. Making the turn onto the road was clearly impossible but he claims he still thought he could "slow her down in the brush along the ditch."

The brush slowed him, all right. It stopped the bike dead in a dazzling, cartwheeling spray of engine, spokes, wheels, frame, and tangled belt. For half a second it was impossible to tell where Harris ended and bicycle began; the whole seemed a jumbled mass of boy and machine.

Then Harris separated. His body high above the brush, spread-eagled—he claimed later he could see for miles—still moving close to fifty miles an hour, then fell down, down in a curving arc to hit the ground and explode in a flurry of willows, leaves, brush, and dirt.

Then silence, broken only by the soft hissing of gas running from the tank onto the engine and the ticking of the brass alarm clock.

"Harris?"

Nothing.

"Harris—are you all right?"

A spitting sound—leaves and dirt being expelled. Then a grunt. "Hell no, I ain't all right. I was stuck in the dirt like an arrow and I'm all over scratches."

"Do you need help?" I couldn't see him for the brush and willows.

"Yeah. Help me find my bibs."

"Your pants?"

"Yeah—they come off me somewhere."

We looked for half an hour and more, Harris hiding twice when cars went by on the road, and we didn't find them and we looked for another half hour and we still didn't find them and we never did.*

The bike ride only lasted about thirty seconds, but in order to explode that moment, Paulsen required more than three pages! By showing students what it looks like to narrow a topic and explode a moment, we will help them gain a stronger vision of success and enable them to do it themselves.

This concept applies to nonfiction writing as well. Consider this passage on the power of a hurricane from Sebastian Junger's (1997) book *The Perfect Storm*:

A mature hurricane is by far the most powerful event on earth; the combined nuclear arsenals of the United States and the former Soviet Union don't contain enough energy to keep a hurricane going for one day. A typical hurricane encompasses a million cubic miles of atmosphere and could provide all the electric power needed by the United States for three or four years. During the Labor Day Hurricane of 1935, winds surpassed 200 miles an hour and people caught outside were sandblasted to death. Rescue workers found nothing but their shoes and belt buckles. So much rain can fall during a hurricane—up to five inches an hour—that the soil liquefies. Hillsides slump into valleys and birds drown in flight, unable to shield their upward facing nostrils. In 1970, a hurricane drowned half a million people in what is now Bangladesh. In 1938, a hurricane put downtown Providence, Rhode Island, under ten feet of ocean. The waves generated by that storm were so huge that they literally shook the earth; seismographs in Alaska picked up their impact five thousand miles away.

Compare this to an encyclopedia article and think which one your students would remember. The intriguing details, a result of a narrowed topic and an exploded moment, create images that students remember. Whether in fiction or informational writing, sharing passages such as these help students understand what they should do themselves. It also helps them understand the trait of *ideas*.

*Excerpt from *Harris and Me: A Summer Remembered,* copyright © 1993 by Gary Paulsen, reprinted by permission of Harcourt, Inc.

Organization

There are a number of components to *organization*, but at the heart lie structure and sequence, leads (as opposed to introductions), and conclusions. The use of transitions and pacing also falls within the boundaries of organization, but I believe that the first three concepts are crucial to success.

To most of us as adults and as teachers who have written dozens if not hundreds of papers over the years, keeping writing structured and in a sequence from beginning to middle to end seems so simple. How else would you do it? But to many of our students, the notion of beginning-middle-end is foreign. Especially the middle part. I've read dozens and dozens of student papers that contained little if any structure. The information was so clearly out of order that I wondered how the students could have possibly missed it. But they did. Whether we show students how to cluster together information related to the same topic, keep a chronological order, or any of a number of other ways to structure, we need to provide them with strategies to organize their writing. Four great sources for this are Vicki Spandel's *Creating Writers* (2009), Ralph Fletcher's and JoAnn Portalupi's *Craft Lessons* (1998) and *Nonfiction Craft Lessons* (2001), and Gretchen Bernabei's *Reviving the Essay: How to Teach Structure without Formula* (2005).

Unfortunately, the tradition of the formulaic structure of the five-paragraph essay is alive and well in our schools. This structure, while easy to follow, creates boring text and causes readers to skim the text rather than read critically. For a fascinating read on the history of this model of writing, I suggest Tom Newkirk's *The School Essay Manifesto: Reclaiming the Essay for Students and Teachers* (2005). Tom's book provides stunning insight as to why and how this model came into use and the inherent problems it creates when students try to use it to craft authentic, dynamic text. Tom points to Lucile Payne's *The Lively Art of Writing* (1965) and John Warriner's *English Grammar and Composition* (1965) as the texts that began the formulaic approach to writing that became the focus of writing in far too many classrooms.

Bernabei's *Reviving the Essay* is loaded with terrific ideas for grades 4–12 on how to teach structure without formula. At the heart of her suggestions is the belief that most school essays "ask students to start with a conclusion, a thesis, and use the rest of the paper to 'back it up.' The real essay offers a journey for the reader, or it doesn't work."

There are many ways to structure an essay. Granted, the five-paragraph essay is one method. But this model does not show a writer's honest, authentic thinking. Successful essays, ones that readers look forward to reading, essays that engage the reader and stir emotions, are not laid out in advance as if the writers knew exactly where they were heading. Sometimes, successful writing takes an unexpected turn that reveals something we never imagined. Formula writing does not allow for these turns. So what is the alternative? Structure without formula begins with strong leads.

Strong Leads

In part, we can thank state testing for the depressing, formulaic, organizational structure that is beginning to dominate so much student writing again, especially in elementary schools. Many states are looking for a bland, clearly stated introductory paragraph that does not appear in any type of professional writing that I've seen. It usually goes something like this: "In this paper, I will explain all about _____ (fill in your own blank!). First, I will tell you about _____. Then, I will tell you about _____. Finally, I will explain about _____. Let's begin."

When was the last time you read a book that began this way? Or a newspaper or journal article? And if you did find writing that began in this manner, were you inclined to keep reading? I certainly wouldn't. Yet, I find many teachers who are using this approach for two reasons. First, they don't know how else to teach openings. Second, papers that begin this way on state writing assessments often receive high scores if the rest of the paper is also clear and organized. While this approach may help some of our students to some degree, for many of our students this formulaic introduction is limiting and boring. It does not lead to writing that engages any reader I know.

I admit that for a number of years, I was guilty of teaching this way. I didn't know how else to teach students to write openings that grabbed the reader's attention. I knew how to teach introductions but not leads. Two questions frame the issue of strong leads: "How should I begin?" and "What goes into a strong beginning?"

Nancie Atwell (1998), in her book *In the Middle,* talks about the SACRED ways to begin.

- **S**etting
- **A**ction
- **C**haracter
- **R**eflection
- **E**vent
- **D**ialog

I love this acronym. It's easy for students to remember and it captures most of the ways a student can begin a piece of writing. By reading the first few lines of a book or an article to your students, you can help them identify quickly which of the SACRED ways the book began. They will also begin to gain a "vision of success" about what a lead looks like when done well. Oftentimes, after such a reading, students realize that a strong lead may incorporate more than one of these options. Here are six of my favorite leads:

1. "Where is Papa going with that ax?" (White, 1952, *Charlotte's Web*)
2. "Zero hit the USS *Yorktown* like a torpedo. On September 21, 1997, while cruising off the coast of Virginia, the billion-dollar missile cruiser shuddered to a halt. *Yorktown* was dead in the water." (Seife, 2000, *Zero: The Biography of a Dangerous Idea*)
3. "If your teacher has to die, August isn't a bad time of year for it." (Peck, 2004, *The Teacher's Funeral*)
4. "I could think of no reason why white people wanted Indian boys and girls except to kill them, and not having the remotest idea of what a school was, I thought we were going east to die." (Cooper, 1999, *Indian School: Teaching the White Man's Way*)

5. "Somehow I knew my time had come when Bambi Barnes tore her order book into little pieces, hurled it in the air like confetti, and got fired from the Rainbow Diner in Pensacola right in the middle of lunchtime rush." (Bauer, 2000, *Hope Was Here*)

6. "It is my first morning of high school. I have seven new notebooks, a skirt I hate, and a stomachache." (Anderson, 1999, *Speak*)

The other issue of what goes into a strong lead is intriguing. Teachers often encourage their students to "write a hook" or "write a grabbing lead" but fail to discuss how this is done! Students walk away from a teacher's desk with as little information as when they approached. *Telling them* to write strong leads does not *teach them* to write strong leads! I often read leads from books, both fiction and nonfiction, to students and have them decide whether or not they like the leads and explain why. Over and over I hear the same responses as to why they like certain leads. Strong leads do some of the following:

- Raise questions in the reader's mind.
- Establish a personal connection for the reader.
- Include an intriguing detail.
- Include humor.
- Paint pictures.
- Use dynamic verbs.

Usually, a strong lead contains some of these items, but not all. When teachers share the leads from a variety of books and then have students practice writing strong leads, they prepare students to write a strong lead when they write a paper or story. (See Appendix A, page 175, for lesson ideas that teach writing leads.)

Strong Bodies

The body (or "middle" for younger students) of a piece of writing is where the direction the writer has begun in the lead takes shape. But before putting pen to paper (or fingers to keyboard), writers need to answer the questions, "What am I trying to say? What is important? How do I get there?" Students often lose direction because they don't have solid answers to these questions. Instead, they're thinking, "What can I say that will fit into my three middle paragraphs?" Or, for younger students, "What am I supposed to say in my middle paragraph?" or "What am I supposed to say in the middle of my paragraph?" The problem is that they're allowing the structure to form the essay instead of the other way around. They are so concerned with meeting the requirements of their understanding of a "correct" essay or piece of writing that they lose sight of what is important to them as the writer.

In the body of a piece of writing, prewriting shows its importance. In prewriting, writers should have determined, to a large degree, their purpose, and what they want to say, what information or ideas are most important, and they should have chunked that content into cohesive manageable parts. Certainly, various graphic organizers, outlines, and pictures, are effective tools to help students find a pattern they want to follow for their writing. And the use of effective, natural transitions connects the key points into a smooth, logical sequence. But these tools are only effective when students know what they want to say because it's important, not because it will give them the required five sentences for their paragraph. If students are more concerned with creating three body paragraphs, the focus of the writing is lost. What if the students have only two main points to discuss, even if those two points are powerful, well developed, and engaging? Should they make up an ineffective third point just to meet the requirements of a five-paragraph essay? Students and teachers should focus on the quality of the writing, not the number of paragraphs.

Strong Conclusions

Strong middle sections of a piece of writing, based on what is important and relevant, lead, eventually, to a conclusion.

Conclusions present another challenge for students and teachers. Young writers simply conclude by writing "The End." This makes perfect sense since so many of their primary books end this way. I'm thrilled to see very young writers add "The End" to their writing because it demonstrates that they are aware that a paper needs to have an ending. This awareness, over time, can be transitioned into knowledge of other ways to end a piece of writing.

One of the reasons students struggle with conclusions is because they have so few chances to write one. The only time they write a conclusion is when they're writing a paper, and how often does that happen? For many high school students around the country, maybe only six or seven times a year! Just as with leads, students need opportunities to examine how professional writers end pieces of writing. What are the strategies they use? The students will rarely if ever see, "So that is the end of my report on _____. I hope you have learned something and that you liked my paper."

When we ask students to examine how professional writers conclude stories, articles, and letters, we help them gain insight into strategies they can use. They'll see summaries, reflections, questions that may lead to future writing, final images, a regret, or something the writer has learned. By reading these and practicing them, they will gain more competence and confidence to write strong conclusions. Here are just a few examples.

- "Glacier's [Glacier National Park] founders left it for each visitor to discover the best way to experience the park. I couldn't say which is best; there are so many still to be tried. But here's my advice for now: Light packs make for light spirits. Don't feed the bears. Save the wolverines. Let it snow." (Douglas H. Chadwick, "Crown of the Continent," *National Geographic,* Sept. 2007: 66–72)
- "And as I looked to the tall pines reaching toward my Louisiana sky, I reckoned that maybe that's the way life is supposed to be. Some days are like Saitter Creek—smooth and calm, letting you stay a child a little longer, and others are like Hurricane Audrey taking hold of you and spinning you above the pines, making you grow up a little quicker—kind of like cutting your hair on a full-moon day." (Kimberly Holt, *My Louisiana Sky,* 1998)
- "Would the whole jungle fall apart if one tarantula species went extinct? No one knows. But one thing's for sure. Without these awesome, regal spiders, the jungle—and our world—would be a lonelier, smaller, less exciting, and less mysterious place." (Sy Montgomery, *The Tarantula Scientist,* 2004)

- "The Supreme Court agrees that focusing on past racial wrongs will not yield solutions for the future—as made clear in June by its ruling against voluntary school-desegregation plans. But there is still a point in remembering how we got here, and remembering how determined some people were to keep Americans apart—if only because it reminds us of why it remains so hard for us to come together." (Ellis Close, "Little Rock: 50 Years Later," *Newsweek* 26 Sept. 2007)

- "For all the sleazebags who will try to lure a kid into a car, there are many Good Samaritans who are just concerned when they see a 12-year-old trudging along the road in the rain. I suppose we live at a time when we can't afford to let them accept the Samaritan's ride. But we also can't afford to have them think that Samaritans no longer exist. All these lectures, lessons and cautionary tales can't be to preserve a lifetime of looking over one's shoulder. As Oscar Wilde wrote, 'We are all in the gutter, but some of us are looking at the stars.' " (Anna Quindlen, "Frightening— and Fantastic," *Newsweek* 18 Sept. 2006)

By reading and discussing these conclusions, and the text that precedes them, students gain an understanding of how to write conclusions. Clearly, teachers need to guide the discussion about these and other conclusions. Then, we need to provide students with opportunities to practice writing conclusions so they can gain more competence and confidence in writing strong conclusions.

Voice

Don Murray (1998) said it best when he wrote, "Voice separates writing that is read from writing that is not read." Most teachers tell me that *voice* is the most difficult trait to teach, but also the one they appreciate the most when it's present in a student's writing. Most of us did not have teachers who talked about voice, other than, "Fred, lower your voice!" Voice is the passion, energy, and enthusiasm present in a piece of writing. When a novel contains strong voice, we're sad when we come to the final pages. We want there to be another chapter. Voice puts a lump in our throat or makes us laugh out loud. It is what differentiates one writer from another and the reason we always buy a new book by our favorite author. Voice tells us that this must be George Will instead of Anna Quindlen. Strong voice results when writers write what they know about and care about. It's that simple. It's a result of strong knowledge about the content. I find this especially true in nonfiction writing. The reports I see elementary students write on a specific state or country leave me gasping for air. I can only be grateful that they tend to be short. When I ask teachers if they enjoy reading these papers, they privately admit, "No!" Most teachers don't enjoy assigning the reports because they know they are going to have to read and grade them. The problem stems from students not truly caring about their topic or fully understanding their topic. Why should fifth-grade students who live in Georgia be excited about writing an entire report on Iowa? The lack of interest is evident in their writing. But ask the same fifth graders to write about something that is extremely important to them and suddenly the paper is alive. Likewise, while students may gather dozens of facts about a state—usually about square miles, population, terrain, resources, and so on—they have little understanding about the significance of the information.

Another challenge with voice in nonfiction writing is that students often lack background knowledge. For most of our students, their experience with nonfiction writing is limited to their textbooks, encyclopedias, and Internet articles. For the most part, these contain horrid examples of what voice should look like in nonfiction writing. But unless they've been shown other models, students merely copy the ones they've seen. Before we assign nonfiction writing, it is helpful to share with students a number of examples from nonfiction writing that have strong voice. Some of my favorite examples for students include *Exploding Ants* by Joanne Settel, *Spiders and Their Web Sites* by Margery Facklam, *The Number Devil* by Hans Enzensberger, *Toni Morrison Remembers* by Toni Morrison, *Bog Bodies* by Janet Buell, *Creepy Creatures* by Sneed B. Collard III, or any of David Macaulay's books. Here are two distinctly different examples of strong voice in nonfiction writing. The first is from *Life on the Color Line* by Gregory Howard Williams:

> I didn't understand Dad. I knew I wasn't colored and neither was he. My skin was white. All of us are white, I said to myself. But for the first time I had to admit Dad didn't exactly look white. His deeply tanned skin puzzled me as I sat there trying to classify my own father. Goose bumps covered my arms as I realized that whatever he was, I was. I took a deep breath. I couldn't make any mistakes. I looked closer. His heavy lips and dark brown eyes didn't make him colored, I concluded. His black, wavy hair was different from Negroes' hair, but it was different from most white folks too. He was darker than most whites, but Mom said he was Italian. That was why my baby brother had such dark skin and curly hair. Mom told us to be proud of our Italian heritage! That's it, I decided. He was Italian. I leaned back against the seat, satisfied. Yet the unsettling image of Miss Sallie flashed before me like a neon sign. Colored! Colored! Colored! He continued. Life is going to be different from now on. In Virginia, you were white boys. In Indiana you're going to be colored boys. I want you to remember that you're the same today that you were yesterday. But people in Indiana will treat you differently. I refused to believe Dad. I looked at Mike. His skin, like mine, was a light, almost pallid white. He had Dad's deep brown eyes, too, but our hair was straight. Leaning toward Dad, I examined his hands for a sign, a black mark. There was nothing. I knew I was right, but I sensed something was wrong. Fear overcame me as I faced the Ohio countryside and pondered the discovery of my life.

Williams's narrative is compelling; a result of his writing about a topic that he knows intimately and cares about deeply.

But what about research writing? Consider this passage from Mary Roach's book *Stiff: The Curious Lives of Human Cadavers*:

> By and large, the dead aren't very talented. They can't play water polo, or lace up their boots, or maximize market share. They can't tell a joke, and they can't dance for beans. There is one thing dead people excel at. They're very good at handling pain.

This passage continues with an exploration of how the auto industry used cadavers as crash test dummies. Roach's writing borders on irreverence. But her book is fascinating as she explores what happens to human cadavers donated to science. The book is very well researched, and she writes with a voice that causes chuckles on almost every page.

Once students have read through these and other texts and discussed the voice used in them, they are far more ready and capable of using an engaging voice in their own nonfiction writing.

Not only do we have to help students find their voice in writing, we also need to teach them to modify the voice to match the purpose and audience for the writing. A letter of complaint to a business leader in the community should carry a very different voice than a thank-you letter to a grandparent. Students need to consider which voice is appropriate to accomplish their purpose. Here is one of my favorite assignments that forces students to practice this concept:

> Find a topic that is of importance to you in school. It could be the wearing of hats in class, use of cell phones, or school uniforms. Write three letters, all on the same topic, to the following people: your school principal, your grandmother, your best friend. Once you have completed the three letters, write a fourth piece that explains how you changed your voice in the letters.

Once students understand that their writing should have voice, that they can define or explain their voice, and modify their voice to match their purpose and audience, their writing gains momentum and energy.

The guide used in reviewing my students' papers was simple. If, paper after paper, I found myself bored and whining, I asked myself if the problem was not with the writer but perhaps with the assignment. If the voice is lacking, we all suffer.

Word Choice

Some teachers confuse *word choice* with vocabulary. Vocabulary is actually a subset of word choice. Strong word choice can bring writing to life, or it can confuse the reader if the language is not accessible. Word choice is about precision in language, finding the exact word to convey one's meaning. Stephen King, in his book *On Writing*, suggests that we tell students not to use adverbs. "If they're using an adverb, it's an indication their verb is not strong enough," he writes. But he continues, "I break that rule all the time, but it's not for a lack of trying to find the exact verb." I always encourage young writers to expand their vocabulary through their reading. While the thesaurus may provide them with words that they may otherwise never encounter, they often do not gain a sense of how to use the word in context.

Some teachers and students believe that word choice is about adjectives, and creating images through description. I encourage both groups to think more about verbs than adjectives. Loads of adjectives can bog writing down, making it tedious for the reader to wade through the text. An avalanche of adjectives is like running in six inches of thick mud. The writing loses steam. But find that just-right verb and the need for glowing adjectives, while not eliminated, is lessened.

As well, the overuse of state-of-being verbs can be the death knell for writing. They make the writing listless, and all the adjectives cannot bring it back to life. Strong, precise verbs need to be our focus. Consider this passage in a book written for third or fourth graders:

> I must have been **born** to play baseball, because Pop says I was only two when I **hurled** a corncob at an old tomcat **chasing** my favorite hen. They say I **threw** so hard, that cob **shot** across the barnyard and **bopped** him on the head. John, the handyman, **whistled** in surprise. "Wouldja look at that, Doc?" he said to Pop. "Your little girl's got some arm on her." And that old cat? He **leaped** like lightning, and never **pestered** my chickens again. (*Girl Wonder: A Baseball Story in Nine Innings* by Deborah Hopkinson)

Think about the verbs: *play, hurled, threw, shot, bopped, whistled, leaped, pestered.* And all within seven sentences! These dynamic verbs bring life and energy to the writing. Compare that to this passage:

> The American Civil War was fought between the states in the north, called the Union, and the states in the south, called the Confederacy. There was an imaginary line called the Mason-Dixon line that separated the north and the south. One of the major issues between the north and the south was slavery. Another issue was states rights versus federal rights. The war lasted from April of 1861 until April of 1865.

This passage is for students of similar age to *Girl Wonder*. But the abundance of dull verbs in this passage leaves the writing flat and lifeless.

Verbs are the heart of word choice, but word choice involves more than just individual words. Success in word choice results when writers use language that they are familiar with and use it in interesting and unique ways. Think about this passage from Roald Dahl's memoir *Boy* (1984) when he writes about the woman who owned the candy store in his town:

> Her name was Mrs. Pratchett. She was a small, skinny old hag with a moustache on her upper lip and a mouth as sour as a green gooseberry. She never smiled. She never welcomed us when we went in, and the only times she spoke were when she said things like, "I'm watching you so keep yer thievin' fingers off them chocolates!" Or "I don't want you in 'ere just to look around! Either you forks out or you gets out!"
>
> But by far the most loathsome thing about Mrs. Pratchett was the filth that clung around her. Her apron was grey and greasy. Her blouse had bits of breakfast all over it, toast-crumbs and tea stains and splotches of dried egg-yolk. It was her hands, however, that disturbed us most. They were disgusting. They were black with dirt and grime. They looked as though they had been putting lumps of coal on the fire all day long. And do not forget please that it was these very hands and fingers that she plunged into the sweet-jars when we asked for a pennyworth of Treacle Toffee or Wine Gums or Nut Clusters or whatever. There were precious few health laws in those days, and nobody, least of all Mrs. Pratchett, ever thought of using a little shovel for getting out the

sweets as they do today. The mere sight of her grimey right hand with its black fingernails digging an ounce of Chocolate Fudge out of a jar would have caused a starving tramp to go running from the shop. But not us. Sweets were our life-blood. We would have put up with far worse than that to get them. So we simply stood and watched in sullen silence while this disgusting old woman stirred around inside the jars with her foul fingers.

While the language is relatively simple, it is precise and effective. Even for nine- or ten-year-old students, there are very few words they will not understand. Because of the word choice—and the details—students gain a clear picture of Mrs. Pratchett. Remarkably, after I read this passage to students as young as seven and eight, they are able to describe Mrs. Pratchett's house, even though it is never mentioned! The language they use to describe her house is spectacular. Here is one from Noelle, a third grader, and this is the child's first draft!

The inside of Mrs. Pratchett's house would have tea stains on the furniture, moldy socks on the floors, old food everywhere. Cobwebs and mudprints linger around the house. Foul smells rise up from disgusting objects. Dust and sour milk give the house something to fear. Ripped chairs and sofas are tipped over. Unchanged sheets lay on the filthy bed. The walls, covered with things you can't identify. Disgusting vermans [sic] crawl around Mrs. Pratchett's house. Bugs, slime and dirt ooze out of the shower. The couch looks as if it had been in a junkyard for many years. The staircase creaks and moans as you walk on it.

Wow! Third grade. Look at the verbs she uses: *linger, tipped, crawl, ooze, moans*. These verbs bring energy and vivid imagery to the writing. Many of us wish our middle school students could produce such work.

Or consider this passage from Kallie, an eleven-year-old, after the teacher prompted the class to write about an illustration of a "kingly looking person in purple robes."

The doors flew open. The wind whipped around the room. The startled men look up. Standing in the doorway was a man. His royal purple cloak rippled in the draft. The room was silent. There was a sudden noise as the men put down their wine goblets. Tink, tink, tink. The room grew hot and sweaty. Some men tried to speak but nothing came out. The gleam of the strange visiters [sic] eyes had frightened the knights who had slain many dragons and fought bravely for the king. The errieness [sic] was unbearable. The visitor's gray beard sparkled in the candlelight, giving it an errie [sic] glow. The windows let the dark seap [sic] in. The large room decorated with banners seemed to get smaller and smaller. The heavy aroma of wine hung in the air like fog on a dull morning. Their dinner bubbled in their stomachs. Their rough fingers grasped their swords stowed under their seats. The round table again fell silent. Then slowly the man spoke. "The king has come."

Kallie's verb usage is remarkable, one strong action verb after another. And her simile is spectacular! Most high school students couldn't craft that simile! How was Kallie able to create such a passage? Simple: she had been an avid reader from a very young age; additionally, her parents, both teachers, read to her all the time. How we wish more students had parents like Kallie's.

Unfortunately, many of our students come from homes in which reading is neither valued nor modeled. This presents an enormous challenge for teachers. We must immerse these children in literature every day, sharing the rich passages that help form an understanding of quality writing in our students' minds.

In addition to teaching the use of strong verbs in writing, teachers also need to stress the importance of precise language. "Elise came out of the tent" can—and should—be replaced by "Elise stumbled out of the tent" or "Elise exploded out of the tent." Likewise, instead of writing "There was a really, really big tree over by the side of the garage that is near the neighbor's big house" we should write, "An enormous tree stood to the left of the garage." Teach students not to use four words if they can say the same thing with one. The days of "word counting"—a practice that encourages wordiness—must end. Keep it simple, clear, and precise. That's word choice in a nutshell.

Sentence Fluency

We know it when we hear it. When fluency is strong, the text flows smoothly to our ears. It tells us that the writing is rhythmic, fluid, and easy to listen to. Strong writing "sounds right." For all of us, when we listen to music, there are pieces that just soothe the soul. So it is with fluency in writing. We enjoy hearing the writing read out loud; in fact, we often want to share the writing with friends, just so they can enjoy it as well. For the great writers, fluency just happens. They hear the music of language in their heads as they write. For example, Diane Ackerman knows how to create passages of science writing that sound like poetry. Consider this passage from her book *A Natural History of the Senses* (1990):

> Nothing is more memorable than a smell. One scent can be unexpected, momentary, and fleeting, yet conjure up a childhood summer beside a lake in the Poconos, when wild blueberry bushes teemed with succulent fruit and the opposite sex was as mysterious as space travel; another, hours of passion on a moonlit beach in Florida, while the night-blooming cereus drenched the air with thick curds of perfume and huge sphinx moths visited the cereus in a loud purr of wings; a third, a family dinner of pot roast, noodle pudding, and sweet potatoes, during a myrtle-mad August in a midwestern town, when both of one's parents were alive. Smells detonate softly in our memory like poignant land mines, hidden under the weedy mass of many years and experiences. Hit a tripwire of smell, and memories explode all at once. A complex vision leaps out of the undergrowth.

Strong fluency is marked by a variety of sentence beginnings and a variety in sentence length. When fluency is weak, it's like the proverbial fingernails across the chalkboard or the chewing of tin foil.

Teachers of upper elementary and middle school students struggle when trying to help their students with fluency. These students have to break years of a bad habit. You see, in the primary grades, students are commended when they write a complete sentence or a few complete sentences. Teachers are thrilled that the sentence begins with a capital letter, ends with a period, and is actually a complete thought! I understand their excitement. But it overlooks the inherent problems in the students' writing structure. The problem is that these same students are actually writing sentences like these: "I like pizza. I like pizza a lot. I like cheese pizza the best."

The problem stems from reinforcing the creation of sentences with a repetitious sentence structure. Subject-verb-object, subject-verb-object. Over and over and over. This redundancy often leads to writing that bores the reader, who may miss quality information because of the monotony. To compound the problem, every sentence begins with a pronoun.

When I work with primary grade teachers, I suggest that if we're going to teach students to write sentences, let's teach them to write quality sentences. Primary-grade students are quite capable of writing sentences that begin with prepositions, adverbs, and adjectives. We need to show our young writers different ways to begin sentences, and point out those beginnings in the literature we read to students. We need to have them practice creating sentences that begin with a designated adverb (e.g., *when*) orally, and then require them to include one sentence that begins with that word when they write. In these ways, we begin to teach them how to craft quality sentences.

As with the other traits, we can use literature to model how to craft interesting sentences. Otherwise, when students arrive in sixth, seventh, or eighth grade, they will struggle to break the habit they've developed over the previous five or six years.

We also need to have our students examine the length of the sentences in their writing. Hopefully, they will find a variety of sentence lengths, and I don't mean nine words, ten words, nine words, eight words, and so on. Ideally, we want to see some four- and five-word sentences mixed in with nineteen- and twenty-word sentences. When I work with teachers and ask them to examine the writing they produce during the workshop, they are often astounded at what they see. Many of them consistently write sentences that are about the same length, but they never noticed it before. I promise them that they will never ignore it again!

Our task is to give students opportunities to listen over and over again to quality passages so they can literally hear how strong fluency sounds. Set the goal, clarify the vision, and then provide them with the tools for being successful.

Conventions

We know how the "blame game" works. High school teachers say, "I don't know what they're doing in the middle school except those teams and things, but they sure don't teach conventions." Middle school teachers say, "I don't know what they're doing in the upper elementary grades except projects all the time, but they sure don't teach conventions." Upper elementary teachers are saying, "I don't know what they're doing in the primary grades except milk, cookies, and recess, but they sure don't teach conventions." And the primary teachers are saying, "If these parents would only send their children to school ready to learn, I could teach a few things!" Finally, the parents are saying, "If my high school teachers had taught me anything, I could better help and prepare my children!"

Punctuation, capitalization, grammar, spelling, presentation. Conventions are the bane of every teacher's existence. We teach these again and again until the veins in our neck are ready to burst. I've never been in a classroom in which the teacher ignored conventions. And still, it appears many students are not learning them. To repeat Einstein's famous quote that Lynna cited in Chapter 2, "Insanity: doing the same thing over and over again and expecting different results." This clearly applies to how we continue to teach conventions. We keep teaching them the same way hoping that maybe this year's students will finally get it. And they rarely do. "It must be the students," we say to ourselves. Perhaps the problem is not with the students.

Our challenge is twofold. First, we are trying to teach too much in too little time. Our curriculum documents require teachers to cover so much material in a given year, and conventions are just one component of that curriculum overload, that we achieve coverage but rarely mastery. So each year a teacher covers the material, but most students master very little. The following year's teacher is then forced to cover two years of material, which the students don't master because there is so much being presented. The following year, now the teacher has to cover three years of material, and the problem continues to compound itself each year. I suggest we focus on teaching fewer skills each year but strive for mastery rather than coverage. The coverage approach has not worked, and to continue the same old trend is fruitless.

The second concern is our approach to teaching conventions. Some things we know. First, in order for the information to move into a student's long-term memory, we need to teach conventions a minimum of three times a week, every week, all year, every year. Second, we must expose students to conventions in a variety of modalities. The day of worksheet after worksheet after worksheet must end. We must incorporate additional approaches such as kinesthetic activities in which students draw physical representations of conventions or act out various conventions, and discussions that engage students and require them to retrieve information, manipulate the information, and then explain the information.

Mini-lessons that are connected to the types of errors we find in our students' writing and that incorporate literature are one way to approach this. For example, the use of punctuation in dialog challenges many students. Traditionally, the teacher explains the rules and then students complete worksheets that require them to insert punctuation into sentences that contain dialog. Unfortunately, the students are neither engaged nor involved in the learning. A better approach would look like this:

1. Discuss how a reader knows when a character is speaking. Talk with the students about dialog and quotation marks, providing merely an introductory explanation. Then, divide the class into three groups.

2. Ask one group to look through books in the classroom library or their personal books and find a minimum of four examples of dialog in which the *John said* format appears at the beginning of the sentence.

3. Ask the second group to look for a minimum of four examples of dialog in which the *John said* format appears in the middle of the sentence.

4. Ask the third group to look for a minimum of four examples of dialog in which the *John said* format appears at the end of the sentence.

Using the book *When Zachary Beaver Came to Town* by Kimberly Holt (1999) as an example, students could find these quotes:

- Cal asks, "What's in the gold box?"
- "Yes I do," the fat kid says.
- "How much do you eat?" he asks Zachary.
- "I better go," she says. "Thanks for the dance, Toby. You're great!"
- "Tobias," Dad says, raising his eyebrow, "the sheriff is waiting for your answer."

Next, ask each group to write their examples on large chart paper and then determine the rules for using punctuation in dialog based on their sentences. Check their work to ensure accuracy, and then place students in groups of three, with one student from each of the original three groups in each new group. (You would have eight new groups of three if you had twenty-four students.) Students should now teach their peers the rules they have discovered for using punctuation in dialog. (An exceptional resource for lessons on conventions is Jeff Anderson's *Mechanically Inclined: Building Grammar, Usage, and Style into Writer's Workshop*.)

The second thing we know about teaching conventions is that a typical student's attention span for conventions is about fifteen to twenty minutes. After that, the student's eyes are spinning and the brain is out the window. Thus, our lessons need to be highly focused and short. Third, what we teach in September will need to be reviewed throughout the year as students require constant attention to each skill. The rationalization "I taught capitalization in October" is no longer acceptable. If we expect mastery, our students require constant review of the conventions they have explored; otherwise, they are often forgotten.

We often ask our students to edit their papers before they turn them in. I discussed the problems with this approach in Chapter 4. Rarely, if ever, do students find any mistakes. Since we know that most students cannot edit their own work and cannot edit the work of others if they're trying to find all the errors, does this mean we have to do all the editing? Good news! The answer is no.

Consider a different approach to teaching conventions and getting the papers edited. Clearly, the two should be connected. The traditional model has been to instruct the entire class on one convention at a time and then have all the students practice that one convention. This method has not produced the results we'd like to see. So what about this: Break your class into three or four groups. Have each group focus on a different convention that is critical at their grade level. Spend four to six minutes with each group providing direct instruction or guidance, and allow them to spend the remaining time finding examples of that convention in literature and explaining why it was used, constructing their own examples, correcting the writing of others for that convention, and similar tasks. When a student has finished a paper that needs editing, one student does not edit the paper. Four students edit the paper, focusing on the one convention they have been studying.

I have found that most students are quite strong at editing a paper for one convention if they have been studying that convention. Eventually, the paper makes its way back to the writer who can examine what corrections were made. Finally, the paper ends up in your hands. Every two or three weeks, rotate the groups into a different convention, so after a period of time, every student has had a chance to come close to mastery of that one convention. After six or eight weeks, they have all had time to focus on three or four conventions and develop a stronger grasp of each of them. Teachers can work through the school year this way, bringing in new conventions every six to eight weeks. I have found this method far superior to the traditional model, which left me frustrated, exasperated, and depressed.

Teaching the Traits

There are four ways we teach the traits, and we want to use each of them during the course of a week.

Making Literature Connections

Once you understand each trait, you will start "seeing" the traits come alive in the books you and your students read. When you share passages from literature, the students begin to understand what the trait sounds like when it's done well. And don't limit yourself just to books at the grade level you teach. Sharing passages from primary books with high school students can be very effective at helping them understand the trait. Likewise, sharing a passage from an adult book with middle school students can also be effective. We need to share a variety of passages, both fiction and nonfiction, from a variety of levels so students acquire the "vision of success." Eventually, our goal is for students to begin to find the passages themselves.

The best places to start looking for these passages are your classroom library, your school library, and your personal library. By examining books you and/or your students love to read, you will find examples of the traits embedded on almost every page. You may find a sentence with a dynamic verb or with a rhythm and flow that resonates in your mind as you read; you may find an opening to a chapter that forces you to keep reading; or you may find a passage that brings tears of sadness down your cheeks. The traits are everywhere in every good book.

Focusing Lesson Ideas

We actually need to teach our students how to craft each skill we discuss. How will we *teach* students to write a strong lead? How will we *teach* students to explode moments in their writing? How will we *teach* them to organize their writing? There are materials available to us that can guide these lessons, such as Vicki Spandel's *Books, Lessons, Ideas for Teaching the Six Traits* (2001), Ralph Fletcher's and JoAnn Portalupi's *Craft Lessons* (1998), and JoAnn Portalupi's *Nonfiction Craft Lessons* (2001). These lessons are often short (fifteen to twenty minutes) and highly focused, providing the students with strategies for achieving quality work.

Assessing Papers

By using clear and consistent criteria (rubrics), students can become quite competent in assessing a piece of writing. Students enjoy the task of reading a piece of writing (written by an anonymous person not sitting in the classroom!) and, in small groups of their peers, determining a score for various traits for the writing. We want students to be able to defend their score, using the rubric criteria and qualifying the score from within the text. If the student finds that the paper has some clear and focused moments but also some fuzzy, underdeveloped, rambling text, then it is incumbent upon the student to show us where those examples are in the paper. Assessing papers is another tool to help students gain a clear vision of success.

T a b l e 5 . 3 **A Few Book Selections for Each of the Six Traits**

Trait	Book Selections
Ideas	*Harris and Me* by Gary Paulsen
	The Perfect Storm by Sebastian Junger
	Spiders and Their Web Sites by Margery Facklam
Organization	*Zoom* by Istvan Banyai
	Yuck! A Big Book of Little Horrors by Robert Snedden
	My Life in Dog Years by Gary Paulsen
Voice	*Stiff: The Curious Lives of Human Cadavers* by Mary Roach
	Fig Pudding by Ralph Fletcher
	Pictures of Hollis Woods by Patricia Giff
Word Choice	*Girl Wonder: A Baseball Story in Nine Innings* by Deborah Hopkinson
	Exploding Ants by Joanne Settel
	From Slave Ship to Freedom Road by Julius Lester
Sentence Fluency	*Out of the Dust* by Karen Hesse
	The House on Mango Street by Sandra Cisneros
	Wait Till Next Year by Doris Kearns Goodwin
Conventions	*The Music of Dolphins* by Karen Hesse
	Your Move by Eve Bunting
	Anguished English by Richard Lederer

Modeling

This is the most powerful and the most frightening teaching tool. Doing, live and in person, what we want our students to do takes confidence and competence on the part of the teacher. But students take greater interest and pay stronger attention when we model what we want them to do. If we expect students to combine short sentences to improve fluency, we need to do it in front of them. If we want students to consider various topics for writing, we should allow them to watch us create possible topics and decide which one is most compelling for us.

Implementing the traits requires significant planning. Again, sharing examples from literature can help. For each trait, prepare three to five literature selections that show what the trait looks like when it is done well (see Table 5.3).

For each trait, develop four to six lesson ideas to help teach the trait and identify papers that students can score and discuss. Finally, for each trait, ask yourself how you will model something for that trait. I know, I know. Time for planning is the one thing we don't enjoy as teachers. But if we utilize the time we do have, work with our colleagues in the planning, use some time in the summer, we gain ground. By dividing the work with colleagues, no one person is overwhelmed. Each teacher at the grade level or department can undertake the task of creating and finding the materials for one trait and share that information with the others. Another approach is for one teacher to find the literature passages for each trait, a second teacher to find the papers to assess for each trait, and a third teacher to create the lesson ideas for each trait. Any way we can lessen the workload on one person, the better for everyone.

I am not suggesting that we incorporate all four of these strategies each day; unfortunately, we don't have that much time. But if we can incorporate one or two of these strategies each day, focusing on one trait for two or three weeks, then students gain the "vision of success" we seek. The alternative is more of what we've been doing for the past thirty years and that approach, by most people's admission, has created serious problems in the quality of student writing. The traits are a method to help our students improve their writing.

Steps to take right now

- Order Vicki Spandel's book *Creating Writers* (5th edition). Read it!

- Think about some of your favorite activities. Dining out? Going to the movies? Hiking? Playing a sport or an instrument? What are the characteristics of that activity that determine whether you've enjoyed yourself? For example, a good hike may require finding outstanding views, breaking a sweat, hearing nothing but the birds and the wind, and hiking at least five hours. How do these requirements relate to the traits of writing?

- Look for examples of the traits in the novel you're reading. Share those examples with your students. Have them do the same!

Lynna's World

The same six traits apply to writing in the workplace. And this is where we can really make the connection between academic writing and professional writing. These traits need to be incorporated into all documents: emails, IMs, memos, letters, and reports. Table 5.4 shows the differences in terminology between academic writing and workplace writing, but as you read through each section you'll understand the many similarities.

THE **Classroom–Corporate** CONNECTION

Match the following sentences with the type of error illustrated.

Completeness

Tone

Conciseness

Active Voice

Fluency

Clarity

a. It has been determined that customer accounts be handled by the sales department.

b. In spite of the fact that the company denied wrongdoing, it agreed to a settlement of the suit for a price of $7.5 million to be paid during a period of time of five years.

c. Ms. Richards argues with her boss because she is incompetent.

d. The report's deadline is June 15. The report will include all requested parts. The report will be professionally bound.

e. Your reimbursement has been delayed because you failed to submit the correct forms.

f. Yesterday we mailed you the book.

Clarity (Ideas)

This is the basic guideline for writing: to write a message that the reader can understand and act on. To achieve clarity in our writing, the message must be accurate, concise, and complete. We also need to use familiar words that are specific, not vague, and to avoid awkward construction, dangling expressions, unnecessary jargon, clichés, and slang. It is essential that students learn to write clearly, so they can avoid making significant errors in their messages. I can't stress enough how crucial clarity is in workplace writing. If we don't write clearly, we, as writers, are setting up a situation for confusion, resulting in lost time, money, and energy.

Table 5.4 Differences in Terminology between Academic and Workplace Writing

Characteristics of School Writing (Six Traits)	Ideas	Organization	Voice	Word Choice	Sentence Fluency	Conventions
Characteristics of Workplace Writing	Clarity	Format	Tone	Vocabulary	Style	Error-free/ Document Design

The following examples illustrate this need.

It is our intention to make every effort to deliver your material by the date of May 15 which you requested.

So does this mean that the supplier is going to "try" but the company probably will not get a delivery? What material are they referring to? This company orders millions of dollars of different types of materials a year. When they mentioned these issues with clarity to the vendor, the next message said:

We will deliver your order of 278 yards of nylon fabric by June 8.

Now this definitely is clearer and shows more confidence, but it backfired on the vendor. The company did not receive the shipment by June 8, and they sued the vendor for breach of contract. Maybe a better way to write this message with clarity and confidence would be:

We will schedule delivery of your 278 yards of nylon fabric for June 8.

That way if the company doesn't receive the order by June 8, the vendor can't be sued because the delivery was *scheduled* for June 8.

I had a boss who used to write emails about meetings that would say,

You are encouraged to attend . . .

Well, we soon found out that when he said *encouraged* he meant *required*. We need to say what we mean, not assume that people will interpret what we *really* mean.

Conciseness of information is important in professional writing as it influences the clarity of a message. People have more access to information at the click of a button, but they have no extra time to analyze the data. Therefore, business people need to receive information in the fewest words possible. Writers also need to include only the relevant information. Readers can't (correction—won't) plough through email messages that are more than three screens long.

Clear ideas are also complete. A message should give readers all the information they need to understand the message and to make a decision. Incomplete messages hurt companies, often resulting in lost time, money, and business.

One employee forgot to include the housing costs in a conference proposal, and the company then had to absorb the $400,000 cost of housing the participants. Unfortunately, the employee lost his job because of this completeness error.

Here's an example of an incomplete message that I see all the time at companies:

The meeting will be held next Thursday on the third floor.

What meeting? This Thursday, May 7, or next Thursday, May 14? What time? Where on the third floor? The writer ends up fielding lots of phone calls and email messages to give readers the information they need.

I love it when students send me an email that says, "I wasn't in class today; what did we do?" (They don't even sign their name.) Who is the student? Which class was missed? What does the student want from me: to leave the handouts at the front office or write out a two-hour lecture?

Here's a common example that you could use in the classroom with your students to illustrate lack of clarity.

A businessman had just turned off the lights in the store when a man appeared and demanded money. The owner opened a cash register. The contents of the cash register were scooped up, and the man sped away. A member of the police force was notified promptly. (www.montgomeryschoolsmd.org/schools/sga/pdf/ga/resources/communications/act.listening.pdf)

This seems like a very simple report. But decide if the following statements about what you just read in the message are true or false.

1. A man appeared after the owner had turned off his store lights.
2. The robber was a man.
3. The man who opened the cash register was the owner.
4. The store owner scooped up the contents of the cash register and ran away.
5. While the cash register contained money, the report does not state how much.

If you answered false to all five of the statements, sorry, but the statements could also be true. Consider the following explanations:

1. It's not clear whether the businessman and owner are two different people or the same person.

2. Does this report describe a robbery even though the words *robber, robbery,* or *crime* are never mentioned? Could it describe a daily occurrence at a business establishment where a male employee was going to make a nightly deposit? He was in a hurry and was a bit angry (thus he *sped* away and *demanded* the money). The police escorted him as he made the deposit.

3. If the businessman and owner are two different people, could the owner be a woman?

4. Because the sentence "*The contents of the cash register were scooped up . . .*" was written in passive voice, it's not clear who did the "scooping up."

5. The cash register may have had no money in it; rather it contained receipts, certificates, food stamps, and so forth.

Are you frustrated? Of course you are; this is what we can't do to our readers. They think they are reading a simple message that they understand, and then find out it means something totally different.

Other ways to revise our work to increase clarity include reducing long sentences and paragraphs, and avoiding legalese and bureaucratese. Ease of readability is important; business people are busy and they appreciate documents that are easy to read and understand.

Format (Organization)

As stated earlier, we have to follow the company's format. Organizing information by doing an outline and checking it out with a colleague or supervisor allow writers to know if they are on the right track before they spend time writing a report. Additionally, various messages require different patterns of organization. Poorly organized messages cause confusion and poor decision making and waste the reader's time. Presenting information logically aids readability, comprehension, and acceptance of the message.

CONNECTION

Clarity, focus, and completeness apply in both academic and professional writing. Consequently, we need to teach students these essential skills in schools so they can apply the skills in workplace writing. To be successful in both settings, writing must be clear in order for it to be effective, giving readers an accurate understanding of the message. When there's clarity, there's no guesswork, which makes it easier for the reader. Also, the clearer the writing, the less time it takes for revision—leaving more free time for other activities.

Direct and Indirect Strategies

Organization also includes where to place the main message in the document. Two common patterns for business documents based on how you think the reader will react to the message are direct and indirect strategies (see Figure 5.1). Use the direct strategy if your reader will be pleased, mildly interested, or neutral. Use the indirect strategy if your reader will be displeased or disappointed, unwilling or uninterested, or hostile.

In the direct approach the main point appears in the first or second sentence, and then the message goes into the background/explanation. This approach has several advantages: It saves the reader time, sets a proper frame of mind, and prevents frustration. The direct

Figure 5.1 **Audience Reaction Determines Organization of Information**

Audience Reaction	Pattern	Organization of Information
Neutral → Pleased	**Direct**	• Main message • Details/explanation/ background
Displeased → Hostile	**Indirect**	• Details/explanation/ background • Main message • Counterproposals/ alternatives

strategy is usually shorter and consequently takes less time to read. With the purpose up front, the explanation can be put in perspective. Readers aren't forced to struggle to figure out the message.

Here's an example of a business message that should have been arranged in the direct approach but wasn't. One day, a company sent an email to employees to announce an upcoming change in the company's voice mail system. Unfortunately, the email was seven screens long. The first few screens described the history of the company and the changes they had gone through during the past two years. Now, most readers weren't interested in this information and didn't have the time to scan such a rambling email. So, they didn't read the entire message.

The next day the employees came to work and realized that their voice mail didn't work. Well, you would have thought that Elvis had come back from the dead! Life as we know it stopped. How could a company operate without voice mail? The place went into a panic mode. People screamed, "Hey, what are we supposed to do? We can't do business! What happened? How do we get it back?"

Finally, a manager reminded everyone about the email, which (eventually) stated that in order to use the voice mail system, the employees would now have to put a 2 in front of their voice mail numbers. So if an employee's voice mail number was 871, it would now be 2871. This whole panic could have been avoided if the email had included the main message (the change in the voice mail numbers) at the beginning instead of burying it on page four.

Compare the letters in Figure 5.2. Note how using the direct approach (a) is easier to read and understand than the letter using the indirect approach (b).

In the indirect approach, the main message is in the middle, buffered by an explanation leading up to the message and by alternatives/counterproposals after the message. This approach works well with three kinds of messages: bad news, persuasion, and sensitive news. You may select the indirect strategy when you think the reader will be unwilling, uninterested, unhappy, disappointed, or hostile. This organizational pattern respects the feelings of the audience by preparing them for the bad news and deemphasizing the negative impact. This strategy also makes a fair reading more likely because when the negative news is up front, the reader may stop reading. Instead, when bad news is delivered gently, a reasonable person will accept the bad news—yes, with disappointment and regret, but not with anger.

I do, however, suggest that this approach does not always need to be used with negative messages. It depends on the relationship you have with the reader. If you're writing to a vendor whom you have a close working relationship with and who likes for you to "shoot from the hip," then by all means use the direct strategy. Figure 5.2c and Figure 5.2d show the difference between a claim letter (negative message) written in the indirect approach versus the direct approach. It's not that one approach is better than the other, but that writers need to select the one that best meets the purpose they are trying to achieve.

It's important that we be proactive rather than reactive when writing our business messages. We can save time and money if we design the message to prevent readers from calling our boss to yell about us or to prevent readers from having their lawyers call us to set up a court date. Using the direct and indirect strategies can help us be proactive in crafting our messages.

Students in your classroom could write different types of messages using the direct and indirect strategies for various situations that they encounter in their daily lives. For example, letters could be written to:

1. *A restaurant.* Address how poorly they and their friends were treated.

2. *Their principal.* Complain about the food in the cafeteria.

3. *A school administrator.* Recommend that students be allowed to leave the school grounds for lunch.

4. *A teacher.* Ask for a letter of recommendation to send to a college.

5. *An author.* Ask questions about their work.

6. *Colleges.* Ask for scholarship opportunities.

CONNECTION

There are times in the workplace when messages will require an indirect organizational pattern. Students need opportunities to practice writing bad-news messages. Whether writers are eleven, sixteen, or forty-four, there will be cases when they have to deliver negative information to a friend, parent, or customer. We need to teach them more effective ways to do this, making their writing very personal and very useful.

Figure 5.2a **Sample Recommendation Letter (Neutral/Positive Message) Using the Direct Pattern**

659 River Drive
San Francisco, CA 74655
March 22, 2009

Ed Parsons
Arlington High School
436 High St.
Akron, OH 45987

Dear Ed Parsons:

States the main message ▶ Clark Morris possesses the potential to become an exceptional teacher. I highly recommend Clark for a position in your science department. Having known Clark since he was in fourth grade, I have been fortunate to follow his growth, challenges, and achievements. His intellectual curiosity, energy, intelligence, and sense of humor provide him with many of the tools that will enable him to make a difference in the lives of young adults. Your students, your teachers, and your school will be improved by Clark's presence.

Clark has always been a curious person. As a student, Clark was able to infuse this curiosity into his fellow students and, thus, was able to enhance the learning for all the students. I am confident that this ability will transfer to Clark as a teacher, and he will be successful in instilling his own love of learning to his students.

Background information; explanation ▶ Clark's energy is infectious. He gets excited about new opportunities and maintains that energy for long periods of time. This energy and commitment will benefit not only his students, but also his fellow teachers. I can easily envision Clark chairing committees within the school as his leadership and energy will keep the committee focused, productive, and successful.

A delightful sense of humor will also help Clark in the classroom. He knows how to laugh and how to create laughter with others. People feel comfortable in Clark's presence as his easy-going manner and sense of humor make others drawn to him.

Please feel free to contact me at 614-987-0087 or fwilson@aol.com if I can provide further information.

Sincerely,

Frank Wilson

659 River Drive
San Francisco, CA 74655
March 22, 2009

Ed Parsons
Arlington High School
436 High St.
Akron, OH 45987

Dear Ed Parsons:

Having known Clark since he was in fourth grade, I have been fortunate to follow his growth, challenges, and achievements. His intellectual curiosity, energy, intelligence, and sense of humor provide him with many of the tools that will enable him to make a difference in the lives of young adults.

> Who is Clark? What is this letter about?

Clark has always been a curious person. As a student, Clark was able to infuse this curiosity into his fellow students and, thus, was able to enhance the learning for all the students. I am confident that this ability will transfer to Clark as a teacher, and he will be successful in instilling his own love of learning to his students.

Clark's energy is infectious. He gets excited about new opportunities and maintains that energy for long periods of time. This energy and commitment will benefit not only his students, but also his fellow teachers. I can easily envision Clark chairing committees within the school as his leadership and energy will keep the committee focused, productive, and successful.

Clark Morris possesses the potential to become an exceptional teacher. I highly recommend Clark for a position in your science department. Your students, your teachers, and your school will be improved by Clark's presence.

> The main message gets lost in the middle of the message.

A delightful sense of humor will also help Clark in the classroom. He knows how to laugh and how to create laughter with others. People feel comfortable in Clark's presence as his easy-going manner and sense of humor make others drawn to him.

Please feel free to contact me at 614-987-0087 or fwilson@aol.com if I can provide further information.

Sincerely,

Frank Wilson

Figure 5.2c   Sample Claim Letter (Negative Message) Using the Indirect Pattern

345 Palmer Rd.
Raines, OH 43068
February 22, 2009

John Larrimer
MMN Health Insurance
4356 Lincoln Ave.
Columbus, OH 43215

Dear John Larrimer:

Positive note ▶ I have been pleased with MMN's coverage in the past. Your coverage and quick response has been impressive over the last ten years that I've had insurance with you. Recently, however, I have a concern that I'd like to bring to your attention.

My daughter's ophthalmologist has referred her to Dr. Mason to have RKJ surgery. After going through the initial screening, Dr. Mason believes that my daughter is an excellent candidate for the surgery. However, MMN has denied coverage for the surgery stating that it is for cosmetic purposes.

Background information ▶ My daughter Marilyn Garrison has a degenerative eye disease and may in the future need a cornea transplant. I assure you, Mr. Larrimer, this RKJ surgery is not for cosmetic reasons. My insurance number is D78857, and the ophthalmologist's number is 614-987-5566.

Main message ▶ I would like you to reconsider your stance on RKJ surgery and grant the claim so that she may proceed with the surgery to correct her vision.

Please feel free to contact me at 614-998-6534 for any further information you may need. I look forward to talking with you and hope that you will see the seriousness of this surgery for my daughter.

Sincerely,

Luanne Garrison

Enclosure: ophthalmologist's report

F i g u r e 5 . 2 d **Sample Claim Letter**
(Negative Message) Using the Direct Pattern

105

Lynna's World
Format
(Organization)

345 Palmer Rd.
Raines, OH 43068
February 22, 2009

John Larrimer
MMN Health Insurance
4356 Lincoln Ave.
Columbus, OH 43215

Dear John Larrimer:

I would like you to reconsider your stance on RKJ surgery and grant my claim
so that my daughter may proceed with the surgery to correct her vision.

My daughter's ophthalmologist has referred her to Dr. Mason to have RKJ
surgery. After going through the initial screening, Dr. Mason believes that my
daughter is an excellent candidate for the surgery. However, MMN has denied
coverage for the surgery stating that it is for cosmetic purposes.

My daughter Marilyn Garrison has a degenerative eye disease and may in the
future need a cornea transplant. I assure you, Mr. Larrimer, this RKJ surgery is
not for cosmetic reasons. My insurance number is D78857, and the
ophthalmologist's number is 614-987-5566.

Please feel free to contact me at 614-998-6534 for any further information you
may need. I look forward to talking with you and hope that you will see the
seriousness of this surgery for my daughter.

Sincerely,

Luanne Garrison

Enclosure: ophthalmologist's report

**Putting the main
message up front is
too abrupt; letter
probably won't get a
fair reading; reader
automatically takes
the stance "We
don't do this."**

Openings, Bodies, and Closings

Organization also includes how writers open, develop, and close their messages.

Openings   *Openings* (what Fred calls *leads*) in emails, memos, and letters need to start on a positive note that leads into the message and that is relevant to the message. Avoid these types of openings:

> My name is Joe Schmoe.
> This letter is about . . .
> Yo, what up?

Openings should provide a positive statement that promotes goodwill. Even if you are writing to complain about a product, you can still start on a positive note:

> I have appreciated your good service in the past.

Not only do openings need to be positive, but they also must be sincere (not sugary). Also, avoid negative words in openings. I generally don't want to read a letter that starts:

> I regret to inform you that . . .

In longer formal reports, the introduction needs to state the purpose and significance of the report, and preview the report's organization.

Bodies   The *body* of the message is organized differently according to the type of message. It includes logical information or evidence. Figure 5.3 contains a few common organizational strategies to use for different types of messages.

So in the classroom, students need opportunities to incorporate different organizational strategies in their writing assignments. For example, a narrative could be organized chronologically, two teachers or colleges could be compared/contrasted, or students could write a persuasive letter to the principal using the AIDA model (attention, interest, desire, and action) recommending a new school policy.

Closings   Like the opening, *closings* (what Fred calls *conclusions*) can have a significant impact on the reader. I would ask you and your students to consider the following when writing closings for emails, memos, and letters.

- The closing should not be a rubber stamp that can go at the end of everything you write, such as "Thank you for your time and consideration."
- The closing needs to leave the reader with a positive impression.

- Negative words should be avoided. For example, instead of writing, "Please don't hesitate to call me," write, "Please contact me at . . . ." However this should not be the only sentence in the closing, as it would then be just a rubber stamp ending. The sentence should include something specific that usually could not be put at the end of other documents you write, such as, "If you have any questions on the proposed solution to the sales vs. commission discussion, please contact me at 755-9836 ext. 4356."
- In longer formal documents, the closing should synthesize the main ideas and give an overview of the significance or conclusions/recommendations.

Figure 5.3   **Organizational Patterns in Body of Documents**

Type of Document	Organization of Information
Routine Requests	1. Main point is up front 2. Follows with details that will allow the reader to fulfill the request 3. Ends in a tactful suggestion of action
Claims Denying the Request	1. Starts with background/explanation that leads into the negative message 2. Continues with counterproposals and alternatives
Persuasive and Sales/Marketing Materials	(AIDA model) 1. Attention—highlight major reader benefit(s) 2. Interest—further explain benefits in detail; appeal to logic and emotions 3. Desire—show how change will make things better, including evidence; anticipate and answer opposing arguments and/or questions; describe how implemented 4. Action—motivate reader to take action; make suggestion convenient for reader; if applicable, include deadline
Formal Reports	Various organizational patterns: 　　Topical 　　Chronological (instruction manuals) 　　Categorical (financial, sales) 　　Spatial (technical description) 　　Compare/Contrast

Tone (Voice)

When we write, we communicate an *attitude* as well as a message. Tone is the emotional atmosphere that surrounds what is said in a document. When we use words that create a positive attitude, we are more likely to get what we want as opposed to when we use negative words.

Positive Tone

Here are three ways to develop a positive tone in our writing:

1. Refer to ourselves in first person, not third person.   In a *Seinfeld* episode, a character named Jimmy always made statements like "Jimmy's glad to be here" or "Jimmy's not feeling good about this" (instead of "I'm glad to be here" or "I'm not feeling good about this").

This becomes a problem when employees don't know whether to say "I" or "the company." The guideline is to write "I" if the writer is actually referring to himself or herself and to write "the company" if the writer is not personally going to take action, but is referring to the company in general. So, for example, the correct use would be "I will evaluate your account" and "The company reviews all applications."

I realize that in many classrooms students are taught to avoid using the word *I*. This actually stems from one author's views in one book that became gospel. In *The Lively Art of Writing,* Payne (1965) wrote that we should never use the word *I* because, in her perspective, it weakens writing. However, as Tom Newkirk, professor of English at the University of New Hampshire, states, "It is not clear how Payne would have students avoid the first person if they were using their own experiences as evidence for an opinion—something most writers do" (Newkirk, 2005). No disrespect, Ms. Payne, but you need to give up on that one.

2. Tell people what we can do rather than what we cannot do.   For example, "We cannot send a representative until Monday" could be more positive if written, "We will send a representative on Monday, May 8."

3. Eliminate as many negative words as possible.   "Your order has been delayed because you failed to include the correct credit information" includes too many negative words. It would be better written, "We will ship your order as soon as we receive the correct credit information."

Another example is the common letter stating that the applicant did not get the job: "Unfortunately, we regret to inform you that you did not get the job." A better way to communicate the information would be, "Although we were impressed with your qualifications, we chose a candidate whose background more closely met our needs. We will keep your resume on file in case another position becomes available." This buffering of the negative message de-emphasizes the impact of the bad news. The reader may not be happy with the message, but a reasonable person will accept the negative with regret and disappointment, not anger and hostile behavior.

Tones to Avoid

The following examples illustrate poor tone. You could use these in the classroom by having the students rewrite them with a more positive tone. (Example rewrites are given after each one.)

- **Critical or Fault Finding Attitude**

    Original: "I wonder if your job description includes monitoring my outgoing email messages to determine if they are business or personal."

    Rewrite: "May I have another copy of the company guidelines used in differentiating business and personal email? Since I also want to follow company policy, it will help me in reviewing my outgoing mail."

- **"I'm Right" Attitude**

    Original: "We clearly indicated in your statement that your monthly payments are $760, not $670 that you mistakenly sent."

    Rewrite: "Thank you for your payment of $670. However, since your monthly payment is $760, please send us an additional $90 so that your account can be balanced."

- **Superior/Condescending Attitude**

    Original: "I would like to offer my deepest sympathy for your efforts in setting an all-time low for sales in your department last week."

    Rewrite: "You're also thinking, I'm sure, about what you can do to offset the all-time low in sales in your department for the week ending September 22. Is there any way I can help?"

- **Angry Attitude**

    Original: "Can't you read??? Can't you follow simple directions??? Why must I keep reminding you over and over and over how to submit your expense reports???"

    Rewrite: "I've enclosed another copy of the instructions for using Excel to submit your expense reports. I strongly suggest that you review the instructions until you know them by heart, thus eliminating costly time for corrections. I would be glad to train you on using Excel or enroll you in an outside training program. Please let me know by Friday, January 18, what would work best for you."

- **Blunt Attitude**

    Original: "You wrote to the wrong department. We don't handle transfers."

    Rewrite: "I would be happy to submit your paperwork to the distribution department to handle your transfer. If you don't hear from them by Monday, May 16, please contact Maggi at extension 2335."

- **Accusing Attitude**

  Original: "You must have dropped your phone. The outside of it is cracked."

  Rewrite: "The outside of the phone is cracked. Your warranty on external parts of the phone only covers the first year of service. However, we would be glad to repair your phone for $45."

- **Sarcastic Attitude**

  Original: "You need this report in two days? Who do you think I am, Boy Wonder?"

  Rewrite: "I understand the urgency in your receiving this report in two days. However, with Robert on vacation, the data analysis will take at least three days. I will drop all other projects I'm currently involved with and submit the report by Thursday. Another alternative would be to bring Mark over from IT. Just let me know what works best for you."

- **Belligerent Attitude**

  Original: "I'm sure your boss won't be happy when I call her explaining your attitude. Maybe I should just let my lawyer take care of this."

  Rewrite: "I'm having a difficult time explaining my concerns to you. Please transfer me to your supervisor."

All of these attitudes will alienate the reader—the most important person.

Not only should we avoid a negative attitude, but we should also avoid these five ways of making readers angry:

1. *Call them stupid.* "If you had read the directions correctly . . . "
2. *Suggest they are lying.* "You claimed that you had contacted them . . . "
3. *Confuse a person's name or gender.*
4. *Blame them.* "Obviously you neglected to . . . "
5. *Write in language that needs interpretation.* "Your application will be given expeditious scrutiny when your financial status ameliorates . . . "

An employee in one of my training programs received from his boss the negative letter shown in Figure 5.4 (names have been changed). I asked the employee if the boss had inquired about the incident, and he said, "No, he just fired off this letter to me."

Now, what was the purpose of this letter: to vent, to flex muscle, to demoralize the employee? Nothing constructive can come out of this type of communication. Actually, the employee was an excellent worker; in this case he had made a professional decision not to follow the standard operating procedure to prevent a $280,000 piece of equipment from blowing up. He had all the qualities I would look for in an employee to work on my staff: professionalism, outstanding communication and problem-solving skills, technical expertise, loyalty, and so forth.

Figure 5.4   Letter with Negative Tone

111

Lynna's World
Tone (Voice)

ABC, Inc.

March 23, 2006

Mr. Mark Dawson
7665 Fallriver Dr.
Columbus, OH 43269

Dear Mr. Dawson:

I find it necessary to write to you regarding your lack of diligence during your shift of March 13, 2006.

You ran a load of heat treatments simultaneously. Both process sheets clearly stated program number 'B6,' but you totally ignored this fact and ran the load to program number 'B27.' If you had bothered to check the program at the start of your shift as you are required to, you would have seen that the actual temperatures were the same—an unnecessary waste of time and effort.

This is totally unacceptable and will not be tolerated, and therefore I find it necessary to issue you with a written warning as to your future conduct.

ABC, Inc. is entering a very important phase during the next few weeks. . . . What possible hope have we of passing an audit with episodes such as this.

I do not expect to see a repeat of the above, ever.

Yours sincerely,

JM Porter
General Manager

C: ABC, Inc. personnel file

His lack of what?

Do you feel the message "stuck your nose up in the air," . . . "bothered to check, you lazy scumbag"?

Don't get hit by the pointed finger that is waving back and forth.

Figure 5.5 **Memo with Negative Tone**

Now there's a positive note that will really make the reader be open to reading the information!

Well, aye, aye, captain!

Dripping with sarcasm!

Yes, let's just step outside to the parking lot.

Obsolete phrasing

Tries to show reader awareness, but then ruins it in the rest of the sentence.

SHOUTING!

Do you hear the clicking of the heels and see the finger pointing?

TO: All Staff
FROM: JM Porter
DATE: April 2, 2006
SUBJECT: Housekeeping/Shop-floor Cleanliness

You guys really need to get your act together!

This morning, the shop floor was again in a disgusting state—just as it has been every day this week.

Here are a few instructions for you all to carry out immediately and until further notice.

1. *Sweeping up.* Do I need to issue a Standard Operating Procedure on how to operate a broom? I expect to see every member of staff keeping the shop-floor tidy AT ALL TIMES. This means picking-up litter (which shouldn't be there in the first place!), sweeping-up debris from whatever source. . . . Anyone not willing to do their fair share can discuss this issue with me at any time.

(This memo continues on to a second page since it's difficult to rant and rave in only one page.)

5. Staging Areas. As stated overleaf, we are currently looking at renewing . . . However, we are not using the current areas correctly. The yellow lines in each area are there so you can put the job inside the lines. I realize this is difficult sometimes due to lack of space, but with a little bit of common sense, this can be overcome. . . . It seems to be common practice at present to leave this work for someone else to do. If a job needs checking-in, it is YOUR job—so do it. And remember—TIDY, TIDY, TIDY.
6. Tools. We have a tool chest—SO USE IT! When you have used a tool, or even the tape dispenser, knife, etc., etc., please please please please put the thing back where it belongs. If you do not, it means whoever wants to use it next has to go searching all over the place.

(The memo continues on, but I think you get the point.)

When I went back to the company two weeks later, the same employee showed me the memo reproduced in Figure 5.5, written by the same boss to all the employees in the department. When we treat our employees this way, the result is almost always negative: reduced productivity, decrease in morale, higher turnover, and increased absenteeism. Or the employees quit or sabotage the company.

Now, I'm not saying that we can't be firm in our writing. It's just that it's not in our best interest to write to people with this tone. We can give people negative news without being blunt, angry, condescending, sarcastic, belligerent, or accusing.

Active Voice

Active voice also affects the tone of our writing. The active voice "I did it" is more direct and concise than the passive voice "It was done by me." Some writers use the passive voice because it sounds more impressive, but it often makes their writing wordy, evasive, or unethical. As stated earlier, many experts think that we should never use the passive voice; I think it's okay to use once in a while. In my writing, I use active voice as often as possible.

Take the sentence, "Unless you pay me within five days, my lawyer will be contacted." Not only does active/passive voice affect the tone, but also the order of the information. What's the difference between these two rewrites?

1. I will contact my lawyer unless you pay me within five days.
2. Unless you pay me within five days, I will contact my lawyer.

The first sentence stresses the threat of a lawsuit. The second sentence focuses more on being paid, which has a better tone.

You-Attitude

Writing with a You-Attitude also improves the tone of our writing. The You-Attitude means considering the reader first when you write. Basic psychology tells us that when people read a message their reaction is "What's in it for me?" The You-Attitude emphasizes what readers want to know and how they will be affected by the message. Keep putting yourself in the reader's position. Try to understand that person's situation, feelings, and viewpoints.

While I was delivering a training program, one participant complained that Dave from IT (who was in the room) always emailed her this message: *"Done."* Each time this happened, she felt as if Dave had stormed into her office, slammed a book on her desk, and declared angrily that the task was completed, further implying that she should not ask for anything else. Dave was shocked to hear her response; he thought he was doing her a favor by letting her know that what she had requested had been completed. She replied that when he sent these emails, she didn't even know what task he was referring to. Then three or four other participants told Dave that they felt the same way when they received his emails. Wow! We need to step into the readers' shoes and ask ourselves, "How would I feel if I received this message?"

Persuasive messages are more convincing if we include reader benefits. If students write a letter to the principal recommending a change in a school policy, they need to incorporate how the change would benefit the principal or the school in general, not just the writer.

Job seekers often fill their cover letters with the word *I*: "I have this degree, I have this experience, I have these certifications," and so on. Instead, they should focus their letter on including what they could do for the company. Prospective employers are more likely to interview the writer if they feel that the applicant can do something for them. I'm not contradicting my earlier statements about the use of *I*. Rather, I am emphasizing that we need to consider when it's appropriate to use *I* and when *I* should be avoided to enhance the You-Attitude.

Nondiscriminatory Language

Writing with nondiscriminatory language also helps the tone of our writing. Using nondiscriminatory language is smart because it's the ethical thing to do, we risk offending others if we don't, and we could be sued for what we put down in black and white. Competent writers in organizations make sure that their writing is free of sexist language and any references to race, religion, ethnic background, age, sexual orientation, and disability. These areas are all protected by federal law. If a supervisor writes in an employee's annual review that "the employee's epilepsy doesn't seem to interfere with her ability to represent the company professionally," the supervisor may as well call the lawyer now and look for a job elsewhere.

Here's another example of discriminatory language:

> Mr. Patterson, a black engineer who is sixty-two years old and has diabetes, denied the charges and said he thought the girls were trying to gyp the company with their demands.

F i g u r e 5 . 6   **Examples of Nondiscriminatory Language**

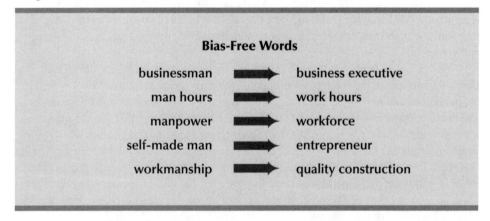

His age, race, and the fact that he has diabetes must be deleted. The employees should not be referred to as *girls*, and the word *gyp* is an ethnic slur. Figure 5.6 contains examples of nondiscriminatory language.

Two ways to avoid sex bias in writing are to make everything plural so the subject can be referred to as *they*, and to reword the sentence so pronouns aren't used. The second option, though, usually results in writing in passive voice. For example, the sentence "The supervisor must submit his time sheets to the HR manager on Fridays by noon" can be revised two ways to avoid sex bias (since all employees aren't male): "Supervisors must submit their time sheets to the HR manager on Fridays by noon" or "Supervisors' time sheets must be submitted to the HR manager on Fridays by noon."

I'm even advising clients not to use titles like Mr. and Ms. Too many people in training programs have told me that they don't like the Ms. title (too feminist-sounding) and too many people with unisex names (like Tracy or Chris) don't like to be referred to in the wrong gender. However, it's a good idea to ask people how they prefer to be addressed. If you can't find out the person's gender or preferred title, use "Dear Chris Brown" or "Dear Tracy Woods."

In summary, it pays to take time to write a well-crafted message. Writing with a positive attitude, using the active voice, incorporating the "You-Attitude," and avoiding discriminatory language all improve the tone of our writing.

> **C O N N E C T I O N**
>
> In both academic writing and workplace writing, writers need to match voice/tone to accomplish their purpose and engage their audience. Teachers need to help students develop an awareness of different types of tones/voice and provide opportunities for students to practice various voices and appropriate tones.

Vocabulary (Word Choice)

Selecting the appropriate word means choosing words that meet the readers' needs and are suitable for the readers' skill level. Writers need to use the correct word and eliminate deadwood constructions.

Conciseness

To achieve conciseness, we need to make every word count by avoiding wordy expressions, eliminating vague words, and using shorter words where possible. No workplace document should contain the wordy phrases shown in Figure 5.7. Here's an example: "It is perfectly clear that meetings held on a weekly basis are most effective." Again, by working with our writing at the word/sentence level, we can make the sentence more concise: "Weekly meetings are most effective."

 Focusing on word choice also includes avoiding double negatives in our writing. Consider this example: "Although the sales returns for May are high in number, experience has indicated that this is not an unusual condition for summer." By eliminating wordiness and double negatives such as "not an unusual," we could rewrite the sentence: "High sales returns for May are normal." When we pay attention to the words we use, our writing becomes easier to read.

Figure 5.7   **Examples of Wordy Phrases and Concise Alternatives**

Wordy Phrase	Concise Alternative
In spite of the fact that	Because
Agreed to a settlement of	Settled
A price of $4.2 million	$4.2 million
Original patent	Patent
In addition to the above	In addition
Made an agreement to	Agreed
A period of ten years in length	Ten years
There are	(Delete this phrase.)
It is	(Delete this phrase.)
Few in number	Few
On a yearly basis	Yearly
A report for which you have no use	A useless report
A program that is designed to save money	A money-saving program
Due to the fact that	Because
The point of the matter is	(Delete this phrase.)
Mutual cooperation	Cooperation
Final outcome	Outcome

Everyday Language

Word choice also includes using everyday language. As Mark Twain said, "Use the right word, not its second cousin."

So why write the word *endeavor* when we can write *attempt*? Well, we can say, "Oh, I'm not going to dummy-down my writing." But the fact remains that it's the *reader* who determines whether or not our message achieves its purpose. So, we can be smug, but when readers don't understand our message, we will lose time when we need to re-explain our message more clearly down the road. Teach students to use short, simple, and common words whenever possible.

Connotative Meanings/Slang/Clichés

The connotative meanings of the words we use also matter. *Criticize* would be a better word choice than *bad-mouth*. *Drunk* or *intoxicated* would be a better choice than *hammered* or *plastered*. Also, we should avoid slang and clichés in our writing. Some people have different meanings for these informal expressions, and others have no idea what the expressions mean. For example, a parent wrote to the school that her daughter was absent from school yesterday because the daughter had a "going over." Many readers would have no idea what happened to the daughter; others would guess that she had a spanking, a physical exam, a slumber party, or an interrogation.

As you know, your students are going to enter a world where they'll be writing to international audiences. Clichés are especially troublesome for international readers. Phrases like "reaching the end of our rope" and "keeping our nose to the grindstone" can confuse English language learners as well as some native English speakers. So students need to practice eliminating idioms and other types of figurative language in writing where the reader may become confused. Writers need to develop an increased awareness of audience and what language that audience will understand.

Some outdated expressions need to be deleted from all writing, not just professional writing. Terms like "as stated overleaf" and "pursuant to your request" are obsolete and, therefore, need to be eliminated from our writing. "Enclosed please find," implies that the information must be hidden and readers have to "find" it. Why not write, "The application information is enclosed."

Precise Words

Precise verbs are also important in business messages. Consider this statement: "Upper management *said* that employees would get a raise." Does that mean that the manager expects that the employees will get a raise or that the employees are guaranteed raises?

We also need to use specific, concrete nouns (which includes avoiding *stuff* and *thing*). Replace "An employee presented a proposal," with "Marilyn Thompson presented a proposal to offer on-site daycare for all employees."

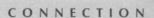

It's also vital to use the *correct* word. Consider this example, from a parent: "Please excuse Joyce from P.E. for a few days. Yesterday she fell out of a tree and misplaced her hip." It sounds like Joyce put her hip someplace and forgot where she left it!

CONNECTION
Academic and workplace settings both require accuracy and precision of language so that readers understand the message the way the writer intended.

Style (Fluency)

We can be effective writers when we use a conversational style, trusting our own natural voice. As mentioned earlier, writers need to develop their own style; they don't need to copy someone else's. Two writers can use different styles to write a persuasive letter yet both be effective as long as they adhere to correct grammar, spelling, clarity, sentence structure, and so forth. Style supports strong clarity and organization, but does not replace them.

Fluent sentences are easy to read because of clear connections, variety, and emphasis. They eliminate choppiness, bluntness, and monotony. Additionally, fluent sentences enhance clarity so that readers don't have to struggle to see what's most important or to sort out relationships between ideas. Therefore, varying sentence structure and using transitions are important in effective professional writing.

For example, read the first four sentences and notice how much more fluent (and economical) the information is when we combine them into the fifth sentence, which is still clear and complete:

1. The company's sales will grow.

2. It will grow from $4 million in 2001.

3. It will reach $6.5 million in 2007.

4. This will be an increase of more than 50 percent.

5. The company's sales will grow from $4 million in 2001 to $6.5 million in 2007, an increase of more that 50 percent.

Transitions such as *consequently* and *however* also help our sentence structure: "Martha is one of my best performers. *However*, she is receiving the lowest raise in the department because of her repeated absences."

Confidence

Writing with confidence means that we believe in what we are saying, that our request is reasonable, and that our information is logical and accurate. Such confidence has a persuasive effect on readers.

Writers in the workplace need to avoid language that makes them seem unsure of themselves. A fifteen-line apology paragraph moves beyond apology into a long-winded wallowing. Instead, if a mistake has been made, create a one-sentence apology, and then use the rest of the paragraph to explain what will be done to rectify the situation.

Job seekers need to write with confidence when they request an interview. Evaluate the following three samples, identifying which one is passive, aggressive, or assertive (the style we want in our writing).

1. Mr. Smith, I would very much like to meet with you to discuss my background and experience. If something would come available that you think I might be qualified for and it wouldn't be too much trouble, please contact me at 769-4293.

2. Mr. Smith, I would very much like to meet with you to discuss my background and experience. I will be calling you early next week to see if we can set up a mutually convenient time for an interview. I am excited to meet with you, as I believe you will be impressed with the contributions I could make to your department.

3. Mr. Smith, I would very much like to meet with you to discuss my background and experience. I will be at your office Monday morning for an interview. Please make sure that you are there.

The first example basically says, "Listen, Mr. Smith, I'm a loser. You know it; I know it. But, if a position comes available and you think, oh, what the heck, and you just happen to have my number ready and five minutes to kill, give me a call." The underlying message in Example 2 is, "I'm confident about my abilities and what I can contribute to your company. Let's get together. I think you'll be impressed." Example 3 crosses the line and is arrogant and aggressive.

As you can see, effective style in workplace correspondence incorporates all the characteristics of effective writing: clarity, voice, conciseness, fluency, tone, completeness, you-attitude, word choice, and confidence.

119

Lynna's World
Error-Free/
Document
Design
(Conventions)

Error-Free/Document Design (Conventions)

I mention writing with correct grammar and spelling in all of my chapters, and Fred does as well. That's how important it is. With the advent of technology (email, Instant Messaging, blogs, etc.) we write more today to communicate than ever before. Poor usage results in confusion, misunderstanding, and loss of credibility.

Consider the following statistics:

- Three-fourths of employers would consider not hiring a job candidate based upon poor spelling or grammar (BBC News, 2006).
- Poor grammar alienates 77 percent of hiring companies (Hertfordshire University, 2006).
- Twenty percent of first-year college students take a remedial writing course (ACT, 2003).

And the one that is really surprising:

- In 2003, college professors ranked grammar as the most important skill; high school teachers said it was the least important (ACT, 2003).

Some critics say that the focus on English usage in the classroom will stymie critical thinking and analysis. But the best idea, the finest plan, is not of much use if it isn't clearly communicated. William Strunk (1979) said, "Unless he is certain of doing well, [the writer] will probably do best to follow the rules." Can the employee who submits a fiscal report to stockholders really be taken seriously when he keeps referring to the "fecal responsibility" throughout the entire written document?

We need to do more that just "cover" the rules; let's teach (not cover) the basic rules of grammar and punctuation. (Do we really need to know that it's a prepositional adverbial clause? Or do we really just need to know how to *use* it?) Teachers, unfortunately, can't assume that students have been taught grammar in previous classes. Therefore, we need to teach it . . . and teach it . . . and teach it again (as well as hold people accountable for writing with correct grammar and spelling). And we can improve grammar instruction—and consequently students' writing—if we teach grammar in context.

Figure 5.8 Most Important Writing Skills, as Ranked by High School Teachers and College Instructors

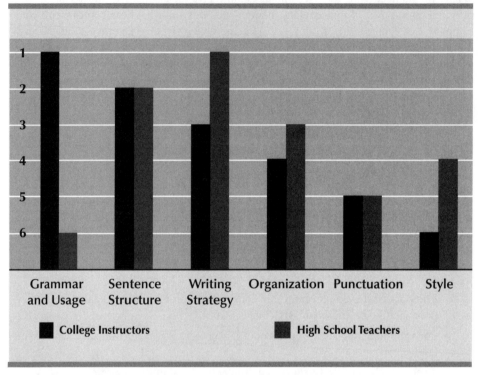

Source: http://act.org/activity/winter2004/survey.html. Reprinted with permission.

Figure 5.8 shows the difference between what high school teachers and college instructors rank as the most important writing skills. The biggest discrepancy occurs in the area of grammar and usage which is ranked as the *most* important skill by college professors but ranked as the *least* important by high school teachers.

Some people believe that incorrect grammar will become standard due to usage. That type of thinking gives us the following headlines:

Miners refuse to work after death

Local high school dropouts cut in half

Police begin campaign to run down jaywalkers

That type of thinking also gives us

Thank God Its Friday

Mens Restroom

12 Items or Less

According to the Association of American Universities, "Grammar is the basis for good writing." Unfortunately, they also state that, "College students make a high level and array of grammatical errors" (www.S4S.org).

The philosophy of writing standards including correct grammar, mechanics, and spelling is not dead—it just needs to be taken off the shelf and dusted. These standards are the nuts and bolts of writing; therefore we must help students master the fundamentals. As Lynne Truss states in *Eats, Shoots, and Leaves* (2003), punctuation is the "stitching of language" and the "traffic signals." And incorrect use of grammar makes an indelible negative first impression. Organizations expect writing to be error-free, clear and accurate. (Notice I didn't say "kinda, sorta, or as close as possible.")

121

Lynna's World
Error-Free/
Document
Design
(Conventions)

Document Design

Not only does our error-free writing make an impression on the reader, but so does the document design. The appearance of our documents says something about us, the organization, and the document's content before the readers read one word. A well-designed document increases our credibility and exudes a positive, professional image.

> ### CONNECTION
>
> **Both worlds must stress the importance of writing with correct grammar, spelling, and punctuation. In the academic setting, students may lose points on their papers. In the business setting, writers may lose customers. As teachers, we need to continue caring that writing should be error-free.**

One of the best ways to enhance the appearance of our documents and to improve comprehension is through graphic highlighting techniques: bullets, underlining, headings, subheadings, italics, boldface, color, boxes, columns, and similar features. Bulleting of information, in particular, is a good technique to emphasize information and/or aid the readability of complex information. Effective document design gives readers breathing space and makes the document appear easier to read.

The key focal points of a document are top and left. So we need to put the most important information of a document at the top and to the left.

Typeface and size of font also make a visual difference. Normally, serif fonts (e.g., Times New Roman) are easier to read than sans-serif fonts (e.g., Arial).

Also, we need to make a balanced use of white space. For example, on a resume, we don't want blocks of white space on the left, with most of the text crammed on the right side of the page.

Workplace correspondence needs short paragraphs. They could even be one sentence. As a general rule, paragraphs should be no longer than eight lines (not sentences). Overall, documents need to look simple and consistent.

One last word on document design: There is a difference in how the layout and design of paper versus Web documents are constructed, read, and evaluated. Online readers' expectations are different from readers of printed documents. Web pages tend to be flashier and more colorful and have more layers to navigate via hyperlinks and menus. To see an example of effective Web page design, go to http://newarkl.com.

Organizations continue to complain about the language skills of employees, from frontline workers to the CEO. The National Commission on Writing (2004) concluded that, "One-third of employees write poorly and . . . remedial training has become a huge industry with more than $3.1 billion spent to help people improve their skills." So, I'm sure we agree that we need to raise the standards and expectations of students/workers to write documents that are clear, concise, complete, and organized, with a positive, confident tone that is reader centered.

Ways to give your classroom the **Corporate Edge**

- Direct students to http://desktoppub.about.com and click on *Basics*. Students should review the information on the site and then design their own business cards, paying attention to how the information is laid out and designed.

- Ask students to analyze documents to decide what information is necessary and what information needs to be deleted. (Feel free to use the sample documents provided throughout the chapters and appendix.)

- Ask students to bring in samples of junk mail or marketing material and analyze the clarity of the letters and the effectiveness of the documents' openings and closings.

- Have students bring in headlines with clarity errors. Richard Lederer's books *Anguished English* and *More Anguished English* are terrific resources for samples of errors that need clarification.

- Create an assignment in which students select one topic of interest and write different documents pertaining to the topic. For example, students could critique a musician's work, write a research paper on the musician, compare and contrast the musician's genre of music with a different genre, write an entry on the musician's blog, and compose a letter to the musician asking specific questions.

Answers to The Classroom–Corporate Connection

Completeness—(f), Tone—(e), Conciseness—(b), Active Voice—(a), Fluency—(d), Clarity—(c)

Assigning Is Not Teaching

An Overview

The assumptions we make about what people know about writing—or what we think they *should* know—often provide us with a distorted reality. Whether we are working with an intermediate grade student who "should know" how to spell *they* (instead of *thay*), a high school senior who "should know" how to use commas, or an adult who "should know" how to use standard grammar, teachers and employers should recognize that people need to be taught, not told. Otherwise, when we assign written work based on assumptions, whether it's an essay for a class or a progress report for a workplace project, the results often don't meet our expectations, which leaves everyone disappointed.

Fred's World

For years, I was under the impression that my early approach to "teaching" had died and was buried with appropriate tributes. However, when I speak with teachers and I look at the school assignments today, I realize that it has either risen from the dead or was never fully buried. Either way, I am saddened and concerned that with all we have learned about teaching writing over the past twenty-five years, some teachers are not basing their instruction on current research. Regardless of what grade we teach, we cannot just assign writing without also providing instruction of how to achieve success.

A Quick Look at the Problem

Perhaps the most egregious examples I've seen lately concern the following crucial steps.

Teaching the Concepts

Approximately a month before the start of school, my friend's daughter Hannah, who was entering ninth-grade honors English, received a letter from her soon-to-be English teacher with the following assignment.

> Read the book *Animal Farm* by George Orwell. Then write a paper, 2 to 4 pages in length, explaining why *Animal Farm* is both a satire and an allegory. Have your finished paper ready for the first day of school.

Hannah, a diligent student, read the book, looked up the words *satire* and *allegory* in the dictionary, and wrote her paper, which covered two and a half pages. Hannah didn't fully understand allegory, satire, or theme (she thought allegory and satire were themes of the novel). The teacher graded the paper, which was weak, as a final draft, and gave Hannah a *D*. In my opinion, the teacher deserved an equal or lower grade. She had done absolutely no teaching, nor did she allow the students to revise their work once they had received her feedback. When Hannah's parents explained to me that their older daughter had received the exact same assignment three years earlier and had also received a *D*, I shook my head.

The first page of Hannah's paper was devoted to a summary of the plot. This was not part of the assignment, but Hannah's decision made perfect sense: "When I finished my paper it was only a page and a half long, so I added the plot summary to make it long enough; that's what we were taught to do last year when we wrote book reports."

Next, Hannah discussed why satire and allegory were themes of the book. Her paper contained basic information, but clearly at a superficial level. It was evident that Hannah, through no fault of her own, did not fully understand theme, satire, or allegory yet. While her paper was reasonably well organized and contained relatively few errors in conventions, the content lacked the depth of thought that she could have included had she fully understood these concepts.

A traditionally strong student, Hannah was very angry about her grade. "I don't understand why I got a *D* because I did everything the teacher told us to do!" I don't blame her.

Teaching the Research Process

My second "favorite" assignment came from a combined seventh- and eighth-grade English classroom. The English teacher, who met with his students two periods a day, assigned the following paper as the class read Arthur Miller's play *The Crucible*.

> Select a group of people that have been persecuted at some point in history. Research what happened to that group, why they were persecuted, if and how the persecution ended, and what the long-term implications were. Write a paper 5 to 8 pages in length including at least three sources.

The assignment sounds more like a master's thesis. I would love to ask this teacher if he ever wrote a paper with these requirements, combined with a lack of direction and instruction, and, if so, what the experience was like for him. He provided no instruction on how to find a topic, how to research such a topic, how to avoid plagiarism, and on and on. The lack of instruction was appalling.

Even when teachers give students a writing assignment sheet filled with requirements about length; a set of expectations for a cover sheet, table of contents, bibliography, illustrations, and other features; and a list of how many points each of these areas is worth; this action does not constitute teaching. A student can easily meet these types of requirements and still produce a very weak piece of writing. If we expect our students to craft quality, interesting writing that is uniquely theirs and not plagiarized, we have to spend time teaching them how to successfully complete the assignment.

Narrowing the Focus

The third weak assignment is from a high school history classroom. The teacher had asked students to write a two-page paper discussing FDR's Four Freedom speech. Students needed to define each freedom, explain its meaning and importance, and provide an example of a nation that does not allow that freedom.

Again, this is a remarkably rigorous assignment for high school students, especially considering they had only two days to complete the assignment! How does such a wide focus provide for depth of discussion? For adequate research of the topics? For an opportunity to write from a strong knowledge base? The students were set up for failure, and based on the finished papers I saw, most students, while they had made a noble effort, had not succeeded in crafting a strong paper.

Identify Purpose and Audience

First and foremost, when we give students an assignment, we should discuss the purpose and audience. Without this prior knowledge, students may well go down a path we never intended. Be sure to discuss the notions of purpose and audience early and often in the school year. These key issues drive our writing.

Three basic purposes for academic writing are to inform, to persuade, and to entertain. All types of writing fall into one of these three purposes. Review the purpose of the assignment and help students explore the implications of that purpose on the approach they take with their writing. Informational writing can also be entertaining, but the humor cannot drown out the information.

Intertwined with the purpose is the audience. Lynna has discussed the importance of audience in previous chapters, but it is worth examining in school writing as well. You may need to remind students to use a different tone in their writing for the teacher than in their writing for their classmates. Provide opportunities for your students to write for a variety of audiences. Students can write to their classmates, the school principal or assistant principal, the person responsible for the school cafeteria, or, obviously, you.

Narrow the Topic

We must also make certain the topics we assign are reasonably narrow or are designed to allow students to narrow the focus. When we ask a third-grade student to write a paper on Ancient Egypt in three pages, we guarantee a paper that is superficial and contains nothing more than a "hit parade" of facts. Our task, once the students have researched information about ancient Egypt, is to help them find a narrow topic on which to focus their writing. Perhaps "The Great Pyramid of Giza" or "The Sphinx" would be a more appropriate topic for a third-grade student.

Provide Models

Students have a right to know what the paper should "look like" when it's done well. Otherwise, they're aiming for a moving target, and they don't even know in which direction the target is moving! When we provide samples of strong, moderate, and weak papers, and we allow students to determine the ranking, we help them gain that vision of success of what it is they're expected to do. Once they've identified which paper is the strongest or weakest, they can identify which elements were essential. This analysis creates the "a-ha" moment we want our students to experience.

We can provide samples from previous years or create our own. Remember that students need models in all genres of writing. They need to see what strong persuasive writing, compare-contrast writing, descriptive writing, and other types look like.

Monitor Points

All too often, especially in middle schools and high schools, we assign a paper and provide students with a due date. While we often help students set up deadlines for various components of their work (research, notes, outline, etc.), we often fail to monitor and look at the students' work at those various points in time. Thus, many students find themselves scrambling like a whirling dervish the night before the paper is due, driving their parents and themselves crazy because they didn't budget their time. Some adults would argue that this is a great learning experience, but when a grade is at stake, I believe we are doing students a disservice. After all, they're just kids, and they need to be guided along their path so they don't go too far astray.

To begin, we need to give students a chance to explore the topic. When we provide a very specific topic, students may not require much time, but if we ask them to find a topic, they will require much more time. Often, students need to explore a broad topic first. For example, students may begin with a general interest in ancient Egypt, but until they've done some research, they may not realize that they are most fascinated by when and why Egypt switched from pharaohs to kings.

As students work their way through the writing process, we should be in a position to examine their work along the way. We need to examine their outline or graphic organizer and add suggestions or raise questions about what they have developed. We need to explore their notes and/or research information before they begin writing, making sure they have enough information. If possible, we should also give students time to make sure at least two or three peers read their writing and provide useful feedback about what is done well and what questions remain for revision.

To give our students the best chance for success, let's do more than just assign. Obviously, we'll end up assigning fewer papers because this process takes time, but the ones we receive will be worth reading. And, by the way, the second example of a poor assignment was mine, from my third year of teaching. I was a VERY slow learner.

Steps to take right now

- Think back to your years in school. How often did a teacher provide you with models of strong and weak papers as part of your writing assignment? If your answer is never, think about how that might have helped—or hindered—you.

- Ask your students how often a teacher assigned a piece of writing but didn't actually teach them how to do it. What challenges did that create for them?

- Start collecting samples of strong, typical, and weak papers that you can share with your students next year. Ask your colleagues if they have any samples they can share with you.

Lynna's World

In the workplace, bosses usually give the assignments, and workers must figure out what to do on their own. That's why it's so important to guide our students to become independent writers. To achieve this, teachers can use monitor points (milestones) and real-world assignments that are meaningful to students.

Match the letter of the writing description with the job title.

Director, Mass Transit

HR Manager, waste management

Pharmaceutical Sales Representative

Project Team Manager, international scales and measurement

Publisher, monthly magazine

Auditor, federal government

Financial Forecasting and Analysis, consumer products

Engineer, aerospace

LPN

Car Installation Technician

Hair Stylist

A. • 15 percent of day spent writing
   • Types of writing: emails
   • Need to be concise and to the point, use grammar and punctuation correctly, write with positive tone
   • I wish my school provided a business writing course.

B. • More time writing than anything else
   • Types of writing: cost analysis, mathematical writing, performance reviews, proposals, technical manuals
   • I wish my school required me to explain thought processes and predictions.

C. • 75 percent of day spent writing
   • Types of writing: emails, agendas, consolidating notes, process/procedural documents, communication bulletins
   • Need to write clearly, concisely, and accurately; addressing international audiences
   • I wish my school required longer reading assignments.

D. • 75 percent of day spent writing
   • Types of writing: audit reports, workpapers, point papers, email, PowerPoint
   • Need to be able to condense volumes of technical information into format for generalized audience
   • I wish my school required me to write continually in a short amount of time.

E. • 75 percent of day spent writing
   • Types of writing: grants, requests, responses to customer complaints, summaries, articles, brochures, handouts
   • Need to be able to write to various audiences
   • I wish my school better prepared me in grammar/mechanics and business writing.

F. • 30 percent of day spent writing
   • Types of writing: email, proposals, requests, narrative descriptions
   • Need to summarize key points, write persuasively, use critical writing and analysis
   • I wish my school focused more on summarized commentary.

G. • 25 percent of day spent writing
   • Types of writing: articles, contracts to advertisers
   • Need effective knowledge of the English language, sufficient vocabulary, organization
   • I wish my school provided more experience in writing.

H. • 50 percent of day spent writing
   • Types of writing: Policies/procedures, performance evaluation, training manuals, company newsletters, reports, emails
   • Need to be able to use extensive vocabulary; audience analysis; outlining; perfect grammar, spelling, and mechanics
   • I wish my school required more audience directed writing, persuasive writing, and citing of sources.

I. • 5–10% of day spent writing
   • Types of writing: completing forms with customer information, descriptions of electronic functions of car, describing problem and specifying what customers want
   • Need to be complete to "save our butts," use correct grammar and spelling so others can understand the information, concise
   • I wish my school provided "a lot more" on how to write, particularly caring about grammar.

J. • Avoid writing; delegate it to others
   • Types of writing: letters to customers explaining charges, tax information to accountant
   • Need to be able to clearly explain information with good tone
   • I wish my school required more realistic types of writing and made me feel more confident in writing.

K. • 75 percent of day spent writing
   • Types of writing: medical charting of patients' condition changes and treatments, employee reprimands
   • Need to be able to write in third person, concise and detailed, accurate, complete
   • Need more format-type of writing skills and better grammar and spelling skills
   • I wish my school provided more opportunities to write using various formats and to improve my grammar and spelling skills.

Source: Great Source Education Group. 2008. Writing Across the Curriculum Participant Binder. Wilmington, MA. Reprinted with permission.

Independent Writers

Businesses need independent writers who know what questions to ask, where to look for help, which communication medium to use, how to critique and evaluate sample written documents and Web sites, and how to write to different audiences. Professional writing today incorporates visuals, applies different rhetorical modes, uses various technologies, and deals with simple to complex issues. To create logical and complete messages, writers must organize material so readers have the required information to make decisions and solve problems. Writers need to support these messages with evidence, which may require different types of research (questionnaires, surveys, interviews, etc.). We must teach all of these skills; we can't assume that writers will pick them up on their own as they get older.

CONNECTION

One of our goals in school should be to create independent writers. Companies expect and *require* workers to write independently. Even with collaborative writing in the workplace, employers expect individuals to come to the table with skills that allow them to participate equally. Therefore, in school we must continually strive to help our students become skilled, independent writers.

Monitor Points

Monitor points, or milestones, are common practice in workplace writing. When corporate officers ask me to write curriculum guides or online instruction manuals, they always give me milestones to complete that break down the project in major stages. That way the manager can check on my progress and make sure that I haven't gone off on a tangent, which would be a waste of time and money. In organizations, workers are usually required not only to meet major milestone deadlines, but also to show the progress in a written report and Gantt chart throughout the life of the project. A Gantt chart is a progress plan and status report, using Microsoft Project or Visio for example, that designates a project's progress. It visually shows all the tasks of the project, due dates, and personnel responsible. A sample Gantt chart is included in Appendix C.

Here's where the classroom environment can teach writers how to get from where they are now to where they need to be by the final deadline. Instead of just saying, "Okay, here's the assignment on project X and it's due March 14," we need to give students the specific parameters required to complete the assignment effectively: topic selection, sources, outline, rough draft, and bibliography all due by specific dates.

When I was training a group of employees on how to write instruction manuals, they initially felt the job was overwhelming. But once we broke the project down into manageable tasks, they could see how to get from A to Z. Whenever I use this approach in training programs (as well as in the classroom), I can see the writers' faces relax and hear their sighs of relief. Invariably, someone says, "You mean that's all there is to it?" (I believe we refer to this in academia as the "light bulb.")

CONNECTION

By establishing monitor points for writing in the classroom, we help our students break the writing into manageable tasks, shorten the time before they receive feedback, and create a legitimate sense of accomplishment. When they enter the workforce, they are better prepared to handle progress reports and meet essential deadlines.

Case Studies

Now, I'm *not* a lover of using case studies for assignments. (Please give me a fair reading here.) A case study is a contrived situation that students pretend they're in and assume a particular role in charge of a specific task. For example:

> You are the supervisor at a pharmaceutical company. Some of your employees are concerned about layoffs. Write a memo to them addressing their concerns about job security.

To me, case studies require students to be somebody they're not, in a pretend situation in which they have no experience or personal knowledge. Hopefully, that will never be the case when they write in the workplace, so why would we have them write like that in the classroom?

I do, however, believe in encouraging students to use their own personal situations and interests in their written work. For example, when I teach students how to write a claim letter, I explain how and why claim letters are written in the workplace. Then, since an assignment of that nature would involve a case study (UGH!), we discuss a claim letter I recently wrote in my personal life. (See Figure 6.1; names have been changed.)

Approximately two weeks later a man from the landscaping company arrived at my house to check into the situation. He was wonderful: He looked everything over, listened to me, and granted my claim, saving us $6500 in tree removal costs. Furthermore, he gave me free lawn treatment for six months and an additional type of application free of charge.

As he was getting ready to leave, I noticed his business card listed him as a regional manager. When I said I was pleased he had checked on this personally instead of sending a lawn technician, he replied, "I just wanted to meet the person who wrote me this letter. Normally I get letters screaming, demanding, and threatening lawsuits." I am convinced that I received the personal attention and positive response because I wrote the letter professionally. (Shoot, I should have been greedy and asked for a condo on the Florida coast!)

When I relate this story to my students, they often start using the positive letter-writing technique with similar success. One student told me, "Professor, every week I hear you yap, yap, yap about how to write in the business world, so I thought, I'm paying a lot of money for this information so I may as well use it." (I think instead of "yap, yap, yap" she meant to say "impart invaluable words of wisdom," but who am I to put words in her mouth?) She tried this approach after some mechanics failed to fix a problem with her car. They resolved the issue to her satisfaction, and she received a free tune-up and a discount on future work.

Not only did she embrace the concept of how to write this type of letter, but her story encouraged others to write their own letters. Two weeks later, another student told me that after hearing her account, he wrote to a local car dealer concerning an unresolved issue, and received a check for $200 for his inconvenience. Students continue to ask me for help in writing claim letters; they're motivated to learn how to write effectively because it involves real-world situations that they care about.

Figure 6.1   **Claim Letter to Landscaping Company**

9213 Carrington Ct.
Pickerington, OH 43147
October 22, 2007

Mark Lansing, Regional Manager
Prime Landscaping
4444 Scotts Rd.
Dublin, OH 43578

Dear Mark Lansing:

Positive note ▶ I have been very pleased with your company's service during the past ten years. Our landscaping has always looked healthy, and your technicians have been prompt and courteous. However, I would appreciate your looking into the recent issue with our pine trees.

Background information ▶ For your reference, our account number is 54667 and Ted is our technician. On October 17, I noticed that practically overnight five of the pine trees in the grove in front of our house died. After an arborist evaluated the situation, he diagnosed the problem as pine bark disease. Furthermore, he said that all five of the trees, stumps, and needles need to be removed immediately to prevent the spread of the disease to the other trees.

Requested remedy ▶ Since we have paid your company to treat our landscaping to prevent these types of diseases from occurring, I would like you to cover the expenses for removing the trees, stumps, and needles.

Please contact me at 614-978-4456 if you need additional information. Due to the urgency of this situation, I look forward to speaking with you as soon as possible.

Sincerely,

Mary Malone

Enclosure: Arborist's report

Assignments like this allow students to select an issue they find relevant, which makes the work more meaningful and interesting. They can write letters to airline companies to request a free ticket because of lost luggage or to school officials to file a grievance or to recommend that you, their teacher, get a bonus. The list of ideas to use as topics is countless.

Ways to give your classroom the **Corporate Edge**

- Give a longer writing assignment, asking students to list the individual tasks involved to complete the assignment, along with realistic due dates for each task. Have students design PowerPoint slides, set up a wiki, or prepare a Gantt chart illustrating the steps involved in completing the assignment.

- Ask students to use situations in their personal lives as prompts to write letters that request information, file a claim, or make a recommendation.

Answers to The Classroom–Corporate Connection

Director, Mass Transit—E; HR Manager—H; Pharmaceutical Sales Representative—A; Project Team Manager—C; Publisher—G; Auditor—D; Financial Forecasting and Analysis—F; Engineer—B; LPN—K; Car Installation Technician—I; Hair Stylist—J

CHAPTER 7

Practice, Practice, Practice

From your perspective

1. *Create a list of opportunities you were given during your college years to "practice" the skills required to teach. Does your list extend beyond student teaching? Analyze your list.*

2. *List opportunities you've created for your students to practice various writing skills. How successful have those opportunities been? List additional writing skills that your students need time to practice. If you provide more time to practice these skills, what will you change or eliminate from your instruction to create the time?*

An Overview

The old adage "practice makes perfect as long as you practice correctly" holds true in writing. Writers—like athletes, musicians, artists, welders, and others—need to practice their craft in order to become highly skilled. Asking a writer—whether twelve years old or forty-two years old—to create a solid story, essay, review, or proposal without first having opportunities to practice each component is likely to frustrate the writer, teacher, or employer. Students and professionals spend hours practicing their crafts before a game, concert, or sales pitch. Shouldn't writing be the same?

The Need for Regular Practice

Every February, hundreds of men, most in their twenties and thirties but a few "oldies" in their forties and making millions of dollars—guaranteed—descend on Florida or Arizona for six weeks to practice the skills they've been honing since they were five or six years old. During that time, they spend seven days a week giving their "body memories" a chance to get into shape again, having spent the previous three or four months doing whatever they pleased in the comforts of their homes. The smart ones have maintained a rigorous workout schedule so spring training in February isn't such a shock to their systems. Even though they have reached the pinnacle of success in their field, professional baseball players understand the value of practice. And their practice continues throughout the season. Before every game throughout the year, the players take batting practice, working to refine some aspect of their swing, trying to reach perfection or to correct a slight error that has prevented them from doing as well as they expect.

So it should be with student writers. They need opportunities on a regular basis to practice their craft. And just as major league ballplayers are not "graded" for their hitting during batting practice, student writers should not be graded for the work they produce when they are practicing aspects of writing. Like batting practice, these "practice writes" should be short and highly focused, honing one skill.

The goal is that when students are faced with a long writing assignment or a prompt on the state writing assessment, they can easily utilize the skills they've been practicing and put them together to form a solid, thoughtful, and engaging piece of writing. It may not be perfect, but it will demonstrate that the student understands how to create writing that is focused, incorporates interesting and unique details, is well organized with a strong lead and conclusion, and uses language that is appropriate for the topic, audience, and writer.

What to Practice

The list of skills students need to practice is long. But the good news is that we have the students in our classrooms for 180 days for thirteen years! So consider this list a beginning:

1. Writing leads
2. Writing conclusions
3. Using supporting details
4. Sequencing information
5. Determining the difference between "everyday" details versus intriguing details
6. Changing voice to match purpose and audience

7. Using dynamic action verbs to replace state-of-being verbs or lackluster verbs
8. Beginning sentences with words other than pronouns and articles
9. Using transitions to connect sentences and paragraphs
10. Finding the one "right" adjective to replace three or four vague adjectives
11. Creating narrowed topics from a general topic

We can begin by exploring the literature in the classroom. If students skim books from the classroom library, they will find numerous examples of great leads and conclusions, sentence structure that varies from sentence to sentence, exploded moments, and language that creates incredible images.

After we have provided focused lessons on these areas, as discussed in Chapter 5 on traits, it is time for students to practice what they have learned. At least we hope they have learned it! This section contains a few examples.

Writing Strong Leads

This exercise comes from my friend Robert Young, and I have used it numerous times with adults and students alike, always with success. First, teach students about the SACRED ways to begin and what goes into strong leads (see Chapter 5). Then, give each student a blank three-by-five-inch card. Ask each student to come up with a story idea on any topic. Have the students write the opening line or opening two lines to their story on the cards, keeping their leads a secret. At the same time, create a card yourself, using one lead you have selected from a published book.

Collect the cards, select three of the better ones and combine them with yours. Read the four leads to the class twice, telling them their task is to determine which is the published lead. Send students who believe it's the first lead to a designated area of the room (e.g., back wall). Do this for each lead and ask people from each group to explain why they believe the lead they selected is the published lead. Don't reveal the answer until the groups are done. Then select another four leads (one from another published book) and repeat the activity. This lesson provides students with opportunities to listen for strong leads and defend their selections. Even our most struggling writers can craft one or two sentences, and, if their lead is read, they can hear positive feedback from their peers about their writing.

Repeat this exercise for a week. Each day when the students enter the room, their first task is to write a new lead they've thought up. Within a week, the students have had a chance to write at least five leads, listen to forty leads, and reflect upon what constitutes a strong lead.

Writing Conclusions

Provide the students with copies of three well-written essays or papers written by students in their grade or within one or two years of their grade. Exclude the concluding paragraphs and have the students write their own conclusions for each essay. Then place students in groups of four to select the best conclusion for each essay from their group. Ask students to read aloud to the class the best conclusion from each group.

You can repeat this activity on a regular basis, two or three times a week with different essays. The students have a chance not only to practice writing conclusions, but also to hear what strong conclusions sound like.

Beginning Sentences with Various Types of Words

Provide students with a paragraph of eight to ten sentences. Be sure seven or eight of the sentences begin with a pronoun or an article. First, have the students count the number of pronouns and articles that begin sentences. Then, teach them how to begin sentences with different types of words (e.g., prepositions, adverbs). Finally, have the students rewrite the paragraph, beginning no more than two sentences with a pronoun or an article.

As we plan a unit, we want to incorporate regular opportunities for students to practice the skills that are essential to the writing they will do for that unit. The intent, just like in athletics, is for students to learn a particular skill; observe others performing that skill; discover, through practice and instruction, what leads to success with that skill; and then practice it over and over and over. Thus, when the time arrives for them to write a complete paper, they can call upon the skills they have rehearsed and successfully bring them to the forefront.

Steps to take right now

- Ask your students to think about a physical activity they participate in on a regular basis. Ask them to write about one aspect of that activity they have practiced numerous times. How often do they practice it? What does the instruction look like? For example, if students play basketball, how often do they practice foul shots? Did they receive instruction on how to shoot a foul shot? What did that look like?

- Decide what component of writing you and your students will begin practicing tomorrow. How will you teach them about that component, and how often will they practice? How will you know when they've "got it"?

Lynna's World

Yes, I agree that our writing does improve the more we write. Heck, I know I'm a much better writer today than I was even ten years ago.

I believe in the rubber band theory: We're all born with a box of rubber bands—athletic skills, intelligence, beauty, musical talent, compassion, and so on. The bad news is some of us acquired bigger rubber bands than others. The good news is that through our experiences and effort we can stretch our rubber bands. So even if people got a smaller written communication rubber band, they can "stretch" it through training and practice to make it bigger than those who received a larger writing rubber band to begin with. And the importance of "stretching" this rubber band is at the heart of most jobs in the workplace.

THE **Classroom–Corporate** CONNECTION

1. Fill in the Blank: "Communication skills are an ever-evolving skill set. You never have enough _____." (Stated by Kevin Jetton, executive vice president of the Association of Information Technology Professionals)

2. True or False: Eighty-six percent of companies surveyed by the National Commission on Writing reported that poorly written application materials would "frequently" or "almost always" be held against a job candidate.

3. Match the purpose with the appropriate type of visual.

   1. To present exact data or a lot of data   A. Bar/Column Chart
   2. To show parts of a whole   B. Line Graph
   3. To compare and contrast   C. Table
   4. To show trends over time   D. Flow Chart
   5. To show steps in a process   E. Pie Chart

Relevance of Assignments

When we make assignments relevant to our students' lives, they take this whole writing concept a lot more seriously. It's important that classroom teachers know what kind of writing is done in the workplace so that they can show students the connection to their writing assignments.

Students need to take the skills we've discussed and apply them to different types of assignments. For example, teachers can show samples of business proposals and discuss how persuasive writing is used, how all the information must be included for the reader, how document design enhances the appearance and readability, and how headings are used properly. Teachers can also show examples of other business documents, such as memos, letters, progress reports, executive summaries, informational reports, instruction manuals, Web pages, and wikis. Together, the class can analyze the organization and examine how rhetorical modes (e.g., compare, contrast, illustration, narration) are used in these documents to make ideas clear.

As well, we need to incorporate various real-world writing assignments periodically or intertwine professional writing characteristics into our students' work. To help students develop the writing skills they will need in the workplace, teachers must provide them with opportunities to explore a variety of career-related assignments, practice editing and revising, analyze data and incorporate visuals, address ethical and legal considerations, and practice multicultural communication. The following section discusses each of these types of assignments, and includes examples of student exercises that relate directly to their lives.

Explore a Variety of Career-Related Assignments

Different Types of Messages

Students should practice writing different types of workplace messages, using different channels of communication. Yes, we live in a world of technology, so students should practice writing emails, blogs, wikis, and other types of electronic communication. But they still need to write a variety of memos and letters, the expected formal channel in the workplace for important documents to be sent to readers and to conduct business, especially internationally. Different types of letters require different formats and strategies: request, reply, confirmation, claim, adjustment, and inquiry. Here are some exercises students might try.

- Write a memo to inform your teacher about the progress of your group or individual project.
- Write a memo to inform your teacher about an upcoming absence and request homework.
- Write a letter of inquiry to a business about a product or service you would like to know more about (e.g., Ford Mustang).
- Write a letter to someone to ask for a letter of recommendation.
- Write a thank-you letter to someone for a gift you've received.
- Write a cover letter for a piece of writing you are submitting for publication.
- Write to a company in the industry that most interests you. Ask for information on industry trends and specifics of the company itself.
- Write a letter to people in professions that interest you, asking them to be a guest speaker to your class.

Students should write sales letters, because in the workplace they may be writing to sell a product, a service, or an idea. They may use persuasive writing to promote an organization's image, to boost employee morale, or to promote goodwill. Here are a few examples:

- Write a persuasive message about something you want changed in your life. For example, write to the principal asking to permit senior skip day or write a letter persuading your teacher that recess should be fifteen minutes longer.
- Write to your parents or other adults to persuade them to let you do something they currently won't allow.

Writing in the workplace requires knowing what the audience needs and supporting the claims with evidence and logical arguments. Students can practice with this exercise:

- Write one simple message to four different audiences (e.g., teacher, grandparent, friend, stranger).
- Write an email to your teacher and to your team members explaining the changes you made in revising and editing a collaborative research report.

CONNECTION

In the workplace, people who are skilled at producing a variety of written documents are extremely valuable to their employer. In the classroom, providing students with regular opportunities to create various types of writing increases their skill set and enables them to demonstrate abilities that may be overlooked if they always write the same type of document.

Throughout their lives they'll be using these skills personally and professionally.

Job Search Documents

It's never too early to help students learn to write job search documents such as cover letters, resumes, application forms, and thank-you letters. (The appendix includes some sample job search documents.) Students can practice the following:

- Write a cover letter and resume.
- In a team, critique sample resumes and select three of the best.

Research Papers

The old "research paper" should also still be practiced. In business, we may manage large projects, and employees will need to research, synthesize information, and work on the project over a relatively long time period. Business reports need to solve problems or answer questions and evaluate, organize, and present information. These formal reports need to be balanced, showing benefits and drawbacks. Students need to practice including higher-level thinking skills in their writing assignments. These exercises can help:

- Research a career that interests you and prepare a report highlighting the job duties, requirements, skills, and so forth.
- Write a report about school problems.
- Write a formal research report on a topic of interest.
- Report on your family's ancestry.
- Write collaboratively to make a recommendation report to your school board.

Career-Specific

Students can examine the different kinds of writing required in specific career paths. For example, students who are considering the field of pharmacy would look at the types of research documents that are required. They may wish to interview someone in the field about the writing they do. Students who want to enter the engineering field could examine technical manuals and lab reports. Then they should have opportunities to practice these types of writing in the classroom.

Practice Editing and Revising

I think what's important for beginning writers is not to see how many papers they can write, but rather to take a few written samples and edit/revise them so they are written correctly. It makes no sense to continue writing incorrectly over and over again. It's like my backhand in tennis. What's the point of getting a ball machine and practicing my backhand stroke two hundred times if each time I hit the ball my form is out of alignment?

Figure 7.1 contains a checklist that students can use to revise business messages. Teachers can review the list with students and provide samples for the students to revise. As well, they can assign the following exercises:

- Compare and contrast business writing with expository writing.
- Critique sample business documents, using the checklist in Figure 7.1.
- Practice editing sample paragraphs from business documents.
- Bring in samples of poor writing you see at school, work, or personal life. The best example of poor writing at the end of the term will win a prize.
- Edit and revise a rough draft of a business document together as a class or small group.
- Examine letters from college admissions offices.
- Bring in a sales letter sent to your home and critique it.
- Collect brochures, advertisements, and flyers from local companies and examine their layout and design.
- Evaluate sample company emails for style and tone.
- Rewrite sample emails to be more effective.
- Evaluate graphic design and layout on Web pages.
- Locate two Web sites for similar products/services and compare and contrast their strengths and weaknesses.
- Put a rough draft on an overhead transparency and edit and revise it together as a class or small group.

Analyze Data and Incorporate Visuals

Since professional writing incorporates visuals, students need to practice analyzing data and then designing visuals to be incorporated into their writing. Visuals give readers breathing space and clarify information. We need to teach students basic guidelines in presenting visuals correctly and introduce them to the most common types of visuals:

Figure 7.1 **Checklist for Revising Business Messages**

Content

- Clarity
- Completeness—sufficient supporting details
- Conciseness—unnecessary information eliminated
- Accuracy of information
- Ethical/legal requirements met

Organization

- Logical sequence of information
- Direct/indirect strategy used appropriately
- Transitions used to connect ideas

Style

- Sentence variety
- Active voice predominates
- Conversational style—pompous language and slang avoided
- Jargon used with discretion
- Concise—no wordy expressions, unnecessary words, or redundancy
- You-attitude is emphasized
- Positive tone throughout
- Bias-free language

Grammar and Mechanics

Check
- Spelling
- Subject-verb agreement
- Verb tense
- Parallelism
- Pronouns—antecedent agreement, reference, case
- Capitalization
- Punctuation—commas, apostrophes, semi-colons, colons
- Spacing

Avoid
- Misplaced and dangling modifiers
- Fragments
- Run-on sentences
- Typographical errors
- Shifts in person and number

Format

Memos
- Appropriate memo style
- TO, FROM, DATE, and SUBJECT included

Letters
- Acceptable letter style (full block, modified block)
- All business letter parts are included (heading, inside address, salutation, complimentary closing, signature block)

Design Elements

- Appropriate use of white space
- Short paragraphs
- Consistency
- Appearance—print and paper, packaging
- Use of graphic highlighting—bullets, lists, headings

- Single-spaced within paragraphs, double-spaced between paragraphs
- End matter if needed (enclosure/attachment, copy notation, distribution list)
- Continuation page headings, if needed

pie charts, bar/column charts, line graphs, and tables. We need to explain how each visual is used for different purposes (i.e., pie charts to show parts of a whole; bar/column charts to compare and contrast; line graphs to show trends over time; and tables to show a lot of data or exact data).

To practice using visuals in written assignments, students might design a pie chart to:

- Depict how classroom time is spent in a typical day (upper elementary)
- Visually show how the students spend their money in a typical month (middle school)
- Illustrate how students get their news each week, such as through magazines, newspapers, television, the Internet, and other sources (high school)

Students might design a bar chart to:

- Compare the number of hours girls and boys read, complete chores, play video games, shop, play sports, sleep, practice a musical instrument, or do homework each week (upper elementary)
- Compare and contrast how students acquire their music—traditional shops, online stores, downloads, and other sources—compared to adults (middle school)

Students could also practice designing line graphs to:

- Show the increased use of blogs and podcasts over the last ten years (upper elementary)
- Illustrate the number of cafeteria lunches served week by week over the last five months and draw conclusions from the data (middle school)
- Depict the number of victories by four sports teams over the last five years (high school)

As a final exercise, students could design a table to:

- Represent the number of items sold at the school store, including type, cost, profit margin, and other features (upper elementary)
- Show results from a questionnaire or survey (middle school)

Teachers may also want to help students explore the visuals that come with Microsoft Office (or Mac equivalent). Gantt charts (explained earlier) are frequently used in business for proposals and progress reports, and students would probably enjoy experimenting with Microsoft Project in designing these project plan and status reports. (A sample Gantt chart is included in Appendix C.) For example, students could develop a Gantt chart for their latest research project they're working on. Also, they could use Microsoft Visio to make a flow chart depicting the steps in a process. This program automatically labels the function of flow chart symbols.

CONNECTION
Because many people are visual learners, student work can and should be displayed visually to supplement and aid in the understanding of the text.

Here are some final examples of assignments that include visuals:

- Create visuals from data. For example, gather information about students' favorite cereals or television programs.
- Design a PowerPoint presentation.
- Construct an organizational chart for your school district.
- Draw a flow chart for a process you do often.
- Write a class newsletter that is distributed monthly.
- Write a brochure about a vacation spot.

Address Ethical and Legal Considerations

In the workplace, legal obligations and ethical considerations often merge. In the world of school, we also need to address and practice these issues in written communication. Students need to be knowledgeable about software duplication, privacy laws, defamation, and fraud. Saying, "Gee, your honor, I didn't know" doesn't go far in a court of law.

Actions, as well as words, have implications and consequences. Philip Kolin, in his book *Successful Writing at Work* (2003), describes the 3 M's in unethical writing: misquotation, misrepresentation, and manipulation. Concealing or omitting the truth, using false advertising, applying bias, lying, and exaggerating information should all be on an ethics checklist for communication in academic and workplace environments.

We should ask ourselves the following questions in dealing with the ethics of our written documents:

- Do I know what I'm talking about or am I just making it up? Do I really believe what I'm saying?
- Do I avoid exaggeration? Do I omit information that leaves the reader at a disadvantage?
- Do I state the information clearly so there's only one way to interpret it?
- Am I being honest and fair?
- Am I respecting all legitimate rights to privacy and confidentiality?
- Would I feel comfortable if my statements were on the front page of the local newspaper?
- Do I give credit to all borrowed material?

These same issues also apply in the classroom. Plagiarism and fabricating information are not uncommon, as we all know. We need to teach our students about these issues and impress upon them the consequences of these practices both in and out of school. For example, a few years ago a student at a prestigious college was expelled during the second semester of his senior year for plagiarizing a paper. Schools should also have in place guidelines for academic dishonesty.

The discussion with students about plagiarism needs to begin in elementary school. As students begin writing reports in third and fourth grades, they often innocently copy material from a book and include it in their report, exactly as they wrote it down. Part of the instructional process of writing a report needs to include *how* to take notes. Discussions about what it means to "borrow" somebody's writing and how to give them credit for what they've written should be part of the unit. Additionally, providing elementary students with opportunities to practice paraphrasing is crucial if students are to avoid plagiarism.

During the 2005–2006 school year, the Londonderry, New Hampshire, School District was concerned about students' knowledge of plagiarism and the ethical and legal use of copyrighted material. As a result, the district created a series of benchmarks, beginning in first grade, that became part of the classroom curriculum. An example from their final document for grade 5 appears in Figure 7.2. The district realized that to ensure that students understand and practice appropriate use of resources and materials, teachers need to begin instruction early.

Additionally, we need to make students aware of legal as well as ethical issues. Seeking the advice of an organization's legal department and knowing state laws can prevent huge liability lawsuits. When we write performance evaluations and letters of recommendation, we need to know the legal implications. If a company calls a customer a "swindler" in a letter, they can be sued for defamation. To explore these issues with students, as well as issues regarding the invasion of privacy and data security, visit www.workforce.com and www.hr.com.

CONNECTION

Legal and ethical issues apply in both the classroom and the workplace. Failure to behave in an ethical manner or adhere to copyright laws can result in significant problems.

Figure 7.2 **Londonderry School District Benchmarks: Grade 5**

Info. Literacy and Comp. Tech.		
5.501	Information Literacy	determine the information needed to solve a problem
5.502	Information Literacy	identify appropriate topics and keywords
5.510	Computer Technology	find information from a given resource alphabetically, chronologically, topically, or numerically
5.512	Information Literacy	with limited assistance, locate information on the Internet
5.513	Information Literacy	identify the parts of a nonfiction book (glossary, index, table of contents)
5.514	Information Literacy	independently complete bibliography cards
5.515	Information Literacy	identify keywords and phrases to record information (note taking)
5.516	Information Literacy	be able to define "plagiarism"

Source: Used with permission of Londonderry School District.

Multicultural Communication

In professional writing, analyzing the audience also entails being able to write for international readers. Most of us may not be bilingual, but at least we can be knowledgeable about and respectful of other cultures and be aware that the conventions of writing change from culture to culture. Again we can't just assume that students know how to write to different audiences or that they have an awareness of other cultures; we need to teach them about cultural differences in communication and provide opportunities to practice writing to people of other countries so that they don't think that everyone in the world communicates like we do.

An example in *Intercultural Business Communication* (2005) by Chaney and Martin describes the following business situation in which the differences in communication led to loss of business:

> Exhibitors at a trade show could not understand why Chinese visitors were not stopping by their booth. The exhibitors were wearing green hats and giving them away as promotional items. They soon discovered that for many Chinese people, green hats are associated with infidelity. The Chinese expression, "He wears a green hat," indicates that a man's wife has been cheating on him. As soon as the exhibitors discarded the green hats and started giving out T-shirts instead, the Chinese attendees began visiting the booth.

One employee at a company told me that his department lost a $10 million contract, all over how they handled the Japanese clients' business cards. He lamented that his boss wished that they had taken the time to learn a little about the Japanese culture before trying to win the contract. (Many Japanese businessmen want people to accept their business cards with two hands, read it, and place it down on the desk; otherwise, the handling of the business card is considered rude.) Many Japanese are offended by American ignorance of business card protocol.

A Fortune 500 company hired me to teach their workers how to communicate with their vendors, who were mostly in the Pacific Rim. They realized that their communication breakdowns were causing loss of sales and a decrease in productivity. I explained that when we write to American readers, we tend to offer direct information. But many Asians prefer information to be more indirect and complimentary. In general, intercultural communication issues can include how information is presented (e.g., the directness and formality, or the document's format and design); the degree of egalitarianism; objective data versus the emphasis on relationships; overall tone; and the importance of time.

Students need this knowledge so eventually they can do business abroad. For American companies to stay competitive, they must be able to compete globally. IBM, for instance, has a global workforce that speaks more than 150 languages. Writers need to know, for example, that people are not referred to as *Oriental*. (People are referred to as *Asians*; objects are referred to as *Oriental*.) Professional communication to international audiences requires writers to adapt to local formats; avoid idioms (e.g., "hit the nail on

CONNECTION

Many classrooms today are culturally diverse. By examining cultural differences, our students are better able to relate to, communicate with, and understand their peers. This helps students succeed in the workplace when communicating with a diverse population.

the head"); cite numbers clearly (the dollar is not the currency used in all countries and most of the world uses the metric system); and, above all, strive for clarity (in both verbal and nonverbal messages). Through practice, the development of intercultural communication skills will help students be more successful communicators in the workplace.

Three Web sites to help us become more knowledgeable of other cultures are www.lonelyplanet.com, www.executiveplanet.com, and www.wtgonline.com/navigate/world.asp. Students can also try these exercises:

- Promote your school to readers from two different countries, adapting your message to the reader's culture.
- Research different communication taboos in at least five other cultures and write a report explaining the taboos.

Ways to give your classroom the **Corporate Edge**

- Ask students to locate and read Internet articles about plagiarism and then write a report defining plagiarism. The report should explain the importance of proper documentation and describe the consequences of plagiarism.

- Create an assignment in which students review sample resumes, read articles on resume writing tips, and write their own resumes. Black out the names and provide copies for all students to review. In small groups, have students select three candidates to interview from the sample resumes. Ask students to write a collaborative report explaining their decision.

- Encourage students to practice identifying legal and ethical issues by asking them to review sample letters, advertisements, emails, and other documents.

- Ask students to research how communication varies from three different countries and write a brief summary of how people in each of the three cultures deal with concepts of time, space, formality, word meanings, and other various communication styles. Have students post their findings on a class wiki.

- Give students practice writing on blogs or in emails to readers from other cultures.

Answers to The Classroom–Corporate Connection

1. practice **2.** True **3.** 1—C, 2—E, 3—A, 4—B, 5—D

A Goodbye from Lynna

The last chapter is geared exclusively toward the school environment, so, I'll give Fred more "air time" to address grading, test preparation, and planning. As you examine these areas, which can seem overwhelming, just keep in mind that those of us in the business world do realize you make a difference, one student at a time. From my role as a mother and corporate trainer, thank you.

from your perspective

1. *Keep a list of the topics of conversations you hear in the teachers' lounge. Is there a common thread? What do you notice about the topics?*

2. *What is a reasonable amount of time to spend grading papers each week? If you're currently teaching, how close are you to that time? If you're not currently teaching, ask some teachers how much time they spend grading papers. If the numbers don't align, determine how to correct this.*

3. *To what extent does the structure of your state writing assessment align with how you teach writing? Do students have an opportunity to plan? To revise? To edit? Have students connected with the topics provided by the state?*

4. *Interview a colleague who has taught for at least ten years. How does that person plan the year? Write down what you can learn from those experiences.*

CHAPTER **8**

Complaints from the Teachers' Lounge

1. How do I grade all these papers?

2. How do I prepare students for local and state tests?

3. What do I do next week?

Grading Papers: An Overview

As teachers, we face a huge dilemma: How can we assign writing on a regular basis without spending our lives grading papers? If we choose to have a life outside of school, we can't assign much writing and our students do not develop the skills required for success later in school and beyond. Is there another option? I believe there is.

Fred's World

A few years ago, while conducting a seminar in Nebraska, a teacher approached me with a simple question. "I love all the ideas you're presenting to us," she said. "But I teach 186 seventh-grade students every day. How do I have my students write and get through all those papers without going crazy and still allow myself to have a life?"

I was stunned. I thought I had a difficult situation when I taught 150 students a day. One hundred eighty-six students a day. I did some quick calculations. She averaged 37 students per class. If each student wrote a two-page paper, she would have 372 pages to read. If she spent three minutes on each page, which is not a significant amount of time, it would take her over eighteen hours of nonstop reading and commenting just to work her way through one set of papers. She was right. If she were going to have her students write on a regular basis and if she were to read each and every paper, providing quality feedback, she would have to sacrifice having any kind of life outside of teaching. This is not something I recommend!

Since my conversation with the teacher from Nebraska, I have met other teachers of middle and high school students who, unfortunately, are teaching even more than 186 students a day. The record I have come across so far is 206. This is simply a disgrace. It is not fair nor instructionally sound to teachers nor is it fair to our students. In an age in which testing is becoming more high stakes every year, and the pressure on students to perform at high levels increases every year, degrading the quality of the instruction they receive by having these numbers pass through a classroom each day is counterproductive to what we are trying to achieve.

Unfortunately, we can't immediately change the systems in which these students attend school. But the very real question for the teacher remains. How do we deal with the mountains of papers that are created when we have our students write on a regular basis?

Different Schedules

As I see it, we have a few options. The first, while not optimal, can work: Have classes write on different schedules. If we spread out the students' writing so that papers from one class are due three or four days later than those of another class, we avoid the massive pile-up of papers. However, this route also ensures that the flow is constant and the teacher almost never gets a break.

Short Assignments

The second option seems slightly more reasonable: short writing assignments. I believe we can teach our students how to write well, provide them with plenty of opportunities for practice, and not bury ourselves under a mound of three-, four-, and five-page papers.

Collaborative Projects

The third approach is to have students work collaboratively (which addresses one of Lynna's goals) in small groups of four or five, researching different aspects of the same topic and each writing one section of the paper. Let's say the topic is tarantulas. The students can conduct initial research to gather information about tarantulas, determine what subtopics are most interesting, and assign one subtopic to each person in the group. Students can then develop questions about each subtopic. For example:

1. *Tarantula hairs:* How many do they have? How far can they fling their hairs? How many barbs are there per hair? Do the hairs grow back after the tarantula pulls them out? What other animals, if any, have barbed hairs?

2. *Mating habits:* Why do the males "tap" the females and how is this done? How do they "transfer" the web sack of sperm? Why do the females often eat the males after mating? How old must the tarantulas be before they are ready to reproduce? How often can the female produce as many as six hundred offspring? Will the female eat the newborn males?

3. *Size:* How large do tarantulas grow in various parts of the hemisphere? Why do they grow larger in some areas than others? At what age/size do they first shed their skin? Exactly how do they shed their skin? How often do they shed their skin? What other animals shed their skin as they grow?

4. *Eyes:* Where are the eight eyes situated on the body? Why do they have eight eyes? Do the eyes have different purposes? How far can they see? What happens if they lose an eye? Can they see colors?

Depending on the size of the group, it would be easy to add other categories. What makes this approach so workable is that each student is actually creating a research paper, even if it is short, and going through all the steps students must undergo to write an entire research paper. Each student has to define a topic, develop questions about the topic, research the topic to discover answers to the questions, create more questions based on the research that has been done, and finally write a section. The group must also learn to write transitions between their sections, just as individual students do for complete research papers.

The benefits are numerous:

- Each student goes through the research process, including the writing.
- Students are involved in both individual and group work.
- Students within the group collaborate and assist each other in their work.
- Students read and review each other's writing and receive feedback about how it can be improved.
- The teacher's workload is reduced to a much more manageable level.

I understand that at some point in students' careers, they need to write a research paper independently, but not every year. In the workplace, almost all research papers are a collaborative effort. Thus, teaching students to research *and* write collaboratively is as crucial as researching and writing independently.

Peer Assessment

The final option to decrease the paper load is my favorite, but it is also the most risky option for teachers: letting students assess each other. I believe the better students become at assessing the work of others, the better they become at writing. By critically examining pieces of peer writing—on different topics, different genres, different modes—students gain a stronger understanding of what good writing looks like. They also begin to see clearly what weak writing looks like. Thus, when they write themselves, they better understand what they need to do.

When students are assessors, they engage in discussions with their peers that otherwise would never take place. Students begin to reflect upon the writing process and think critically not only about whether a piece of writing is strong or weak, but also about what makes it strong or weak, and in what areas is it strong and in what areas is it weak. Explaining their thinking to their peers requires thought, sensitivity, and honesty. Of course, younger students may have a more difficult, if not impossible, time assessing writing than high school seniors. So the age of the students needs to be taken into account.

Clearly, the teacher should assess and grade students' writing. But does the teacher have to be the one to assess every draft of every piece of writing the students produce? Instead, when a student has completed a draft of writing, or a portion of a piece of writing, why not allow two or three students to review and react to it? The writers' workshop model involves peer discussion and review, but we can take this one step further. We can allow students to score the paper, using very specific analytic rubrics, and defend the score they arrived at, sharing that thinking with the writer.

Unfortunately, the reality is that teachers will need to spend significant time grading papers. But there are reasonable ways to trim this back. Remember, if you sacrifice your own personal life in order to grade papers constantly, you'll eventually burn out and look for a new career. So before you assign those seven- or eight- or ten-page papers, make sure you plan sufficient time to respond to them in a quality fashion. If the students take the time and energy to write a ten-page paper, they have the right to expect more than a brief perusal of the paper and a grade without any comments. Assign smart. Work smart.

Steps to take right now

- Keep track of how much time you spend reading and/or grading papers during the next three weeks. Make sure to include time on the weekends! Monitor how much time is spent "correcting" and how much time is spent commenting. There is a difference!

- Ask your students what they would like to see when you return a paper to them (besides an *A*!). What is most interesting and useful to them?

The World of Testing:
An Overview

Yes, the testing craze is here to stay for the foreseeable future.
We can complain all we want, and many of our complaints are
legitimate. But that does not eliminate the reality that many
politicians, school board members, superintendents, parents,
and even some teachers place an enormous emphasis on
the results of these tests.

Fred's World

With the advent of No Child Left Behind (NCLB), the results have taken on
new meaning. Now, those results often determine whether or not individual
students will be promoted to the next grade, receive a high school diploma, or have the
flexibility to attend different schools. The results can even determine whether teachers
and administrators will keep or lose their jobs. High-stakes testing has arrived.

On the plus side, because many tests now require students to write in response to a
prompt (versus the old system of multiple-choice questions), students now spend more
classroom time on writing than ever before. Students write more often; teachers try, with
various levels of success, to evaluate that writing; and teachers talk with students about
how to improve their writing. Students are beginning to understand that writing will be an
important aspect of their lives after school, whether they go directly to work, into the military, or on to college. Teachers are examining how to teach writing and how to meaning-
fully assess the writing their students produce. All of these are positive benefits of NCLB.

Then there are the negatives. In states in which writing is not being tested, teachers
have openly admitted to me that the amount of writing students do for class is minimal.
Why? Because teachers are smart people. They teach what will be tested! If the school's
reputation hinges on the test results, and if the tests focus only on reading and math, why
focus attention on writing? After all, the state has, in its own way, said that writing is not
important. (If it were, they would test it.) This is indeed a sad commentary on today's
educational priorities.

In some states, the only writing being assessed is four- to seven-sentence responses
to questions in reading or math (e.g., "Explain how you solved the problem"). When
teachers focus only on how to answer those types of questions, students may not learn
how to create a cogent, cohesive, focused, and interesting piece of writing. Thesis
statement? Why teach a thesis statement if it will not be included on the mandated
state test?

The next concern is that when tests require students to create a longer response to an open-ended prompt (extended constructed response), the writing process is totally eliminated. Students have no time to reflect upon their topic (which is often something they know little if anything about), to write a draft, to receive feedback about their draft, and then to revise or edit their work. We have to question what the test actually measures. What happens to students who, in order to produce their best work, need time just to think? What if we told adults, "Tomorrow I'm giving you a writing test. You won't know the topic until your time begins; you can't ask anyone for assistance; you can't ask for clarification, or receive an answer to a question if you have one. And, by the way, the quality of your work will determine whether or not you keep your job." Sound like fun to you? Then imagine you're only nine or thirteen or sixteen years old!

Clearly, there are significant problems with this system. However, for the time being, we need to do all we can to prepare our students to be as successful as possible with the system in place. So how do we teach students to become competent writers *and* do well on the tests? Here are a few suggestions.

Rule #1:
Don't Teach to the Test

To help students perform well on tests, hundreds of teachers now only teach writing as direct response to prompts. No other writing takes place in their classrooms. Their students have no surprises when test day comes, but are they learning how to write well? Are they learning the process by which real writers write? Are they learning the components of good writing? Are they learning how to ask questions about their writing or the writing of others? And are they learning how to hold a conversation about writing? If all they do is practice responding to a prompt, they will not be prepared for the writing they will be asked to do when they leave school.

So is it possible to teach the students to write well, for a variety of purposes and for a variety of audiences, and also do well on the state test? I believe the answer is yes, if strong writing is imbedded in the curriculum beginning in kindergarten, where writing instruction looks *very* different than it does in fourth grade (when the first writing test usually occurs), and weaves its way through every grade. If students enter fourth grade with a strong background in writing and discussing writing, then the fourth-grade teacher can pick up on the process and content developed in the four previous years, continue that process, and prepare students to write well and be successful on the test.

Please, teach your students to write well. If we can do this, then they can utilize those skills in any situation, including a prompt situation.

Rule #2:
Don't Start Talking about the Test during the First Month of School!

(Unless, of course, you live in a state like Indiana in which the testing takes place during the first month of school!) If our focus on writing is strictly about the test, beginning on Day 1 of school, we give students this message: Writing is about testing, not about being an educated person who uses writing as a tool to communicate ideas, information, and emotions. Instead, we want our students to think of writing for the real reasons, not an artificial reason such as a single test.

Focus instead on teaching students that we write for different purposes and different audiences. As the year progresses, and as testing time gets closer, we can discuss how one purpose for writing is to respond to a prompt to demonstrate to people who don't know us (as often happens with writing outside of school!) that we are competent writers. If we have focused all year on writing well for different purposes and different audiences, students will approach the task with a strong understanding and minimal dread.

Rule #3:
Model, Model, Model

As with all styles of writing, students need to acquire that strong vision of success. Teachers can help students by demonstrating how they would approach a prompt. Allow students to develop a prompt on any subject. (The toughest my students came up with was "alternative uses of toilet paper.") Use an overhead projector or a computer with a projection device, and allow the students to watch you plan, consider various topics on which to focus your writing, use some type of organizational tool to organize your writing, and then actually write your piece. You don't have to create the entire piece, but letting students see how you would use your first ten minutes can be invaluable. If you get stumped, discuss what to do when the brain freezes! This is teaching at its finest.

During the three weeks prior to the test, let students watch this process three or four times each week, and then practice it numerous times themselves. Their understanding of what they should do will become clear. Once again, it's the "vision of success."

Rule #4:
Have Students Assess Prompt Responses from Previous Years

Each year, most states release samples of student writing that were written in response to that year's prompt. These samples demonstrate what the writing looks like at each score point, whether the rubric is a four- or six-point scale. Provide students with copies of these samples and ask them to determine the strengths and weaknesses of the writing. Students can score the writing using the state's rubric, and, to really develop their skills, revise the weaker papers to look more like the stronger ones. They will begin to understand further what they should do when confronted with a prompt.

Rule #5:
Practice, Practice, Practice

As suggested earlier, if we expect our students to perform well at any task, we need to give them a chance to practice before the task begins. If we have spent our year, and the years prior to the test year, teaching our students to write well, they now can practice applying those skills to a new situation. Specifically, we need to create prompts, ask students to respond, and give them feedback about their writing. These practice writes do not need to be counted for a final grade.

Our feedback should focus on the key traits on state tests: ideas (what some states call topic development); organization; and conventions. This is not to say that word choice, voice, fluency (the combination being what some states call *style*) are not important, but most states focus heavily on developing the topic by adding details and including an introduction or lead and a conclusion.

So as we provide students with feedback about their work as they prepare for the state test, let's target those areas. Our instruction helps students focus, relax, and understand what they need to do in order to succeed on the state test. It makes their lives—and ours—far less stressful.

Steps to take right now

- Go online to your state Web site and access the state writing rubric and samples of student writing. If you can't find them, ask your building administrators if they have copies. What does the rubric emphasize? Do you teach those components to your students? What do you notice about the student papers? What can you learn from them?

- Provide your students with some of the student papers and rubric. Have them score the papers and determine if their scores match the scores assigned to the papers. Have the students select a weaker paper and revise it to create a stronger one.

Planning a Year:
An Overview

For many novice teachers, planning means trying to figure out what
they're going to do tomorrow, not next month or even next week.
Yet long-range planning is crucial if we expect to provide quality,
coherent, and meaningful instruction. So what questions and issues
do we need to answer and consider—knowing the unexpected
will arise—in planning our instruction? This section contains
a few hints for framing our work.

Fred's World

As a young teacher, trying to plan out your year is like learning how to drive.
When we first received our learner's permit and started driving, most of us were
in panic mode. Our mother or father, in the passenger seat, a look of pure terror frozen on
their face, yelled at us and we realized we'd never tried to multitask like this before. We
didn't see much beyond the dashboard. We saw the speedometer, the hood of the car, and
maybe ten feet in front of us. Anything to the side or behind us ceased to exist. The traffic
light fifty yards down road was invisible as was the sign on the side of the road saying
"slow down, construction ahead." Who knew there was an ambulance on our tail, lights
flashing, siren blaring, trying to get by us? Likewise, our first few years of teaching can
be overwhelming. We are asked to accomplish more than we ever dreamed of, perhaps
more than is realistically possible. Most important, it is crucial to stay focused. It is easy
to become distracted by the blur of activity and the whirl of demands and requests flung
upon us. We need to stay focused on what is best for our students.

During these first years, "planning" means trying to figure out what to do the next
day; sometimes it means how do I get through *this* day! Next week exists only because
we've been told there is an assembly on Wednesday at 9:00 and that we have lunch duty.
Next month does not exist. We're just trying to get through the day without crashing.
Thus, I realize planning for something when you have little idea about what you'll be facing is a daunting task. However, if you set time aside during the summer, you can develop
a basic approach and strategy for how you will help your students improve their writing
and still maintain your sanity.

As I have written earlier, I was overwhelmed my first few years. Part of the problem I
encountered in teaching writing was that I had no reference point. As papers started to arrive on my desk, I was constantly questioning just how strong or weak a paper was. With
each paper I wondered whether this was typical or weak for ninth grade. I wondered how

much and what types of improvements I should see between my ninth graders and twelfth graders. Initially, I treated all the students the same, maintaining the same expectations for the ninth grade students that I had for the twelfth grade students. In retrospect, that was foolish. Would I expect the same level of quality from a third grader as I would from a sixth grader? Fortunately, as time progressed I began to figure everything out, or so I thought. By the middle of my second year, I thought everything was under control and I was clear about what strong, typical, and weak writing looked like. Until my department chair threw me an unintended curve ball.

For my first three semesters of teaching, I taught only average and low level classes. Thus, the "strong" writing I was seeing was strong all right, but only on a level of my other students in the average and low level classes. But second semester of my second year, I was assigned an honors class. Suddenly, with the arrival of the papers from the first writing assignment, my understanding was turned upside down. I was seeing a level of writing I had not seen during my first three semesters. What I had come to believe was "strong" writing, in comparison to what I was now receiving, was only mediocre. Because I lacked a reference point about strong, typical, and weak writing at various grade levels, I had arrived at an erroneous understanding of what these levels looked like. It required a number of additional years of teaching a variety of students from different grade levels before I finally arrived at a point where I felt comfortable with my expectations and understanding about the quality of students' writing.

If you're about to start your teaching career, have a couple of years under your belt, or are a veteran teacher working to improve your teaching skills, you probably will face or have faced the same situation I did. As you plan your upcoming year, do yourself a favor and consider a few suggestions.

Identify Reference Points

Whether you're teaching third grade, seventh grade, or twelfth grade, you'll need some reference points. Just as our students need a "clear vision of success" for good writing, we do as well. A close friend of mine, who had taught sixth grade for seven years, was transferred to a first-grade classroom. She called me after the first few days of school in a state of shock. "You won't believe it," she said. "Most of them make their threes backwards and they don't know it! And some of them can't even spell their names!" Experienced first-grade teachers expect this and are prepared for it as well as other challenges. My friend, lacking a clear reference point of what to expect, was forced to revamp much of what she had planned to do during the first few weeks of school.

I strongly recommend that you speak with your grade-level colleagues before the year begins. Ask them for some samples of student writing (some might call these *exemplars*) that represent strong, typical, and weak writing at the beginning of the year and the end of the year. By examining these papers, you will gain a strong understanding of what you'll see in September and, more important, what you should strive for during the course of the year. The students' writing can serve as a compass for what to teach *if* we pay close attention.

I understand and agree with the general philosophy that we "take students from where they are when they arrive and work to improve their writing over the year." However, we still need to have a clear understanding of our goal. What should a "typical" student's writing look like at the end of the grade? What does "strong" writing look like at the end of the grade? If we don't know the answers to these questions, we can't plan how to get there.

With papers in hand, ask yourself some basic questions. What do the strong papers contain that the typical or weak ones do not? What impresses you about these papers? What skills do these writers show? How will you teach your students to develop similar skills? What types of errors are present in the weaker papers? Assume you will see these in the writing of your own students. How will you teach them about these errors so they can avoid making these same mistakes?

When you compare the writing from the beginning and the end of the year, what improvements do you see? How will you help your students make these same changes? Once you have a clear vision of what you are trying to achieve, you're ready to move on with your year-long plan.

The Curriculum

After you've looked at student writing from the grade(s) you'll be teaching, review the school or district curriculum document that clarifies what students should know and be able to do at each grade level. Alternately, look on your state's Department of Education Web site or ask your principal to provide you with a copy of your state's curriculum document. Every state has developed content area and grade-level standards that are used as a basis for state testing.

Explore a couple of areas. First, look at the grade level prior to yours. It is helpful to know what the students were supposed to be taught (no guarantee they were!) the previous year. You'll need to know whether or not students are coming with some understanding of paragraphs, or how to begin sentences with words other than pronouns and articles, or how to write a bibliography. Create that skill checklist and, shortly after your school year begins, give a brief assessment to see how well your students have learned these skills. Be prepared to provide some review!

Also identify what types of writing students have focused on. Narrative writing? Descriptive writing? Informational writing? How about research writing? You will want to know what types of writing experiences your students encountered before entering your classroom.

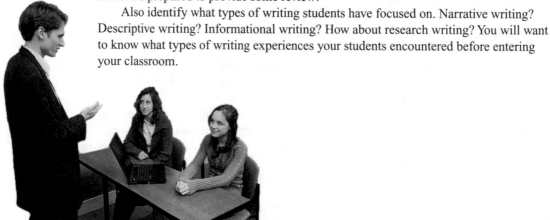

Then examine your own curriculum. Again, what skills are you expected to teach, and what genres of writing are the students to explore? Then, in conjunction with either your grade-level peers or your teammates, you will want to begin mapping out when you will teach each of these skills and concepts. Here is a quick breakdown.

Upper Elementary

These grades are exciting times for students and teachers. Most students are able to write sentences fluently, develop unique and creative ideas in their writing, and incorporate an amazing sense of humor. Most students still love to write.

If you are fortunate enough to teach in a self-contained classroom in which you are responsible for all subjects, you possess far more flexibility in managing your students' writing than other teachers. The more you can incorporate writing into all the content areas—including science, math, and social studies—the more likely you are to provide quality writing instruction, and the more likely students are to acquire the skills, knowledge, and confidence about writing that we desire. With careful planning, you can engage your students in a variety of types of writing, as dictated by your curriculum, during each unit of study.

For example, a friend of mine teaches a fourth-grade social studies unit called "Explorers." As part of their study, students complete various writing assignments, which he models and teaches during Language Arts. Using a combination of journal writing and historical fiction, students complete six entries in a "Captain's Log." Each entry must incorporate historical data to demonstrate the students' knowledge of the content being studied. This assignment provides the students with opportunities to focus on the traits of *ideas* and *voice*.

Another focus of many Language Arts curricula in third grade is the development of an interesting, cohesive paragraph, and the development continues into fifth grade, when students are usually writing longer reports and research papers. You will probably want to identify time early in the school year to determine how well your students can write a paragraph and then have time built into your daily schedule to help students improve their level of success. If your students are going to write longer papers throughout the year, they will need to be able to craft a solid paragraph.

As you look at your year, determine when you will teach various units from science, social studies, and math, and then consider what types of writing experiences you can connect to each unit. Which pieces of writing would you like to see go through the entire writing process? Why? What can you use as models in those areas to show the students what strong writing looks like? Will you need to create your own models, or do you have some from a previous year or a colleague?

While much of the students' writing can revolve around content areas, they also need time just to write. Given time and freedom to write, kids love to write poems, short stories, anecdotes, letters, cartoons, captions for photographs, reactions to incidents in school, revised versions of fables and fairy tales, and on and on. The opportunity to try out new modes of writing excites kids and produces some terrific thinking and writing. It keeps the love of writing alive in our student writers.

Secondary Grades: Middle School

Consider yourself lucky! Working in a middle school, you have the good fortune of having not one but two support groups: your fellow content area teachers and your teammates. With their help, you can better plan the units of study the students will undertake during the year and how you can lead the writing that will connect to these units of study. The challenge, if you are the Language Arts teacher, may be that your teammates will try to convince you that you are solely responsible for the writing that will take place. Hopefully, most content area teachers are cognizant of the importance of writing in the content areas and of their role in helping students improve their writing. If this is not the case, you may be in a position of teaching your students *and* your colleagues! If so, tread slowly but do take the steps.

Before the year begins, decide whether you want to focus only on one genre for a block of time (a grading period of nine weeks) or to incorporate a variety of genres each grading period so the students can continue to grow in each genre as the year progresses. Each approach has its advantages and disadvantages, so speak with your colleagues to see if the school has an approach it prefers. If not, speak with the other English teachers about what they suggest and their reasons for thinking as they do.

You may want to begin your year by having each student complete a writer's survey such as the one developed by Nancie Atwell (2002) (slightly modified here):

1. Are you a writer?
2. If you answered *yes* to #1, how did you learn to write?
3. If you answered *no* to #1, how do you think people learn to write?
4. Why do people write?
5. What do you think a good writer needs to do in order to write well?
6. How does a teacher decide which pieces of writing are strong?
7. How do you feel about writing?
8. What kinds of writing do you like to write?
9. How do you decide what you'll write about?
10. How often do you write at home?
11. In general, how do you feel about what you write?

Imagine the wealth of information you'll gain from your students' responses, which can help drive your instruction, telling you some of the obstacles you'll need to overcome as well as some of the strengths you can build upon.

My experience with middle school students leads me to believe that most of them love to write, provided they have some say about what they write. Middle school students are very funny, although most of them don't see the humor in their lives. They are also concerned with self-exploration—trying to determine who they are, why they're changing, what's up with these people of the opposite gender, and all the other joys that accompany adolescence. They'll love you one day and hate you the next for reasons known only to them and their invisible twin. We can turn these moments into remarkable writing opportunities, as long as we ensure that they feel they're in a safe environment. When we provide students with guided writing time and also free writing time, they will produce volumes of work, and from these drafts we can help them produce exploded moments of laughter, thoughtfulness, and sensitivity. So your planning needs to incorporate regular opportunities for the students to write freely, using some of that writing as the springboard for conferences and revision.

Determine what skills and genres students need to focus on at your grade level. Connect these to the literature you'll be teaching and/or content from science, math, and social studies. Determine when your colleagues will be teaching different units of study and discuss how writing can be incorporated into those units. Keep in mind that the writing can take place as part of the content area or Language Arts or both! If we want students to make connections, this is one way to ensure it happens.

Unfortunately, many of our students lack experience writing in content areas. They often complain, "Why do we have to write in here? I thought this was science, not English." In time, they will learn what we understand: writing in the content areas actually increases their understanding of the material being discussed.

In planning, lay out broad concepts and topics for the year, but determine the specifics for only a month. Life in middle schools changes constantly, and if you plan specifics too far out, you'll only frustrate yourself when you have to change everything. Remember, in middle school the only constant is change!

Secondary Grades: High School

Teaching writing to high school students is dynamic. For many students, this is their last exposure to formal education. After they leave high school, they're off to the military or work. For others, it's the final gateway that hopefully prepares them for success in college. Either way, teaching high school students is a fascinating and unique opportunity to help them improve their writing as we write with them.

At the high school level, planning is often a solitary act. The autonomy that exists for teachers in many high schools is both a luxury and a problem. In a tightly knit department, assistance and guidance may be close at hand. But in a department that does not function as a team, you will feel isolated and lost. If you're in a very small high school, you may be the only English teacher, and there may not be anyone around to guide you.

In high school, you could easily be facing four or five different preps, teaching American Literature first period, Creative Writing second period, Junior English third period, and so forth. As a result, planning is imperative or you will be totally overwhelmed.

First, carefully examine your curriculum. What does it tell you about what you are expected to teach? Years ago, high school curricula were nothing more than course descriptions, and teachers maintained total freedom about what to teach and how long to spend on each unit. That has changed. Most high school curricula today are very clear and specific about what is to be taught and, oftentimes, how long to spend on each unit of study. So examine the curriculum and take careful notes about what it dictates and, equally important, what it leaves out. If it does not state what genres to focus on, you need to start asking questions. If it does not suggest a time line for each unit, you need to seek advice from colleagues or administrators. You clearly need some advice about how much time to spend on each topic or unit within the course. For example, a course on American Literature should not focus so heavily on drama that poetry and short stories get left out. This type of imbalance will come back to haunt you.

Second, seek out the texts that are available for you to use with your students and read them! These may be novels, anthologies, plays, collections of poetry, student handbooks, and grammar books. Become familiar with all of the material available to support your instruction.

Third, break your course into manageable chunks. Take into account the curriculum and the time you will spend on each section within each course, and then lay out in broad terms the focus of your teaching for each month. Next, work to plan specifics a full month ahead, listing what literature you will use and what writing the students will produce. At the end of each week, when you're exhausted at home, look at the plan and determine which materials you will need and what actions you will take in order to transition smoothly from one week to the next. Somewhere in all of this, try to get a few hours of sleep; you'll need it!

In high school, like in all other grades, we should connect the literature the students are reading to their writing and to their own lives. For example, your curriculum may require that students work on compare/contrast papers in tenth grade. If students are reading *Romeo and Juliet* and you've shown them the film *West Side Story*, you have a perfect opportunity to combine literature, writing, and the students' own lives. Teach the students how to write a compare/contrast paper, and then ask them to select one of the main characters from the play along with the corresponding character in the film. Assign a paper in which students compare and contrast those two characters and include personal connections from their own lives. In what ways have they experienced similar conflicts to the two characters they're writing about? How did they address the situation, and what can they learn from the writings?

If your curriculum calls for persuasive writing, there are a host of approaches teachers can use to connect this writing to literature or content area studies. Again, after we have taught students how to write persuasive essays—giving them opportunities to examine, assess, and discuss a few—they can write their own essay that connects either to content area studies, literature, or their daily lives. If they're studying the world's energy crises, they can write a persuasive essay on the value of building more nuclear power plants or a call for a moratorium on the building of additional ones. If they're studying the current war in Iraq, they can write a persuasive essay on whether or not the United States should set a deadline for the removal of American troops. Students often write most powerfully about an issue in their own lives in which they have a conflict with a teacher, school, parent, or society. Remember, if your goal is for students to become competent with persuasive essays, they will need to write more than one! If you decide that one of their persuasive essays should be focused on English class, then they might choose to focus on whether or not George was justified in killing Lenny in Steinbeck's classic *Of Mice and Men*. The opportunities are endless. Let's not miss them.

Lesson Planning for Teachers of All Grades

The following guidelines for lesson planning will help enhance and enrich your instruction and your students' learning.

1. I have a narrow focus for the lesson.

2. I have a passage from literature to model the concept.

3. I have samples of student writing for students to assess.

4. I have an activity planned that, while challenging, allows for success.

5. I have created opportunities for students to work in small groups during the lesson.

6. I have a way to model the concept I'm trying to teach.

7. I know how to tell which students understand the lesson and which ones don't.

Trust me, I made every mistake possible my first few years. I never asked for or looked at a curriculum document. (I later found out there wasn't one.) I never asked for help. I never planned more than a week ahead. My students paid the price. While we had fun and they enjoyed being in my classroom, their learning lacked focus, connections, and depth. The time you spend planning now will save you time and tears later on and will enhance the education of your students. That should be reason enough.

Steps to take right now

- Look at your school calendar for the dates of your next weeklong vacation. Pick three days you are willing to devote to planning how you will teach writing for the month following the vacation. Promise yourself you will use that time to plan . . . and do it!

- Set aside one week from your next summer vacation. Don't schedule anything for that week. Use that time to plan your writing instruction for the following school year. See if you can convince a colleague to work with you that week (and don't work longer than eight hours a day!).

- Based on your local and/or state curriculum documents, your knowledge of your students, and input from your colleagues, create a checklist of essential skills for the students you'll be teaching. Additionally, create a checklist of curriculum content that you want to work on with your students.

Conclusion

Both Our Worlds

If the world, as Thomas L. Friedman, Pulitzer Prize winning columnist for the *New York Times*, suggests, is flattening, the ability to write well will take on a new and more important role in students' future opportunities for success. All of us—teachers, parents, and employers—want our young people to become competent and confident writers. How we approach the teaching of writing in our public schools during the next twenty years may well determine our children's future. By basing our instruction on best practices and by providing time for students to write on a regular basis, we can give them the tools for a successful future. But writing instruction needs to change, and fast. The preparation of our future teachers on how to teach writing needs to change even faster.

We need to demonstrate a closer connection between school, college, and the workplace. Businesses are voicing their concerns about the deficiency in the writing skills of their employees. As educators, we need to establish rigorous yet reasonable expectations of the writing skills of high school graduates. We also need to provide students with opportunities for real-world learning. This will allow them to become more confident writers and prepare them for the skills expected in the workplace. We can't be using the same old philosophy when it comes to writing assignments, because writing in the workplace is continually changing, particularly due to technological advancements and the increasing need to communicate internationally.

According to the Hart Research and Public Opinion Strategies (2005), who surveyed high school graduates, employers, and college instructors:

- College instructors estimate that 42 percent of their students are not adequately prepared.

- All groups called for higher standards. Only 24 percent of high school graduates say they faced high expectations and were challenged in high school.

- Knowing what they know today, 65 percent of college students and 77 percent of non-students say they would have worked harder in high school.

- Employers estimated that 45 percent of recent high school grads are not prepared with skills to advance beyond entry level jobs.

There needs to be a new collaboration involving meaningful dialog between schools, colleges, and the workplace. One suggestion to help bridge this gap is for educators to get feedback from industry to see exactly what needs fixing. Then, we can assess the information in our committees and decide how to address these issues in the classroom to prepare students better for writing in their lives beyond school. As teachers, we need to develop an awareness of the characteristics and types of workplace writing. When we incorporate these aspects into classroom assignments, students begin to see the relevance and application of their writing skills.

We also need to collaborate with school districts so that they don't set students up for failure. We as teachers know that students need the opportunities to be successful. Consequently, administrators need to be concerned about class size, unrealistic expectations, and lack of updated training for teachers.

Students need to understand that good communication skills are essential for job performance and success in the workplace. We are judged by our writing even before we are hired. Interviewers form opinions about us from our pre-visit documents: application forms, cover letters, and resumes. Consequently, hiring decisions and promotions are based on our writing ability. If people want to look proficient in the workplace, they need to write well. Teaching our students to become competent and confident writers will help them perform their job duties more effectively. In the workplace, employees are writing more than ever and must effectively employ different mediums in their communications.

The College Board's National Commission on Writing (2004) has issued a number of reports addressing the critical concern of employees being unprepared to write in the workplace (available at www.writingcommission.org). "In most cases, writing ability could be your ticket in… or it could be your ticket out," stated one human resource director who responded to their survey. Gene Budig (2006), in "Writing: A Necessary Tool," states, "To remain competitive in an increasingly global economy and to meet the needs of an ever-changing workplace, America needs to pay new and special attention to developing the writing skills of all students at all levels in school."

Teachers require quality professional development in order to better teach students to write well; students need better instruction to help them become better writers, and they need the opportunities to write more often. Good writing takes plenty of practice and hard work. Teachers can provide the opportunities to learn and practice; parents can encourage their children to work hard. Our students don't need to be great writers, but they do need to be—and can be—competent writers.

APPENDIX A

Lesson Plans

Lesson 1

Focus Area: Incorporating details into text

Time Needed: Approximately 45 minutes

Literature: *Boy* by Roald Dahl

Procedure:

1. Ask students to discuss with a neighbor what they believe a woman who owns a candy store would be like.

2. Ask students to share their perspectives with the class.

3. Read pages 33–34 ("Her name was Mrs. Pratchett . . . . stirred around inside the jars with her foul fingers.").

4. Ask students their reactions to Mrs. Pratchett.

5. Have students think (no discussion) for thirty seconds about what Mrs. Pratchett's house would look like and then share their ideas with a neighbor for one minute. Next, share ideas with the whole class. Write all the ideas on the board/overhead.

6. If time allows, ask students to draw a quick sketch of one room in Mrs. Pratchett's house.

7. Share your own writing—which you have prepared prior to class—about the room you selected in Mrs. Pratchett's house.

8. Ask students to write about one room in Mrs. Pratchett's house, incorporating as many intriguing details as they can.

9. Have them share their writing in small groups and then allow some students to share with the whole group.

10. Discuss with the students which details were the most intriguing and how incorporating details also applies to more academic writing.

Lesson 2

Focus Area: Language Acquisition (synonyms)

Time Needed: 45–60 minutes

Literature: Poem "Big" by Colin McNaughton

Materials: Five to eight paint swatches from your local paint store or hardware store of different shades of blue (or any other basic color)

Procedure:

1. Display and read the poem "Big" to the class.

2. Review any words that students may not fully understand.

3. Explain that students are going to write a "Small" poem.

4. Provide two minutes for students to write down individually every word they know for *small*.

5. Provide two minutes for them to share with neighbors and write down additional words that their neighbors had on their lists.

6. Provide five minutes for students to use any resource in the room to acquire additional synonyms for *small*. They may use a thesaurus, dictionary, textbooks, or computers for a synonym search, or they may ask adults in the room.

7. Going around the room, have students offer one word from their lists. Add each word to a list on the board/overhead/computer projection. Continue until all words are displayed.

8. Review the meanings of any words students may not know.

9. Display one paint swatch and ask what color it is. Students will respond "blue." Display another paint swatch and ask what color. Again, students will respond "blue." Continue through each swatch. Explain that while each swatch is blue, they are different shades of blue; each is slightly different. Likewise, while all the words that have been listed mean "small," they are different "shades" of small and have different connotations. Discuss how students cannot just select any of the words and use them in their writing to replace *small,* as it may be a large enough difference in "shade" or connotation to change the meaning.

10. Ask students to write a "Small" poem using their favorite words. They may use the same format as McNaughton or they can use their own style.

11. Share the poems with the class.

Explanation:

To develop students' vocabulary, we often give them lists of new words and ask them to memorize the definitions. Most students remember the definitions for the quiz and then the words and definitions disappear into a black hole. With this activity, students become familiar with new words but only have to memorize one definition. I find it remarkable how many students will continue to use some of the words for months afterwards. You can repeat this activity each week, using a new word each week, especially those words we would like to bury (e.g., *nice, good, fun, awesome, pretty, thing*).

Lesson 3

Focus Area: Practicing Voice

Time Needed: 30–45 minutes

Literature: Short Story "Eleven" by Sandra Cisneros

Procedure:

1. Read the story "Eleven" with your class.

2. Working in small groups, have the students discuss what it would be like to be Rachel. Then have them discuss what it would be like to be the red sweater. Finally, have the students discuss why Mrs. Price may have acted as she did.

3. Individually, students should select either Mrs. Price or the red sweater (pretending it can talk and write). From that perspective, in the voice of that character, students should write a journal entry about what happened in school that day.

4. Have the students share their writing in small groups and select a few students to share their writing with the class.

5. As follow-up for homework or in class the next day, ask the students to write in the voice of either Sylvia or Phyllis. Then, compare the voices of the two characters from whose perspective they wrote.

6. As a final follow-up, students can pretend they were in Mrs. Price's class that day and write in their own voice about what happened.

Lesson 4

Focus Area: Fluency in Writing

Time Needed: 15 minutes

Procedure:

1. Ask the students to select a piece of writing they have crafted in the past two weeks. It can be a first draft or a final draft, but a first draft is preferable. The writing should be at least ten sentences long.

2. Ask the students to count and write down the number of words in each of the first ten sentences.

3. Ask them to determine the average sentence length, the range of length (e.g., from seven words to twenty-three words), and how many sentences are longer and shorter than the average.

4. Ask the students to write down the first word of each of the first ten sentences and the part of speech of each of those words. (I know, I know. Many students will need help figuring out what part of speech each word is.)

5. Students then report on how successful they have been in varying their sentence length and sentence beginnings. Using seven different words to begin sentences may not be a positive if all seven are pronouns!

6. Work with students who lack variety in sentence length or beginnings, and teach them how to change their writing to improve in these areas.

Lesson 5

Focus Area: Writing Leads

Time Needed: 20 minutes

Literature: Opening three or four lines from six or seven different books (Don't tell the students what the book titles are, but make sure they are books your students would read.)

Procedure:

1. Ask students to number a sheet of paper from one to six (or seven). Tell the students that you're going to read the leads to six or seven different books, and that after you read each lead, they should mark their numbered paper with a + sign or a – sign to help them remember whether or not they liked the lead.

2. After you have read all the leads, go back to the first lead. Ask how many students liked Lead 1 and how many disliked Lead 1. Ideally, there will be some students on both sides. Reread the lead and ask students to tell you what they liked or disliked about the lead. The class does not need to discuss who is "right" or "wrong." The key is for students to explain specifically what they liked or disliked about the lead. After the students explain what they liked or disliked, tell them the name of the book.

3. Go through each of the leads in this fashion.

4. Once you have completed all the leads, ask the students to identify the most common reasons why people liked certain leads. Students may point out that the leads raised questions, created visual images, evoked personal connections, contained details, and included humor.

5. Next ask students the most common reasons why people disliked certain leads. Most likely you will hear that these leads lacked any personal connections, contained clichés, were boring (I always ask, "What made them boring?"), did not inspire further reading (Why not?), or lacked general appeal.

6. Talk with your students about how they can incorporate this information into writing their own leads. Then provide them with chances to practice writing leads.

Lesson 6

Focus Area: Narrowing the Topic (Part A)
              Collaborative Writing and Research Writing (Part B)

Time Needed: 40 minutes (Part A); numerous periods (Part B)

Literature: *Harry the Tarantula* by Leigh Ann Tyson or any other short
              informational book

Procedure (Part A):

1. Explain that you are going to read a book to students and you want them to re-member as many details as possible.

2. Upon completion of the reading, ask students what details they remember about tarantulas (or the topic your book addressed). Write these details on the board/overhead/computer. With this book, students usually recall eighteen to twenty-three details.

3. Ask the students to review the details and select their five favorites.

4. Provide each student with five small stickers (colored dots, small sticky notes).

5. In groups of five at a time, ask the students to place a sticker next to each of their five favorites. Each student must select five; a student cannot place three stickers on one detail.

6. You will now have a visual representation of what the class feels are the most in-teresting details. Circle the five to seven details that received the most votes.

7. The class will now create a "How To" poem: "How to be a Tarantula." Call for a volunteer and ask that student to pick one of the circled details and create the opening line for the poem. Require that the first word of each line be an action verb. For example, students may say, "Grow three to ten inches long" or "Paralyze your prey with your poisonous fangs" or "Birth up to six hundred babies at a time."

8. Continue adding lines until all the circled details are used.

Explanation:

When writing reports, students often gather dozens and dozens of pieces of information. Unfortunately, students often believe they should use all the information in their report, which prevents them from developing any information in depth. Their reports become a series of facts. This begins the process of showing students how to narrow the scope of their writing, focusing only on the most intriguing pieces of information. They can now develop depth of discussion on the five or six or seven pieces instead of just covering information at a superficial level.

Procedure (Part B):

1. Divide your class into groups so that the number of groups is equal to the number of lines in your poem.

2. Assign each group one line of the poem.

3. Explain that each group's task is to develop a series of questions related to their line. For example, if a group is assigned the line "Fling your barbed hairs at your predators," then their questions may include the following:

    a. How many hairs does a tarantula have?

    b. How long are the hairs?

    c. Do all tarantulas have the same-colored hair?

    d. How many barbs on a hair?

    e. How long are the barbs?

    f. Do the hairs grow back?

    g. Do they have hairs at birth or do they grow later in life?

    h. How far can they fling their hair?

    i. Why do they fling their hairs at their predators?

    j. Do other animals have barbed hairs?

4. After you have approved their list of questions, and possibly added a few, ask them to research the answers.

5. Once they have gathered the answers, ask them to write a solid paragraph or two explaining their line of the poem. Students may need assistance on how to organize themselves to craft the writing.

6. Once all the groups have completed their writing, assign these additional tasks: One group will need to create an opening paragraph; one a closing paragraph; others will create transitions between paragraphs.

Explanation:

Learning to write a quality research paper is a daunting task for many students and grading them is often a less-than-pleasurable task for the teacher. This approach to teaching students how to write a research paper incorporates all the components but does so in manageable chunks. Each student is involved in narrowing down a topic, developing questions, researching, writing, and revising. Additionally, all students are writing collaboratively (please refer to Lynna's section on teaching collaborative writing in Chapter 3), and the teacher is not inundated with thirty research papers per class that are tedious and painful to read. Granted, there are times when students need to write research papers independently, but this exercise teaches them what they need to do when that time arrives.

Lesson 7

Focus Area: Writing Leads (a chance to practice!)

Time Needed: 30 minutes

Literature: *Creepy Creatures* by Sneed B. Collard III and *Animals Nobody Loves* by Seymour Simon

Procedure:

1. Explain to the students that both books contain fascinating information about various animals, but that you think they will find differences in how the authors write leads. Fortunately, some animals (vultures, hyenas, piranhas) are discussed in both books.

2. Read the opening line about piranhas from the two books. Ask the students which lead is stronger and why.

3. Do the same for hyenas and vultures.

4. Discuss with your students why Collard's leads are so much stronger than Simon's. What strategies does Collard use to create his leads?

5. Show the students the picture of a skunk from Simon's book. Ask the students to write the opening line (or two!) that should accompany the picture. Write one yourself as well! Share the leads aloud.

6. Continue showing photographs from Simon's book and have the students write the opening line for each photograph. The photos of the rattlesnake, shark, and crocodile are especially dynamic.

Explanation:

This activity provides students with opportunities to practice writing leads. While their early attempts may not by exceptional, they are able to hear how their classmates and teacher approach the task, which eventually enables them to write stronger leads themselves.

Lesson 8

Focus Area: Word Choice for Descriptive Writing

Time Needed: 45 minutes

Literature: *Boy* by Roald Dahl

Procedure:

1. Make sure the students are already familiar with the passage about Mrs. Pratchett (Lesson 1) and have written with details about one of the rooms in her house.

2. Read the passage again, asking the students to listen for words they particularly enjoy.

3. Once you have finished the passage, ask students which words they liked. Write these down so all the students can see them. Add some of your favorite words if the students have not mentioned them. You may well have fifteen to twenty words on your list. Discuss the meanings of words students may not know (e.g. *sullen, loathsome, hag, splotches, foul*).

4. Have the students vote to select the ten strongest words from the list. Make sure the final list includes verbs, nouns, and adjectives.

5. Ask students to select a different room in Mrs. Pratchett's house than their first writing and describe it, using at least three of the words from the list.

Lesson 9

Focus Area: Crafting Sentences

Time Needed: 15 minutes

Materials: Seven pieces of oak tag, approximately ten-by-thirty-six inches

Procedure:

1. Write one of these phrases without punctuation on each piece of oak tag: the flying saucer; after circling; the wheat field; landed; three times; of flashing lights; in a blaze.

2. Ask seven volunteers to come to the front of the class.

3. Provide each student with a piece of oak tag on which a phrase is written.

4. Ask the students to arrange themselves in order to create a sentence. The subject and verb must be the first words of the sentence. The results may look like this:

the flying saucer	landed	in a blaze	of flashing lights

after circling	the wheat field	three times

5. Now ask other students to identify different ways to craft the sentence using all the phrases each time. Call on a student who will direct the students in the front to rearrange themselves. For example, a student may arrange the students in front this way:

after circling	the wheat field	three times	the flying saucer

landed	in a blaze	of flashing lights

6. Continue to call on students who can arrange their friends in a different order. See how many ways they can craft the sentence. (A hint: There are at least seven ways to craft the sentence.)

7. In order to work on conventions, you can provide a small stool for the first person to stand on each time as a reminder to capitalize the first word. You can also have someone hold a card with a period as a reminder of end punctuation marks. If your students have worked with commas, you can provide two students with comma cards that can be used in certain phrasings.

8. Discuss varying sentence structure when we write so that we do not always have subject-verb-object sentences.

Lesson 10

Focus Area: Show Don't Tell

Time Needed: 45 minutes

Literature: *Today I Feel Silly and Other Moods That Make My Day* by Jamie Lee Curtis

Procedure:

1. Read the book.

2. Ask the students to identify at least twenty emotions (e.g., happy, melancholy, worried, fear, etc.). Create a list so the students can see them.

3. Call on individual students who are willing to stand in front of the class and pantomime one of the emotions. Go first to model how this is done. Students should guess which emotion is being acted out. Once the correct emotion is determined, ask the students, "How did you know? What actions showed that emotion?"

4. Allow four to seven students each to act out a different emotion, always discussing what actions helped identify the emotion. How *does* one show fear? How *does* someone show anger?

5. Write each of the emotions on a piece of scrap paper and put them into a hat.

6. Have each student select an emotion from the hat. Each student should craft a brief piece of writing—less than twenty-five words—describing a person displaying that emotion. They may not use the word or any of its synonyms in their writing. Again, I encourage the teacher to participate. Collect the passages, read them aloud, and ask the students to determine which emotion is being described.

7. Discuss with the students why showing is more powerful than telling.

8. As a follow-up, ask students to skim their novels to find examples from literature in which the author shows instead of tells.

APPENDIX B

Business Writing Lesson Plans

Upper Elementary

Focus Area: Grammar and Spell Checkers

Time Needed: One class period

Procedure:

Have the students:

1. Use a computer to examine the following sentences, which you have previously typed into a word processing document (including the errors).
   a. my farther and I tasted the contraption we built
   b. The students crated the sign for memorial high school.
   c. They was about to ask what.
   d. Once up on a time there were a little lamb, whose fleece was white as snow and ate allot of wool.

2. Use the grammar and spell checkers on the sentences. Print a copy.

3. On the paper version, underline errors the software identified and circle any errors missed.

4. Write an email to their classmates that explains their findings.

Focus Area: Intercultural Communication

Time Needed: Three class periods after completion of the book

Procedure:

Have the students:

1. Read a book that has a character from another country. Examples could include *Becoming Naomi Leon* (Ryan), *Snow Treasure* (McSwigan), or *Iceberg Hermit* (Roth).

2. Brainstorm a list of ideas about themselves, their class, school, and community that the character might be interested in learning about.

3. Using some of these ideas, write a rough draft of a letter to the character, being sensitive to using language appropriate for an international reader.

4. Exchange the rough drafts with other students in the class for them to proofread and make comments.

5. Revise the letters based on input received.

6. Display the letters in the classroom.

Grades 6–8

Focus Area: Designing a Flow Chart

Time Needed: Five class periods of 45 minutes each

Procedure:

Have the students:

1. Research what a passport is and how and why it is used by American citizens.

2. Research what is needed to apply for a passport.

3. In small groups, design flow charts depicting the steps involved to apply for a passport.

4. Create a brochure for other students in the school informing them of the purpose and requirements of passports. The brochure should also explain how to obtain a passport and include a flow chart that shows those procedures.

Focus Area: Writing Instructions

Time Needed: Two or three class periods plus work at home

Procedure:

Have the students:

1. Examine a variety of instruction manuals to determine what they look like; what is included and what is not included; the language that is used; how they convey information; and how, when, and where illustrations are used.

2. Write an instruction manual on how to operate a piece of equipment (e.g., iPod, digital camera, cell phone) or how to play a video game. Have them include at least five features (e.g., how to download music from the computer to an iPod or how to download a picture from a camera to the computer).

3. Write the instructions for a different audience, such as a third grader or a grandparent who is not technically savvy.

4. Include at least one visual that is labeled, numbered, and titled.

5. Evaluate each others' writing based on clarity, conciseness, completeness, and logical order.

Focus Area: Writing Recommendations

Time Needed: Three 45-minute classes or one class and homework for two nights

Procedure:

Have the students:

1. Research the Grammy Awards. They should explore the following:

   What are the Grammy Awards?

   How often are they held? Who sponsors the Awards?

   Why are they important? What is the benefit to the winners?

   How are individuals/groups nominated?

   How are the winners determined?

2. Write a letter to the Recording Academy nominating a favorite group or singer for a Grammy Award. Include an introduction, description of the artist(s) and their music, the reasons why the artist(s) should win (or be nominated), and a conclusion.

Focus Area: Evaluating Web Sites
Writing Feedback Letter

Time Needed: Three class periods or one period and homework for two or three nights

Procedure:

Assist the students in constructing an evaluation template that identifies and measures components that measure validity. This template, at a minimum, should examine the authors' expertise, credentials, and affiliations; date created/updated; links; and clarity and accuracy (e.g., graphic design principles, sources cited, biases, grammar and spelling errors). Then have the students:

1. Find five Web sites about a topic of interest and print the home pages.

2. Evaluate the Web sites using the template.

3. Write a letter to the authors/publishers of one of the Web sites telling them, from a student's perspective, what was useful or not.

Focus Area: Writing Position Letter

Time Needed: Two class periods of 45 minutes each

Procedure:

Have the students:

1. Write to a state legislator who is considering passing a new law prohibiting the use of speaking and texting on a cell phone while driving. Explain their support or opposition to the proposed legislation, including research data to support their positions.

2. As an extension activity, create a PowerPoint presentation that states the position and includes charts and graphs that support the position.

Sample Gantt Chart

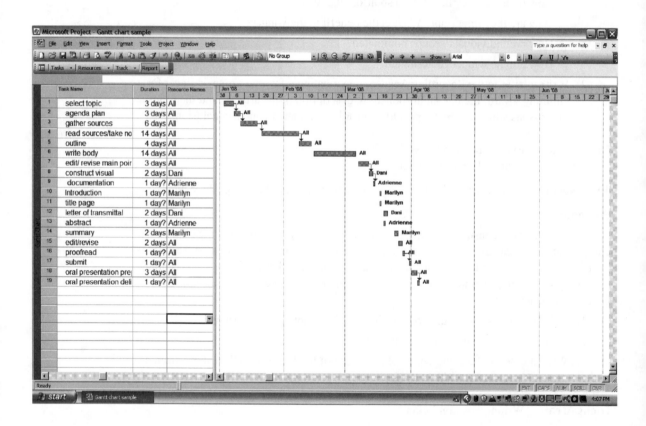

Sample Job Search Documents

Charles R. Hilburn

Email: chilburn@wcollege.edu   Cell: (603) 784-0844

School Address: Box 786, Washington College, 654 N. Hill Rd., Chelsea, NY 13323

Permanent Address: 984 Cherry Bottom Rd., Lee, NH 03825 (603) 784-8777

EDUCATION

Washington College, Chelsea, New York
Bachelor of Arts Degree, projected graduation May 2010
Prospective majors: Public Policy and Economics; Cumulative GPA 2.8/4.00 (82.9%)

St. Mark's School, Southborough, MA; Graduated June 2006

SKILLS

Computer: Microsoft Word, EXCEL, SPSS, PowerPoint, iWeb, Academic Databases
Languages: Intermediate-level French

ACTIVITIES AND HONORS

Washington College
    Men's Varsity hockey team, *member* (2006–2007)
    Theta Delta Chi fraternity, *member* (2006–Present)
    Alpine Ski Team, *member* (2008)
    Investment Club, *member* (2007–Present)

St. Mark's School
    Varsity Hockey team, *Captain*, (2006), *member* (2003–2006)
    Varsity Baseball team, *member* (2004–2006)
    Varsity Soccer team, *member* (2003, 2005)
    EV Club, member (2006)

EMPLOYMENT

Washington College Library, Chelsea, NY
    Interloan Library Assistant 10/06–5/07, 10/07–present
    Record lending and borrowing of books using OCLC; search for and copy articles

J. Crew, Kittery, Maine
    Sales Assistant, 5/07–8/07
    Assisted customers, stocked merchandise, handled sales at register

Juniper Hill Landscaping, Barrington, NH
    Laborer 5/06–8/06, *Team Leader* 5/07–8/07
    Assisted mason installing walkways and walls; planted shrubs and trees; responsible for supervising two other crew members.

C&J Trailways, Portsmouth, NH
    Grounds Maintenance, Summers 2004 and 2005
    Mowed and raked lawns, maintained perennials, trimmed shrubs, planted annuals

JOSEPH PERKINS

196 Stonecreek Dr., Watkins, PA 43567   jperkins@comcast.net   876-943-2878

OBJECTIVE

To obtain a part-time or summer internship position in a newspaper, magazine, or Web organization where I can demonstrate my writing, Web architecture, and computer graphics skills

EDUCATION

Completed three years at Watkins High School; expected graduation June 2008
G.P.A. 3.6/4.0 (Top 10% of class)

EXPERIENCE

Watkins High News, Watkins High School

- **Web Designer,** deployed Web server using Apache, PHP, and MySQL for school newspaper, 11/07–present
- **Editor** of school newspaper, 6/05–10/07

Watkins Yearbook, Watkins High School

- **Web Developer**, developed yearbook Web site using HTML, Flash, Java Script, and PERL, 1/06–6/06
- **Staff member**, experience with interviewing, page layout and design, and writing editorials, 3/05–11/05

CURRICULUM HIGHLIGHTS

Advanced senior writing seminar; debate; photography; computer classes working with desktop publishing, Front Page, and other Web software.

HONORS, AWARDS, AND MEMBERSHIPS

- **APA Scholarship recipient**
  Based on academic achievement, community service, and contributions to high school communications projects
- **Newspaper Design winner, 2007**
  Washington College Communications Contest
- **President of high school chapter of Web Designers Council (WDC), 2007–present;**
  Member, 2004–present
- **Secretary of National Honor Society, 2006–present**

References Available Upon Request

Jordan Casey

1360 Kemery Rd., Akron, OH 43678   (330) 432-1445   jcasey@hotmail.com

OBJECTIVE

Dependable high school senior with strong work ethic and excellent customer service skills seeking a part-time retail sales position with an electronics company/department to gain technical experience for a future career in electronics engineering

WORK EXPERIENCE

Fairfield Country Club, Tennis Instructor, Summers 2006 and 2007

- Taught tennis lessons to a diverse group of members
- Assisted in maintaining tennis facilities and equipment
- Supervised junior tennis activities sponsored by country club
- Organized tournaments

Minute Man Press, Delivery Driver, part-time 2005–2006

- Picked-up and delivered supplies to local businesses
- Assisted printer in preparing customers' orders

VOLUNTEER WORK

Big Brothers/Big Sisters, 2005–present, volunteer big sister for 10-year-old girl

Slate Elementary School, Ohio School for the Blind, 2000–2001, book reader

EDUCATION

Akron High School, expected graduation June 2009

College Prep Curriculum including AP classes; Currently top 5% of class

National Merit Scholar

School Organizations:

National Honor Society
Pep Squad, Decorations Committee Chair — 2006
Latin Club, Secretary 2006, Treasurer 2007
Senior Student Council Representative

References Available Upon Request

1350 Shoreline Drive
Ada, NH 46709
September 3, 2008

Paul Tackett
Maxzone Inc.
1350 Sunbury Dr.
Westerville, NC 78944

Dear Paul Tackett:

I am a senior at Boston University, majoring in computer science, and am interested in the programmer position you have advertised in the *Eagle Gazette*. After researching your company, I am very impressed with your software documentation practices and focus on research and development of virtual technologies. My technical expertise, leadership abilities, and communication skills would make a valuable contribution to your IT department.

I have the following skills to contribute to the continued success of Maxzone's vision.
- Developed projects in five different programming languages
- Designed web pages using HTML
- Set up wikis for professors' classrooms
- Worked on senior project team to develop data base for local manufacturing company

Please refer to the enclosed resume for additional information concerning my background and experience. I've also included letters of recommendation for your review.

I would be delighted to meet with you to discuss how I could benefit your department. I will be calling you early next week to see if we could set up a mutually convenient time to meet. If you would like to contact me, I can be reached at 675-989-8761 or at bshort@aol.com. I look forward to speaking with you about this exciting opportunity.

Sincerely,

Bob Short

Enclosures (4)

468 Coventry St.
Angola, NY 14006
September 3, 2008

Robert Smith
ABC Company
21 Court St.
Anytown, Ohio 43068

Dear Robert Smith:

I am interested in the part-time position listed on your Web site. Please accept this letter and accompanying resume as evidence of my interest in applying for the summer camp Counselor II position at Tall Timber Ranch. I am interested in your organization because of its focus on outdoor sports and team activities. My previous camp experience, athletic abilities, and communication skills would be a valuable asset to your counselor team.

In addition to my camp counseling experience during the past two summers, I also have an aptitude for working with pre-teens and motivating them to excel and develop their self-esteem. My past experience has also afforded me the opportunity to work with a diverse group of people. I am a dependable worker who is willing to go the extra mile. My people skills, partnered with my ability to relate to pre-teens, makes me an ideal candidate for your outdoor education staff.

Please refer to the enclosed resume for additional background information.

I would appreciate the opportunity to meet with you and discuss how my skills would meet the needs of your company. You can contact me at *xxxxxxxx*. I look forward to hearing from you.

Sincerely,

Howard Marshall

Enclosure

APPENDIX E

Suggested Books on Teaching Writing

Anderson, Jeff. *Mechanically Inclined: Building Grammar, Usage, and Style into Writer's Workshop*. Portland, ME: Stenhouse Publishers, 2005.

Atwell, Nancie. *In the Middle: New Understanding about Writing, Reading, and Learning*. Portsmouth, NH: Heinemann, 1998.

Bernabei, Gretchen. *Reviving the Essay: How to Teach Structure Without Formula*. Shoreham, VT: Discover Writing Press, 2005.

Calkins, Lucy McCormick. *The Art of Teaching Writing*. Portsmouth, NH: Heinemann, 1994.

Elbow, Peter. *Writing Without Teachers*. 2nd ed. New York: Oxford University Press, 1978.

Fletcher, Ralph, and JoAnn Portalupi. *Craft Lessons: Teaching Writing K–8*. Portland, ME: Stenhouse Publishers, 1998.

Graves, Donald H. *A Fresh Look at Writing*. Portsmouth, NH: Heinemann, 1994.

Graves, Donald H., and Penny Kittle. *Inside Writing: How to Teach the Details of Craft*. Portsmouth, NH: Heinemann, 2005.

Lane, Barry. *The Reviser's Toolbox*. Shoreham, VT: Discover Writing Press, 1999.

Lane, Barry. *After the End: Teaching and Learning Creative Revision*. Portsmouth, NH: Heinemann, 1993.

Liner, Tom, Dawn Kirby, and Dan Kirby. *Inside Out: Strategies for Teaching Writing*. 3rd ed. Portsmouth, NH: Heinemann, 2003.

Murray, Donald M. *A Writer Teaches Writing Revised*. 2nd ed. Boston: Houghton Mifflin Company, 2003.

Murray, Donald M. *Write to Learn*. 8th ed. Boston: Heinle, 2004.

Newkirk, Thomas. *Misreading Masculinity: Boys, Literacy, and Popular Culture*. Portsmouth, NH: Heinemann, 2002.

Portalupi, JoAnn, and Ralph Fletcher. *Nonfiction Craft Lessons: Teaching Information Writing K–8*. Portland, ME: Stenhouse Publishers, 2001.

Ray, Katie Wood. *Wondrous Words*. Urbana, IL: NCTE, 1999.

Romano, Tom. *Crafting Authentic Voice*. Portsmouth, NH: Heinemann, 2004.

Spandel, Vicki. *Creating Writers Through 6-Trait Writing*. 5th ed. Boston: Pearson, 2008.

Spandel, Vicki. *Creating Young Writers: Using the Six Traits to Enrich Writing Process in Primary Classrooms*. Boston: Pearson, 2008.

Spandel, Vicki. *The Nine Rights of Every Writer*. Portsmouth, NH: Heinemann, 2005.

Recommended Web Sites on Writing

http://owl.english.purdue.edu
The English Department at Purdue University maintains this site, which is loaded with ideas and resources for both teachers and students in grades 7–12. Along with their monthly topic, the site includes information on writing process, grammar, technical writing, citations, and more.

www.nwp.org
This is the home site for the National Writing Project and will direct you to state-by-state sites and the contact information for each site. Additionally, it provides up-to-date information about the teaching of writing as well as resources that can assist classroom teachers.

http://writingfix.com
Maintained by the Northern Nevada Writing Project, this site provides some lesson ideas, texts, and great ideas for teaching writing.

www.ncte.org/about/over/positions/category/write/
This site is maintained by the National Council of Teachers of English and provides a current listing of articles, publications, and positions about the teaching of writing.

www.nwp.org/cs/public/print/resource/922
This site is part of the NWP home site and provides thirty teacher-tested ideas for helping students improve their writing. Each of the thirty topics is accompanied by a succinct lesson idea for addressing the specific issue.

www.worldlingo.com/en/products_services/worldlingo_translator.html
English language learners in your classroom? This site allows the user to input up to 150 words in any language and have the text translated into another language!

www.englishcompanion.com
Maintained by Jim Burke, a high school English teacher in California, this site lists recent reports, Web sites, and resources designed to answer teachers' questions and provide information about the teaching of English/Language Arts.

www.geocities.com/ljacoby_2000/6traits.html
Developed by a classroom teacher in Arlington, Massachusetts, the site lists numerous other Web sites, most of which address Six Trait writing. The links include lesson ideas, literature, explanations of the traits and a host of other information.

www.nwrel.org/assessment/
The Northwest Regional Educational Lab maintains a strong Web site about the Six Traits. At this portion of their site, students can explore sample papers while teachers can practice scoring papers for individual traits.

www.usingenglish.com/teachers/html
This site is geared toward teachers of English Language Learners but does include resources for teachers of native English speakers as well. The site lists resources, lesson ideas, and other links for helping students who are learning to write in English.

www.writesite.org
This interactive site, created by the Think Network in Dayton, Ohio, focuses on middle school journalism. The site provides instruction and direction for writing various types of journalism articles, including features, news, and editorials.

www.abcteach.com/directory/basics/writing
For those days when you just need help, this site offers a wide variety of printable forms of writing prompts, lessons, and resources.

www.easybib.com
This site allows you to enter data on a source and will provide the correct bibliography listing for both APA and MLA.

www.discover-writing.com/archive-index.html
Barry Lane is a terrific writer and presenter. If you're not familiar with his work, read some of his books. This link from his home page provides approximately fifteen lesson ideas. Each lesson has modifications to meet the needs of various grade levels.

189

References

ACT. "National Curriculum Survey Calibrates ACT's Assessment Tools." 2004. Online: http://act.org/activity/winter2004/survey.html.

Ackerman, D. 1990. *A Natural History of the Senses.* New York: Vintage Books.

Anderson, J. 2005. *Mechanically Inclined: Building Grammar, Usage, and Style into Writer's Workshop.* Portland, ME: Stenhouse.

Anderson, L. 1999. *Speak.* New York: Penguin Putnam.

"As Many as 40 Percent of American Public High School Graduates Are Unprepared for College and Work." 07 February 2005. Achieve, Inc. Online: www.achieve.org/node/96.

Atwell, N. 1998. *In the Middle: New Understanding About Reading, Writing, and Learning.* Portsmouth, NH: Heinemann.

Atwell, N. 2002. *Lessons That Change Writers.* Portsmouth, NH: Heinemann.

"Bad Spelling Puts Off Employers." *BBC News.* 8 April 2006. http://news.bbc.co.uk/go/pr/fr/-/1/hi/education/5243098.stm.

Bauer, J. 2000. *Hope Was Here.* New York: Penguin Group.

Bernabei, G. 2005. *Reviving the Essay: How to Teach Structure Without Formula.* Shoreham, VT: Discover Writing Press.

Budig, G.A. 2006. "Writing: A Necessary Tool: Mr. Budig Issues a Call to Policy Makers, Educators, and Business Leaders to Get Serious about Improving Our Students' Writing Skills." *Phi Delta Kappan.*

Chaney, L.H., and J.S. Martin. 2005. *Intercultural Business Communication.* Upper Saddle River, NJ: Prentice Hall.

Clark, R. 1987. *Free to Write: A Journalist Teaches Young Writers.* Portsmouth, NH: Heinemann.

"Communication Skills—Start Here!" *Improve Your Communication Skills.* 2008. Online: www.mindtools.com/commskll/communicationintro.htm.

Cooper, M. 1999. *Indian School: Teaching the White Man's Way.* New York: Houghton Mifflin.

Cose, E. 2007. "Little Rock: 50 Years Later." *Newsweek* 24 September, 41.

CTER. "Expository Writing." http://wik.ed.uiuc.edu/index.php/expository_writing.

Culham, R. 2003. *6+1 Traits of Writing: The Complete Guide.* New York: Scholastic, Inc.

Dahl, R. 1984. *Boy: Tales of Childhood.* New York: Penguin Putnam.

"Employers: Workers Need Better Writing Skills." *The America's Intelligence Wire* 14 Sept. 2004.

Fletcher, R. 1998. *Craft Lessons: Teaching Writing K–8.* 2nd ed. Portland, ME: Stenhouse.

Fox, M. 1993. *Radical Reflections: Passionate Reflections on Teaching, Learning, and Living.* San Diego, CA: Harcourt, Inc.

Graves, D. 1994. *A Fresh Look at Writing.* Portsmouth, NH: Heinemann.

Holt, K. 1998. *My Louisiana Sky.* New York: Dell Yearling.

Holt, K. 1999. *When Zachary Beaver Came to Town.* New York: Dell Yearling.

Hopkinson, D. 2003. *Girl Wonder: A Baseball Story in Nine Innings.* New York: Atheneum Books.

Jacobs, Paula. 1998. "Strong Writing Skills Essential for Success, Even in IT. (Industry Trend or Event)" *InfoWorld.* 6 July.

Junger, S. 1997. *The Perfect Storm.* New York: HarperCollins.

Keizer, G. 1988. *No Place But Here: A Teacher's Vocation in a Rural Community.* New York: Penguin Books.

King, S. 2000. *On Writing: A Memoir of the Craft.* New York: Pocket Books.

Kolin, P.C. 2003. *Successful Writing at Work.* Boston: Houghton Mifflin College Division.

Lederer, R. 1987. *Anguished English: An Anthology of Accidental Assaults upon Our Language.* New York: Dell.

Lederer, R. 1993. *More Anguished English: An Expose of Embarrassing, Excruciating, and Egregious Errors in English.* New York: Dell.

McSwigan, M. 1942. *Snow Treasure.* New York: Scholastic, Inc.

Montgomery, S. 2004. *The Tarantula Scientist.* New York: Houghton Mifflin.

Murray, D. 1998. *Write to Learn.* Fort Worth, TX: Harcourt Brace College Publishers.

The National Commission on Writing for America's Families, Schools, and Colleges. 2008. CollegeBoard. www.writingcommission.org/report.html.

"NCTE Beliefs about the Teaching." 2004. *NCTE Guideline.* Writing Study Group of the NCTE Executive Committee. (November) www.ncte.org/about/over/positions/category/write/118876.htm.

"The Neglected 'R': The Need for a Writing Revolution." 2003. *The National Commission on Writing in America's Schools and Colleges.* The College Board. (April) www.writingcommission.org/prod_downloads/writing.com/neglectedr.pdf.

Newkirk, T. 2005. *The School Essay Manifesto: Reclaiming the Essay for Students and Teachers.* Shoreham, VT: Discover Writing Press.

Paulsen, G. 1993. *Harris and Me.* San Diego, CA: Harcourt Books.

Payne, L. 1965. *The Lively Art of Writing.* New York: Penguin Putnam Books.

Peck, R. 2004. *The Teacher's Funeral: A Comedy in Three Parts.* New York: Dial Books.

Portalupi, J. 2001. *Nonfiction Craft Lessons: Teaching Information Writing K–8.* Portland, ME: Stenhouse.

Quindlen, A. 2006. "Fantastic—and Frightening." *Newsweek* 18 September, 72.

Roach, M. 2003. *Stiff: The Curious Lives of Human Cadavers.* New York: Norton and Company

Roth, A. 1974. *Iceberg Hermit.* New York: Scholastic, Inc.

Ryan, P. 2004. *Becoming Naomi Leon.* New York: Scholastic, Inc.

Sawyer, R., and J. Schiel. 2000. "Posttesting Students to Assess the Effectiveness of Remedial Instruction." *ACT Research Report Series.* (June) Online: www.act.org/research/researchers/reports/pdf/act_rr2000-7.pdf.

Schotter, R. 1997. *Nothing Ever Happens on 90th Street.* New York: Scholastic, Inc.

Seife, C. 2000. *Zero: The Biography of a Dangerous Idea.* New York: Penguin Books.

Spandel, V. 2005. *Creating Writers Through 6-Trait Assessment and Instruction.* 4th ed. Boston: Allyn & Bacon/Pearson.

Standards for Success Website. www.s4s.org.

Strange, W. 1996. "STRANGE WORLD: Wack Facts from Planet E." *Campus Life* Sept.-Oct. 1.

Strunk, W., and E.B. White. 1979. *Elements of Style.* 3rd ed. New York: McMillan.

Technology Initiative Grants Program. 23 April, 2008. Online: http://tig.lsc.gov/techglossary.php.

Truss, L. 2003. *Eats, Shoots, and Leaves.* New York: Gotham Books.

Warriner, J. 1965. *Warriner's English Grammar and Composition.* San Diego, CA: Harcourt, Inc.

White, E.B. 1952. *Charlotte's Web.* New York: HarperCollins.

Wikipedia. "Wiki" (definition). 5 May 2008. http://en.wikipedia.org/wiki/wiki.

"Wikis in Plain English." May 2007. Common Craft. Oneline: www.commoncraft.com/video-wikis-plain-english.

Williams, G. 1995. *Life on the Color Line.* New York: Penguin.

Wiseman, R. 2007. "A Quirky Look at Our Quirky Species: The Power of Positive Thinking." *New Scientist.* May 12.

Wong, E. 2001. "Chief Executive Is Criticized After Upbraiding Workers by E-Mail." (Business/Financial Desk). *New York Times.* 5 April.

"Writing: A Ticket to Work . . . Or a Ticket Out." September 2004. CollegeBoard. www.collegeboard.com/prod_downloads/writingcom/writing-ticket-to-work.pdf.

Writing Across the Curriculum Participant Binder. 2008. Wilmington, MA: Great Source Education Group.

"Writing, Clear, and Simple." 12 Dec. 2007. Online: http://rmjacobsen.squarespace.com/notebook/2007/12/12/programming-readers.html.

www.montgomeryschoolsmd.org/schools/sga/pdf/sa/resources/communications/act.listening.pdf, 10 Dec. 2007.

www.oe2u.com/courses.php?lang=en, 10 Mar. 2008.

Index